SPIRITUAL INTEGRITY
Christ Followers & Their Leaders

A Pragmatic Exposition of Second Corinthians

Jim Crain

Published by Jessup University Press
2121 University Avenue
Rocklin, CA 95765

The views of the author do not necessarily reflect the views of the Publisher.

Library of Congress Cataloging-in-Publication Data
Crain, Jim.
Spiritual Integrity: Christ Followers and Their Leaders (A Pragmatic Exposition of Second Corinthians)
ISBN-13: 978-1530949762 (paperback)
ISBN-10: 1530949769

1. NT Commentaries — English. 2. Second Corinthians.

Cover: Bev Cotton Designs
Portrait: "Head of Christ" by Antonio da Correggio (1489 – 1534)

Printed in the United States of America.

Table of Contents

Introduction

THE NEED FOR INTEGRITY

If something has integrity, it is whole; all the parts fit. It's complete, honest, and consistent. Every time. All the time. Individuals with integrity are what they should be. When people are looking and when they aren't. There is no pretending or posturing. Integrity is having a consistency of character. It is what we do and why we do it. It is who we are.

Integrity is the opposite of hypocrisy. A hypocrite is not a person without faults, but someone who pretends to be. The term comes from the stage plays of ancient Greece. The actor portrays himself to be something everyone knows he isn't. He holds the mask of his character on a stick. At the end of the performance, he lowers the mask to reveal his true identity to the applause of the audience. Someone without integrity is like that; they are play-acting. The only difference is that the crowd doesn't know it. If the person is good at it, the people are applauding. But, they shouldn't be.

Integrity is in limited supply these days. Too often, there's a discrepancy about our lives. Despite our intentions to be congruent, we aren't. Like the Christ followers in first century Corinth, there's a dissonance about us. Faith and practice are out of tune.

The truth is, at any given moment, we either have integrity or we don't. To the extent that we act according to the values, beliefs, and principles we claim to hold, we have integrity.

Integrity finds its roots in the Latin term *integer,* which describes a complete entity. Mathematicians use the word to designate whole numbers. It is an apt description of Christians too, since the word for salvation itself means to be made healthy and whole. But, like the Corinthians, many Christ followers today are saved, but they aren't complete. They are integrity-deficient.

The Apostle Paul's letters to the Corinthians address the issue of integrity. They are a deep reservoir of spiritual insights, principles, and practices still relevant for contemporary Christians and the churches they attend. First Corinthians exposes the errant beliefs and behaviors of integrity-deficient Christians. Second Corinthians exemplifies the characteristics and conduct of leaders who have the integrity their followers need. The following exposition of Second Corinthians is intended to be pragmatic; i.e., dealing with things sensibly and realistically in a way that is based on practical rather than theoretical considerations—all in the pursuit of spiritual integrity.

THE INTERPRETATION OF SCRIPTURE

Basic to proper biblical interpretation is discovering the meaning of Scripture. This is known as exegesis, which is a transliteration of the Greek term that means "to draw out." This is where we start. Once we carefully extract the truest meaning we can from a biblical text, we have its interpretation. Then we can turn to the business of applying it to our lives. We put it into practice for everyone to see, understand, and appreciate. Application is built on interpretation.

The first task of the exegete, then, is to interpret. This begins by investigating the context of the text we are seeking to understand. Like a diamond in a wedding ring, every biblical text has a setting— a context. Actually, it has two contexts.

First is its *literary context*; i.e., the verses and chapters that precede and follow the specific passage being studied. This also includes seeing the text's place in the section of the writing in which it appears and how it contributes to the argument or narrative of the book as a whole.

The second context is the *historical context*. Here, the exegetical obligation is to reconstruct the circumstances that caused the document to be written in the first place. What situation is the writer addressing? This is a tough assignment, but essential. The true interpretation of many biblical passages is context-dependent. Our goal is to ascertain what happened there and then, so that we can properly apply what is being said here and now.

HISTORICAL CONTEXT

The historical context of many of the epistles in the New Testament can be traced back to the narrative of the Book of Acts, including First and Second Corinthians.

In this case, it all starts in Acts 16. Paul is in the middle of his second mission trip. He and his companions are on the west coast of the Roman province of Asia (modern day Turkey) in the city of Troas. But not for long—dramatic divine intervention is about to change all that. Luke reports, *"During the night, Paul had a vision of a man of Macedonia standing and begging him, 'Come over to Macedonia and help us'"* (Acts 16:9).[1]

Paul, Silas, and Timothy have been traveling around Phrygia and Galatia (also modern day Turkey) running into one obstacle after another. Their itinerary was being blocked. By God! Luke records:

> *Paul and his companions traveled throughout the region of Phrygia and Galatia, having been kept by the Holy Spirit from preaching the word in the province of Asia. When they came to the border of Mysia, they tried to enter Bithynia, but the Spirit of Jesus would not allow them to. So they passed by Mysia and went down to Troas.* (Acts 16:6-8)

The next morning, they headed west. Luke joins the team and adds this entry to his journal: *"After Paul had seen the vision, we got ready at once to leave for Macedonia, concluding that God had called us to*

---

[1] Unless otherwise noted, all scriptural quotations are from the New International Version (NIV), 2011 edition.

preach the gospel to them" (Acts 16:10). The mandate in which Jesus commissioned the original apostles to be his witnesses *"in Jerusalem, and in all Judea and Samaria, and to the ends of the earth"* (Acts 1:8), was now being extended to Paul and his colleagues. Another concentric circle was added to the evangelistic trajectory of the gospel. For the first time, Europe will hear the good news.

The foursome take a boat across the Aegean arm of the Mediterranean. Disembarking in northern Greece, they head to Philippi, the leading city in the district, named after Philip of Macedon, the father of Alexander the Great. There the team happens upon a handful of godly women just outside of town, by the riverside, praying. Lydia is the one we are introduced to by name. Luke notes, *"The Lord opened her heart to respond to Paul's message"* (Acts 16:14).

A little while later, still in Philippi, another incident occurs. This time Paul's preaching was substantiated by an exorcism — he casts a demon out of a slave girl whose masters were selling her fortune-telling talents. They squawk. Paul gets jailed. He and his friends are charged by the town magistrates with *"throwing our city into an uproar"* (Acts 16:20).

After being flogged, Paul and Silas are released from custody and the civic leaders insist that the apostle and his companions leave town. Luke stays put, but Paul, Silas, and Timothy head south about a hundred miles to Thessalonica. There, in rapid order, a church is planted in the city whose namesake is Alexander the Great's half-sister. Predictably, hostile Jews start trouble. In an unintentional compliment, they complain to the city officials: *"These men who have caused trouble all over the world have now come here...defying Caesar's decrees, saying there is another king, one called Jesus"* (Acts 17:6-7). True enough. Turmoil ensues. A quick decision was made to hustle Paul out of town before things got uglier. *"As soon as it was night, the brothers sent Paul and Silas away to Berea"* (Acts 17:10).

In Berea, Paul preaches. As usual, people get saved. Then the Jews from up north arrive, *"agitating the crowds and stirring them up"* (Acts 17:13). For his own protection, the beleaguered apostle is once again whisked away; this time, to Athens. Silas and Timothy stay in Berea, while our lone fugitive from injustice arrives in the intellectual capital of the ancient world. The metropolis was the proud hometown of Socrates, Plato, and Aristotle — the geographical birthplace of Greek philosophy itself. Oddly enough, at the same time, the city was also rife with pagan religious superstition.

Waiting for his coworkers to arrive, Luke reports of Paul, *"He was greatly distressed to see that the city was full of idols. So he reasoned in the synagogue with the Jews and God-fearing Greeks, as well as in in the marketplace day by day with those who happened to be there"* (Acts 17:16-17).

As Providence would have it, Paul attracts the curiosity of the Areopagus, the civic council of academics who had the power to let him speak or shut him up. They courteously invite him to explain himself. Not one to miss an opportunity to preach the gospel, Paul does a masterful job of making a case for the philosophical logic of the Christian worldview (Acts 17:22-31). But, his effort to make the good news appealing to this erudite audience is met with mixed reviews. Luke summarizes the three-fold response of the philosophers. *"Some of them sneered, but others said, 'We want to hear you again on this subject'"* (Acts 17:32). He adds, *"Some of the people became followers of Paul and believed"* (Acts 17:34). Then he notes, *"After this, Paul left Athens and went to Corinth"* (Acts 18:1).

Shortly after arriving in Corinth, the commercial hub of Greece, Paul meets two Messianic Jews, Aquila and his wife, Priscilla. They are dedicated evangelists. All three are tentmakers. They form a partnership — the original bi-vocational team of coworkers. Every day they made tents and preached the gospel too. Luke says, *"[Paul] stayed and worked with them. Every Sabbath he reasoned in the synagogue, trying to persuade Jews and Greeks"* (Acts 18:3-4). Later, *"When Silas and Timothy came from Macedonia, Paul devoted himself exclusively to preaching, testifying to the Jews that Jesus was the Messiah"* (Acts 18:5).

In no time at all, opposition arose again. Once more, it was the Jews. *"They opposed Paul and became abusive"* (Acts 18:6). Frustrated, the apostle follows the biblical precedent of what to do when a prophet's preaching is stubbornly rejected. *"He shook out his clothes in protest and said to them, 'Your blood be upon your own heads! I am innocent of it. From now on I will go to the Gentiles'"* (Acts 18:6).

It will be non-Jews who get saved this time. Luke proudly reports that *"Many of the Corinthians who heard Paul believed and were baptized"* (Acts 18:8). It gets better. Jesus himself assures the apostle of his prospects for success. *"Do not be afraid; keep on speaking, do not be silent. For I am with you and no one is going to attack and harm you, because I have many people in this city"* (Acts 18:9-10).

In approximately eighteen months the church in Corinth was firmly planted (Acts 18:11, 18). In the process Paul was assisted by Aquila and Priscilla, Timothy, Silas, and two converted synagogue leaders — Sosthenes and Crispus. Then, for reasons Luke leaves unexplained, Paul packed up and left town.

THE CORINTHIAN CORRESPONDENCE

After leaving Corinth, the apostle returned to the congregation in Antioch, Syria that had originally commissioned him to be their cross-cultural representative (Acts 13:1-3). Sometime later he embarked on another evangelistic campaign, commonly known as his third missionary journey. On foot and on his own, he arrives in Ephesus in the Roman province of Asia (Acts 19:1). From there he writes three of his four letters to the troubled and troubling

Corinthian Christians, some two hundred and forty miles to the west, across the Aegean Sea.[2]

Corinth's moral infamy remains legendary. To *Corinthianize* was to be a profligate playboy. Corinth was a populous, cosmopolitan, prosperous, materialistic place. Ignominiously, it was the hedonistic capital of the Mediterranean world, known as the city "where the vices of East and West meet." Without a doubt, it was a tough town in which to be consistently Christ-like.

Sadly, the church was in Corinth and Corinth was in the church. It was in response to the prevalence of sexual promiscuity that Paul first wrote to the Corinthians. That original letter is lost to history. We only know of it by his passing reference to it when he says, "*I wrote to you in my letter not to associate with sexually immoral people*" (1 Corinthians 5:9).

As for First Corinthians itself, two factors combined to compel Paul to write it. First, there were oral reports. "*My brothers and sisters, some from Chloe's household have informed me that there are quarrels among you*" (1 Corinthians 1:11). Second, the leaders of the church had written a letter itemizing many of the problems they were facing. This letter was most probably hand-delivered by three men, who surely added even more details about the multidimensional crisis in Corinth (1 Corinthians 16:17). Paul responds. "*Now for the matters you wrote about*" (1 Corinthians 7:1).

The problems in the church at Corinth were not incidental. A divisive spirit was defusing itself throughout the congregation. Strained relationships, in some cases had become litigious. Add to that, shocking sexual laxity, marital discord, compromise with

---

[2] All the letters of the New Testament have one thing in common; they are occasional documents. In other words, some circumstance caused them to be written. Biblical scholars call this "occasionality." Usually, the situation was generated by the readers, not the writers. In this case, it was the Corinthians' confused beliefs and unacceptable conduct that compelled Paul to respond.

idolatry, gender conflict, worship improprieties, the misuse of spiritual gifts, doctrinal confusion, and a host of attendant issues.

Paul is their spiritual father. He responds in kind. *"I am writing this not to shame you, but to warn you, as my dear children. Even if you had ten thousand guardians in Christ, you do not have many fathers, for in Christ Jesus I became your father through the gospel"* (1 Corinthians 4:14-15).

Like a good parent, the apostle admonishes his children, tackling their problems one by one. But, it is clear from the start that he attributes the entire malaise in Corinth to a single undesirable disorder. In a word, the source of the trouble in the Corinthian church was worldliness.

You can sense Paul's exasperation. *"Brothers and sisters, I could not address you as people who live by the Spirit, but as people who are still worldly"* (1 Corinthians 3:1). With impassioned concern, he identifies the tell-tale signs of the carnality that had come to characterize the congregation. In the process, he outlines the principles and procedures by which a worldly Christian can become a spiritual one. His response to their troubles has transcendent value and relevance.

To understand the conceptual framework of the Corinthian correspondence, consider the three circles in the following diagram.

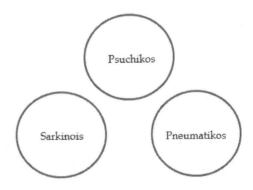

In the top circle, is the Greek word "psuchikos." Psuchikos transliterates into English as "psyche"; i.e., the human soul or mind. Paul uses this term when he says, *"The person without the Spirit does not accept the things that come from the Spirit of God, but considers them foolishness, and cannot understand them, because they are discerned only through the Spirit"* (1 Corinthians 2:14).

What the NIV specifies as *"the person without the Spirit"* is a translation of two Greek words, "psuchikos anthrōpos." More literal versions render it, "the natural man." This is the biblical description of the vast majority of earth's human inhabitants; they are without the Holy Spirit. They are doing the best they can to live their lives by the perceptions and energies of their own psyche; mind, emotions, and will—that's it. No supernatural presence, power, or wisdom. They are "natural" men and women. On their own. Non-Christians.

In contrast to "psuchikos" the Apostle Paul talks about "pneumatikos," or *"the person with the Spirit,"* as depicted in the circle to the bottom-right. He asserts, *"The person with the Spirit makes judgments about all things, but such a person is not subject to merely human judgments"* (1 Corinthians 2:15).

Here we have the exact opposite of a non-Christian. This is a Christ-follower who is filled with the Holy Spirit. Everything is said and done under the influence of the Spirit of God. This individual is an integer, with a Christ-like consistency of character—the embodiment of spiritual integrity.

In the remaining circle is the Greek word "sarkinois." This term is typically translated *"worldly."* Paul says, *"Brothers and sisters, I could not address you as people who live by the Spirit, but as people who are still worldly"* (1 Corinthians 3:1).

This was precisely the problem with the church in Corinth. There wasn't an observable distinction between them and their fellow Corinthians. Their values and subsequent behavior was not noticeably different from what it was before they decided to become Christ followers.

Little progress has been made. In spite of being Christians for upwards of five years, the Corinthians were still *"mere infants in Christ"* (1 Corinthians 3:1). Reflecting back on his eighteen plus months with them, Paul says, *"I gave you milk, not solid food, for you were not yet ready for it. Indeed, you are still not ready"* (1 Corinthians 3:2). Their behavior is confirmation of their childishness. Paul confronts them with the evidence of his diagnosis. *"For since there is jealousy and quarreling among you, are you not worldly? Are you not acting like mere human beings?"* (1 Corinthians 3:3). It was a blunt rebuke.

The Corinthians were Christians, but they were behaving like non-Christians. They were integrity-deficient. It was embarrassing. And unacceptable. Like any leader with integrity, Paul will not ignore it. He won't look the other way. Instead, he lovingly forces them to face their immaturity.

Finally, we place one more item in our three-circled diagram: a horizontal line separating the top circle from the bottom two.

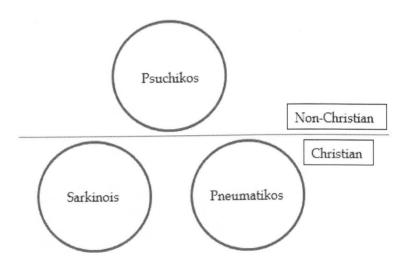

People in the top circle are not Christians. It's our responsibility to change that if we can. The two circles below the line represent those who have put their faith in Christ. In the right circle are individuals for whom Christ is Lord as well as Savior. Those in the left circle are the ones for whom Christ is only Savior. Such believers are justified, but not sanctified. The salvation process has been truncated. They are not integers. Our task as leaders with integrity is to do what we can to move people like this from left to right—from worldly to spiritual.

THE CHALLENGE OF SPIRITUAL LEADERSHIP

This schematic represents the challenge before Paul and his co-workers in their ministry to the Corinthians. For all of us, it is nothing less than carrying out the Great Commission. *"He said to them, 'Go into all the world and preach the gospel to all creation'"* (Mark 16:15). We evangelize the lost. Then we make disciples of those who respond in faith.

> *Then Jesus came to them and said, "All authority in heaven and on earth has been given to me. Therefore, go and make disciples of all nations, baptizing them in the name of the Father and of the Son and of the Holy Spirit, and teaching them to obey everything I have commanded you."* (Matthew 28:18-20)

It's an astounding assignment. Thankfully, Jesus promises to be with us while we do it. *"And surely I am with you always, to the very end of the age"* (Matthew 28:20).

Now, let's see what spiritual leaders with integrity can do to inspire and instruct those under their influence to become integers themselves—whole and healthy Christ followers, experiencing him as both Savior and Lord.

Chapter 1

Making the Most of Unavoidable Distress

2 Corinthians 1:1-11

"Sorry for your troubles" is a phrase often repeated in Frank McCourt's 1996 bestseller, *Angela's Ashes*. In that gritty memoir about his impoverished childhood in Limerick, Ireland, there were troubles aplenty for McCourt, his alcoholic father, his mother (Angela), his two younger brothers, and only sister. It's a heartrending tale of intense grief, anguish, and distress. Though perhaps less dramatic, it seems that there are plenty of troubles for most of us too.

Job, who had more than his share of heartaches, summarized the human condition when he bemoaned, *"Mortals born of woman, are of few days and full of trouble"* (Job 14:1). It's life. Painful, disappointing things happen to us. Scripture commonly calls them "trials." They are inevitable, unavoidable, and uncontrollable circumstances. Loss of health, prolonged illness, permanent injury, unemployment, unrequited love, a broken marriage, a wayward child, the death of someone dear to us—all qualify. Troubles.

I have a theory about such distress. Accepting the dismal premise that we are all totally depraved creatures, sharing the same precarious environment, we are not going to escape the consequences of our own sins or someone else's. Thus, each of us, at any given time, is either in the middle of a trial, coming out of a trial, temporarily out of a trial, or going back into another trial. Sounds fatalistic, I know. It is. Disappointment, pain, and the distress they bring are inescapable. Make no mistake about it. Become a Christ-follower and it gets worse. That's Paul's thesis in the opening paragraph of Second Corinthians. Matter-of-factly, he asserts that *"We share abundantly in the sufferings of Christ"* (2 Corinthians 1:5). Given that reality, how will we respond?

Before we answer that question, let's review the situation at Corinth and the letters Paul has already written to the congregation. The apostle founded the church around 51-52 AD, as documented by Luke in Acts 18. Doing so took more than a year and a half (Acts 18:11). It was no easy task. As nearly everyone knows, Corinth was a wickedly sinful place, especially when it came to sexual immorality.

Shortly after he left town, Paul hears that some of the Corinthians have succumbed to the promiscuous temptations of the city; and even done them one better. *"It is actually reported that there is sexual immorality among you, and of a kind that even pagans do not tolerate: a man is sleeping with his father's wife"* (1 Corinthians 5:1). This shocking report comes with word of further misconduct in Corinth. *"My brothers and sisters, some from Chloe's household have informed me that there are quarrels among you"* (1 Corinthians 1:11). Then, a letter from the church leaders arrives, containing several questions about even more serious improprieties going on (1 Corinthians 7:1).

Paul responds to this troubling information with what is our canonical First Corinthians, which is actually his second letter to them (1 Corinthians 5:9). He confronts, he chastises, he coaxes, he encourages. While news of their reaction to this written exhortation hangs in the air, we discover that some forceful outsiders, most likely Jewish Christian preachers from Jerusalem, have arrived in Corinth and are sowing doubt about the authenticity of Paul's apostleship.

Concerned about a congregational revolt, Paul made an emergency trip to Corinth. It didn't turn out well. Seemingly, in some kind of face-off, the ringleader of the rebellion publically insulted Paul and challenged his credibility. The people listened to the accusations, but no one stood up in his defense.

Stung by this lack of loyalty, the apostle left town and soon writes what has come to be called the "stern letter"[3] in which he reprimands the church for their indecision and deficient support. Like his original letter, it too is lost to us.

Still worried, Paul dispatches his young assistant Titus to see what was going on in his absence. Titus returns from his reconnaissance of the situation with news—both good and bad. Gladly, most of the Corinthians have renewed their devotion to Paul and have repented of their sinful immaturities.

> *See what this godly sorrow has produced in you: what earnestness, what eagerness to clear yourselves, what indignation, what alarm, what longing, what concern, what readiness to see justice done. At every point you have proved yourselves to be innocent in this matter...by all this we are encouraged.* (2 Corinthians 7:11-13)

Most of the church, then, has become what you could call the Compliant Majority. But, there remains a Defiant Minority, continuing to undermine Paul's leadership in the congregation. In Second Corinthians the apostle rejoices at the repentance of the majority and assures them he will return to resolve the controversy over his leadership once and for all. And, if necessary, by a dramatic display of apostolic authority. *"This will be my third visit to you...On my return I will not spare those who have sinned earlier or any of the others"* (2 Corinthians 13:1-2). Until then, this fourth letter to them will have to suffice.

Paul begins in the customary style of all first century correspondence, with a greeting. *"Paul, an apostle of Christ Jesus by the*

---

[3] Some scholars argue that 2 Corinthians 10-13 is the "stern letter" appended to the original text of Second Corinthians. Though there is no manuscript evidence to support this theory, the tone of those chapters is similar to the stern letter.

will of God and Timothy[4] our brother, to the church of God in Corinth, together with all his holy people throughout Achaia" (2 Corinthians 1:1).

In his letters, Paul typically describes himself as an apostle[5] to underscore his spiritual authority.[6] Nowhere was such a reminder more apropos, or necessary, than in Corinth. In this church his

---

[4] Seven apostolic assistants were associated with Paul's ministry in Corinth. First is Sosthenes. We know little about him. He is mentioned in the greeting of First Corinthians (1 Corinthians 1:1) and is likely the same man identified as the former leader of the Jewish synagogue in the city, now a Christian (Acts 18:17). Second is Luke, who seems to have had occasional contact with the Corinthians. He may be the individual anonymously described as *"our brother who has often proved to us in many ways that he is zealous"* (2 Corinthians 8:22). Third is Timothy, who served as an envoy to Corinth on Paul's behalf. He says, *"I have sent to you Timothy, my son, whom I love, who is faithful in the Lord. He will remind you of my way of life in Christ Jesus which agrees with what I teach everywhere in every church"* (1 Corinthians 4:17). Timothy is included in the greeting of Second Corinthians, which indicates his ongoing ministry with the church. Fourth is Titus, who acts as Paul's apostolic emissary after First Corinthians, perhaps delivering both the "stern letter" as well as Second Corinthians. Fifth is Silas, Paul's chief companion on his third missionary trip, who was instrumental in the initial preaching of the gospel in Corinth (2 Corinthians 1:19). Finally, Priscilla and Aquila were there at the start of the Corinthian church. Paul lived with them when they all simultaneously arrived in town (Acts 18:1-3). The couple served as crucial co-workers in the establishment of the congregation.

[5] Greek: "apostolos" (ἀπόστολος). Literally, a "sent one." This term is a title primarily reserved for those original men handpicked and commissioned by Christ himself. This is the source and character of their spiritual authority. In Paul's case, Jesus said of him on the day of his conversion, *"This man is my chosen instrument to proclaim my name to the Gentiles and their kings and to the people of Israel"* (Acts 9:15). Paul would later say, *"I thank Christ Jesus our Lord, who has given me strength, that he considered me trustworthy, appointing me to his service"* (1 Timothy 1:12). This apostolic destiny was ordained by God before he was born (Galatians 1:15). He further verifies his apostleship, identifying himself as *"Paul, an apostle – sent not from men nor by a man, but by Jesus Christ and God the Father"* (Galatians 1:1). Speaking of the gospel he preached, he declares, *"I did not receive it from any man, nor was I taught it; rather, I received it by revelation from Jesus Christ"* (Galatians 1:12).

[6] Philippians and First and Second Thessalonians are the only exceptions to this rule. Most likely his amiable rapport with these healthy and compliant congregations didn't require that he mention his office.

apostolic authenticity was being vociferously challenged. Paul firmly reasserts the authority of his office. He mentions it, but does not pound them over the head with it. Leaders with integrity know the source of their prestige, but they maintain that high status with humility. We know where it comes from. And, we know that God does not share his glory with another (Isaiah 42:8).

In greeting the congregation, Paul establishes something that we should be clear about from the start. Despite their embarrassing immaturities and characteristic carnality, the Corinthians were Christians. Paul addresses them as *"The church of God in Corinth"* (2 Corinthians 1:1). He does not hesitate to identify these worldly and wayward believers as an assembly *"of God."* It was a Laodicean-like church (Revelation 3:14-22) to be sure; but it was the church. Like all churches, it was one that Jesus himself was building (Matthew 16:18). In this case, it was still very much under construction.

It is interesting to note that Paul does not have just the Corinthians in mind when he writes this letter. He has a broader audience in view. *"Together with all his holy people throughout Achaia"*[7] (2 Corinthians 1:1). It is unclear just why the apostle addresses a larger number of Christians in an embarrassingly revealing letter about the problems in Corinth. Perhaps, it's because what goes on in one congregation is typically known by surrounding congregations anyway; so he might as well be open about it. Better facts than gossip. Plus, to know that your dirty laundry is being aired for everyone else to see is disconcerting enough to motivate you to own up to your deficiencies.

---

[7] Northern Greece was named Macedonia. Southern Greece, was called Achaia. Both were first century Roman senatorial provinces, governed by proconsuls. In Paul's day, the proconsul of Corinth was Gallio (Acts 18:12). The major cities of Achaia were Athens, Corinth and Sparta. Adjacent to Corinth was Cenchrea, the Aegean seaport slightly to the south, mentioned in Romans 16:1.

Still, let's say it again, the Corinthians were Christians. Without question, worldly ones, but Christians nonetheless. Paul calls them *"holy people"* (2 Corinthians 1:1), or saints.[8] Unholy saints! It's a contradiction in terms, but in Corinth it was also a reality. Paul's intention is to change all that.

Next, in the traditional greeting of first century letter writing, Paul expresses a prayer-wish. It's more than a wish; it is a prayerful wish. It is something he sincerely hopes and prays will become a reality. *"Grace and peace from God our Father and the Lord Jesus Christ"* (2 Corinthians 1:2).

This standard style of saying hello is packed with doctrinal truth and spiritual implications. Subtly, Paul reminds his readers that the Christian experience starts with grace; the undeserved, unearned, and unconditional love of God. It is the water in which the fish swims. It is the air in which the bird flies. It is the atmosphere of the Christian life. The sequence of the phrase is theologically significant too. Peace[9] is the settled serenity that comes with being the recipient of the lavish unmerited favor of God. Grace creates a rightness between us and our Creator; peace is the experience that follows that reality. Typically, Paul describes this double blessing as coming from

---

[8] Greek: "hagioi" (ἅγιοι). To be a Christian is to be a saint. In apostolic vocabulary, the terms are synonymous. The word describes "holy ones," i.e., those separated from sin and devoted to God. It is regrettable that over the course of church history this simple concept has been distorted with layers of unbiblical teaching.

[9] Greek: "eirēnē" (εἰρήνη). This word does not presume the absence of trouble or struggle. Instead, it conveys the sense of unthreatened security and blessing in spite of one's circumstances. It is the experience of Christ's promise when he said, *"Peace I leave with you; my peace I give you. I do not give to you as the world gives. Do not let your hearts be troubled and do not be afraid"* (John 14:27). And, *"I have told you these things, so that you may have peace. In this world you will have trouble. But, take heart! I have overcome the world"* (John 16:33). Peace is the result of justification; being declared right with God. *"Therefore, since we have been justified through faith, we have peace with God through our Lord Jesus Christ, through whom we have gained access into this grace in which we now stand"* (Romans 5:1-2).

God, the Father and the Son.[10] The inclusion of this gracious greeting reminds the troublesome Corinthian congregation of God's love for them. The expression of good will towards those we serve is an essential quality of leadership with integrity.

THE PRESSURE OF SUFFERING

Greetings extended, Paul quickly turns to the substance of the things he wants to say. The initial topic is the reality of trouble. In life, painful, disappointing, and even depressing situations, are inevitable and unavoidable. Paul now explains how we can survive the trials[11] that God allows to come our way. Surprisingly, he starts with a doxology. *"Praise be to the God and Father of our Lord Jesus Christ"* (2 Corinthians 1:3).

There is an inextricable pressure to living in this world; but let's keep it in perspective. Paul starts where we should all begin when it comes to inescapable trouble — worship. At the moment he is smack-

---

[10] There are exceptions to this rule. Paul says to the Colossians, *"Grace and peace to you from God our Father"* (Colossians 1:2). To the Thessalonians, he writes, *"Grace and peace to you"* (1 Thessalonians 1:1). To Timothy he modifies the phrase a little further. *"Grace, mercy and peace from God the Father and Christ Jesus our Lord"* (1 Timothy 1:2; 2 Timothy 1:2).

[11] Greek: "peirasmos" (πειρασμός). This word is alternatively translated "trial" or "temptation." Context is what determines the proper understanding of it. Temptation comes from the devil, the world around us, or from within ourselves. God does not tempt us and is incapable of doing so (James 1:13-14). By contrast, trials happen to us, often without warning or fault on our part. While God does not and cannot tempt us to sin, he certainly can and does allow us to be tried. Some might presume that God causes trials. Maybe. But one thing is certain; he does let them happen. After all, there isn't a trial we have ever faced that God couldn't have prevented. The good news is that though God may not exempt us from trials or extract us from them, he has promised to always see us through them.

dab in the middle of a painful trial himself; one caused by the Corinthians. Still, the first word out of his mouth is *"Praise."*[12]

Paul typically credits both Father and Son for the blessings of the Christian life.[13] Implicit in his theology is the New Testament axiom that the revelation and blessings of God are known and experienced through Christ. Here, with the use of a three-fold title, *"Lord Jesus Christ"* (2 Corinthians 1:2), Paul identifies his role (*"Lord"*), his person (*"Jesus"*) and his office (*"Christ"*). In Scripture, Jesus shares the Father's glory. In this instance though, the Father is the focus of adoration. Paul proceeds to describe him in ways that remind us of the consolation that is ours in any and every troubling situation. God is *"The Father of compassion"*[14] (2 Corinthians 1:3). It is God's nature to be compassionate. As someone once observed; if God is our father, that changes everything.

Paul adds another phrase to this opening expression of praise: *"The God of all comfort"*[15] (2 Corinthians 1:3). It is God's compassion that gives rise to his comfort. In the original text, the word comfort is in the plural. Simply put, there is not a situation in which God is not there to encourage and console us. He *"comforts us in all our troubles"*[16] (2 Corinthians 1:3). The comfort is all-encompassing – exactly what we need when we are feeling afraid and vulnerable.

---

[12] Greek: "eulogētos" (εὐλογητός). This is a compound word coming from a verb that literally means to "speak well of." It is the origin our term eulogy. In the middle of trouble, Paul speaks well of God.

[13] We can rest assured that though the Holy Spirit is not usually mentioned in such benedictions, his presence and part in the blessings of God is presumed by Paul and confirmed by historical Christian orthodoxy.

[14] Greek: "oiktirmos" (οἰκτιρμός). As a Jew, it is quite natural for Paul to use this Hebrew idiom that means "all merciful Father." The term connotes feelings of pity.

[15] Greek: "paraklēsis" (παράκλησις). This term means "called alongside." It connotes comfort, encouragement, and support. It is the very word used by Jesus to describe the Holy Spirit as our *"Advocate"* (John 14:26).

[16] Greek: "thlipsis" (θλῖψις). Paul chooses yet another word for trials, sometimes translated *"troubles"* (2 Corinthians 1:8). The term suggests

In praising God for comforting his people in all their troubles, the apostle speaks with fresh recollection of unbearable difficulties of his own. *"We do not want you to be uniformed, brothers and sisters, about the troubles we experienced in the province of Asia"*[17] (2 Corinthians 1:8). While the details of this ordeal are unknown to us, evidently the Corinthians were privy to what their spiritual father had recently been forced to withstand. Whatever the specifics, it was severe. *"We were under great pressure, far beyond our ability to endure, so that we despaired even of life itself"*[18] (2 Corinthians 1:8).

I've faced some hardships in my day, but none life-threatening. Despair comes in varying degrees, but each trial carries with it the sense of being trapped with no way out. Paul presumed that this particular predicament was going to cost him his life. *"Indeed, we felt we had received the sentence of death"* (2 Corinthians 1:9). If we take what he says literally, then this was an instance of governmental persecution, perhaps referring to a magistrate somewhere who sentenced Paul to some kind of execution. Maybe it was lions in the arena (1 Corinthians 15:32). Whatever the particulars, the apostle concluded that he was good as dead. But, he didn't die; God delivered him from it.

---

increasing and seemingly unbearable pressure; sometimes of a pack animal whose legs buckle under a load beyond its strength to bear. Paul refers to such crushing burdens three times in these opening sentences of Second Corinthians.

[17] Scholars are forever guessing about the details of this event so vivid in Paul's mind. Presumably, he is speaking of some overwhelming experience in Ephesus, located in the *"province of Asia."* The episode recorded in Acts 19:23-41 is traditionally referred to as a possibility. We know too though, from 2 Corinthians 11:16-33, that Paul had been through numerous life-threatening situations. We can't say with certainty which experience he refers to here.

[18] It is tantalizing to match this statement to 1 Corinthians 15:32 where Paul speaks of fighting *"wild beasts in Ephesus."* Again, reconstruction of historical events referred to in the epistles is often educated conjecture; we can only suppose.

There is an unyielding reality to times of trouble. Life is hard. But, if distress is unavoidable, then let's follow Paul's example and make the most of it. The apostles were partners in pain. They didn't expect anything else. Peter says, *"If you suffer for doing good and you endure it, this is commendable before God. To this you were called, because Christ suffered for you, leaving you an example, that you should follow in his steps"* (1 Peter 2:20-21). They presumed it and they rejoiced in it (Acts 5:41; 16:25). They even welcomed it. Paul told the Philippians *"I want to know Christ – yes, to know the power of his resurrection and participation in his sufferings"* (Philippians 3:10). Suffering is part of drinking the cup of Christ (Matthew 20:22-23).

THE PROVISION OF COMFORT

There's a mystery to suffering. It's inexplicable why some people suffer more than others. Why are some martyrs for Christ, while the rest of us have barely been insulted for being a Christian? Still, to one extent or another, we all experience pain in this world. Moses was right. *"Our days may come to seventy years, or eighty, if our strength endures; yet the best of them are but trouble and sorrow"* (Psalm 90:10).

Sometimes in the depths of despair we ask: Why me? Why now? Why this? To console ourselves, we presume there is a purpose to our trials, but typically, we aren't sure what it is. Rarely does God disclose that information. But here, we are kindly told one of the reasons why he lets us experience times of distress. Paul asserts that God *"comforts us in all our troubles, so that we can comfort those in any trouble with the comfort we ourselves have received from God"* (2 Corinthians 1:4). We are channels then, of God's compassionate consolation. What we have received from him, we pass on to others.

There's nothing quite like one cancer patient telling another about the goodness of God. Whatever the trials he has allowed into your life, you now have a ministry with people who are facing the same kind of misery. There's unassailable authority in that kind of testimony. To those who are hurting, we can sincerely say, "I feel your pain." We have been comforted; we are now comforters. We are Christ to others. *"Because he himself suffered when he was tempted, he is able to help those who are being tempted"* (Hebrews 2:18).

Paul's distress, allowed or ordered by God, had a purpose; the comfort he received was to be passed on. *"If we are distressed, it is for your comfort and salvation; if we are comforted, it is for your comfort, which produces in you patient endurance of the same sufferings we suffer"* (2 Corinthians 1:6). Without distress we would need no comfort. God allows suffering for transformational purposes. We suffer; we are comforted. Others suffer and we pass on the comfort we have received to them; they are comforted. It is a classic "Pay It Forward" sequence. The end result is *"patient endurance"* (2 Corinthians 1:6). This is a fundamental element of God's all-loving sovereign plan for our lives.

Early in his service to Christ, Paul was stoned, dragged outside of town, and left for dead. But miraculously, *"After the disciples gathered around him, he got up and went back into the city"* (Acts 14:19-20). Right away he resumed preaching. Shortly thereafter, he pronounced his perspective of the whole ordeal and what similar experiences portend. *"We must go through many hardships to enter the kingdom of God"* (Acts 14:22).

There would be no need for endurance if there were nothing to endure. As we endure, we will be comforted. *"And our hope for you is firm, because we know that just as you share in our sufferings, so also you share in our comfort"* (2 Corinthians 1:7).

When the pressure of a distressful situation is about to crush us, God intervenes to relieve it. Or, at least, to console us while we outlast it. There's a transcendent truth here: God's comfort is always equivalent to our troubles. Always! *"For just as we share abundantly in the sufferings of Christ, so also our comfort abounds through Christ"*[19] (2 Corinthians 1:5).

When we are feeling confused, fragile, hurting, and heartbroken, God's consolation and encouragement are extended to us—freely and in abundance. His is a father's compassion. Deliverance will come. Paul speaks from experience. *"He has delivered us from such a deadly peril, and he will deliver us again"* (2 Corinthians 1:10).

I have known people in deliverance ministries. It is their calling to pray for the afflicted, asking God to rescue them from their suffering. Sometimes it happens—the trouble doesn't just dissipate, it disappears. That's the essence of Paul's testimony here. Literally, he says that God delivered him "out"[20] of deadly peril. But deliverance isn't always immediate or dramatic. Nor is it guaranteed. In fact, sometimes we are never relieved of our suffering.

God does not promise to deliver us *from* our troubles, but one thing's certain; he will be with us *through* them. Ultimately though, deliverance will come—for all of us. *"Never again will they hunger; never again will they thirst...for the Lamb at the center of the throne will be their shepherd; he will lead them to springs of living water. And God will wipe away every tear from their eyes"* (Revelation 7:16-17).

God will never fail to deliver his people. We join Paul in confidently saying, *"On him we have set our hope"* (2 Corinthians 1:10). Distress is inevitable. Pain is inescapable. Hardship is unavoidable.

---

[19] Jesus starkly predicted our sufferings for him when he warned: *"If the world hates you, keep in mind that it hated me first. If you belonged to the world, it would love you as its own. As it is, you do not belong to the world, but I have chosen you out of the world. That is why the world hates you. Remember the words I told you: 'A servant is not greater than his master. If they persecuted me, they will persecute you also'"* (John 15:18-20). The pain Christ endured is passed on to us. Hence Paul enigmatically says, *"I fill up in my flesh what is still lacking in regard to Christ's afflictions"* (Colossians 1:24). More plainly he asserts, *"We share in his sufferings in order that we may also share in his glory"* (Romans 8:17).

[20] Greek: "ek" (ἐκ). This term is the root of our English word "exit." When God provides a way out of our pain, let's be sure to take it.

But God's comfort is incomparable — and dependable. Suffering and comfort coalesce into hope.

THE PURPOSE OF PAIN

Paul now reveals something else about trials and troubles; there is a purpose to pain. Bad things happen. Bad things happen to good people. But, why?

I think of Dennis Mitchell, age 38. On March 3, 2000, his wife, Sandy, lost control of her Ford van near Livermore, California. The vehicle swerved off the road, rolled over several times, smashed into an oak tree and burst into flames. In a single day, Dennis Mitchell lost his wife and all six of his kids. Explain that!

Philosophers and theologians call it the "Problem of Suffering and Evil." Why is there so much wickedness and calamity in this world, often randomly inflicted on those who don't deserve it? Hinduism says it's Karma; you suffer because you have it coming. In a previous life you were bad; now you are paying for it. What goes around, comes around. For monotheistic religions, the problem gets personal. If God is all powerful and all loving, how come he lets awful things happen? Doesn't he care? Or is he helpless to do anything about it? It's a problem. Either way, the critics say that it's his fault.

I'm not sure there is a satisfactory answer to the problem of pain and suffering. But, here Paul gives us the second of three reasons why God would allow anyone, especially the righteous, to suffer. Every trial we ever face has been allowed or ordered by God for some good, loving, and constructive purpose.

Speaking of his own recent deadly adversity, Paul testifies, *"But this happened that we might not rely on ourselves but on God, who raises the dead"* (2 Corinthians 1:9). God allows us to suffer to make sure we remember the limits of our own strength, and to learn to trust him instead.

In his thought-provoking book, *The Jesus I Never Knew,* Philip Yancey reminds us of the irreversible nature of death.[21] We can't undo death. But the resurrection of Christ underscores the fact that God can. He did, and he will. In the face of death, self-reliance is ridiculous. In much lesser situations, relying on ourselves is also ineffective. The intended outcome of every trial is *"patient endurance"* (2 Corinthians 1:6). Trusting God is the key to achieving this level of perseverance. To that end, it is God's intention to bring us to the point of total dependence on him.

Finally, there's one more way to make the most of unavoidable distress; we should pray. In the face of menacing situations, we turn to God. Trouble gets God's people on their knees and keeps us there. Petition and intercession unites us as it strengthens us. God delivers us through it. Again, Paul testifies:

> *He has delivered us from such a deadly peril, and he will deliver us. On him we have set our hope that he will continue to deliver again, as you help us by your prayers. Then many will give thanks on our behalf for the gracious favor granted us in answer to the prayers of many.* (2 Corinthians 1:10-11)

Prayer reminds us of the synergistic nature of spiritual transformation. God doesn't do it all. And certainly, we can't do it on our own. Together though, we can accomplish the impossible. Prayer unifies us with God and each other in doing great things. Not all the requests we make of him are granted; we acknowledge that. But, prayers answered create an outpouring of worship. Paul promises that *"many will give thanks."*[22] Prayers are prayed and

---

21 Yancey, Philip. *The Jesus I Never Knew.* Grand Rapids, MI: Zondervan, 1995.

22 Greek: "ek pollōn prosōpōn" (ἐκ πολλῶν προσώπων). The phrase translated *"many"* is literally "out of many faces." It is a pictorial expression of human faces lifted up toward God in gratitude.

answered; *"the gracious favor"*[23] of God is bestowed on us (2 Corinthians 1:11). The result is polyphonic praise. Praise always makes pain purposeful.

Growing up as an only child, I lived under the delusion that I could control my personal environment. Most of the time I could; there was no one around to mess it up. But, one day that fantasy was shattered once and for all. I was about eleven, playing football with a few friends in front of our house, when suddenly, staggering up the driveway came my drunken father. I was mortified. And, there was nothing I could do about it. With my friends snickering, I threw the football down and ran away as fast as I could. It was a lasting lesson in what life is really like oftentimes — out of control.

Hardships happen. Running away from them is not the answer. A better alternative is to decide in advance how we are going to respond to them. The good news is that as Christians with full access to the grace of God and the wisdom of his Word, we have all the resources we need to make the most of unavoidable distress.

Paul has now laid down the general response we should all take toward the unwanted, unexpected, unavoidable, disappointing, difficult, painful circumstances that happen to us — often without warning and due to no traceable fault of our own. Next, the apostle will turn to the specifics of the distress between himself and the Corinthians. He will face the tension and attempt to resolve it. After all, that's what leaders with integrity do.

---

[23] Greek: "eucharisteō" (εὐχαριστέω). This is the verb form of "charisma," typically translated as "grace." Favor is God's grace. Here we find the source of our word "eucharist." The Lord's Supper is a ceremonial portrayal of the gospel itself.

THINK

1. Have you come to grips with the fact that life is filled with painful, disappointing, and unavoidable distress? If so, how did you accept that conclusion? Are you at peace about it?

2. What terms does Paul use here to describe his own unavoidable distress?

3. In 2 Corinthians 11:24-28 Paul itemizes some of the troubles he's endured. What were they?

4. Suffering as a Christian is inevitable. True or False?

5. Have your sufferings ever caused you to *despair even of life*?

6. What's God's answer to the problem of inescapable pressure?

7. What motivates God to comfort us in our distress?

8. What is the first purpose of pain found in 1:4?

9. What is the second purpose of pain found in 1:9?

10. What is the third purpose of pain found in 1:10-11?

ACT

1. Evaluate your current situation. Right now, are you in a trial, coming out of a trial, out of a trial, or anticipating another trial coming your way? Find a friend you can trust to pray with you about it.

2. If you are in the middle of an escapable trial right now, practice praising God for allowing it to happen to you and for eventually seeing you through it.

3. Ask God for the opportunity to pass on the comfort you have received from him to someone else in pain. When that chance comes, take it.

4. Do some research on the problem of pain and evil. There are some rational answers as to why God allows bad things to happen to good people. Find out what they are.

5. Does your church have a 24-hour prayer ministry, so that people can call or text their prayer requests with the assurance that someone will be praying for them within minutes? Pledge yourself to make sure one gets started.

Chapter 2

Accepting No Substitute for Sincerity

2 Corinthians 1:12-22

In 1992 when Bill Clinton was first elected President of the United States, 57% of the electorate voted against him. In 2000, the presidential contest between George W. Bush and Al Gore was hanging in the balances. Literally! The voters in the pivotal state of Florida gave Bush the election by only 537 ballots. Indignant Democrats squawked, but the Supreme Court ruled against a recount, so George and Laura moved into the White House for eight years. Bush and Clinton both entered office without a clear majority of the people on their side. Even today, office-holders are ecstatic with approval ratings of over fifty percent. Every politician knows disapproval goes with the territory. Spiritual leaders know it too.

Living with disapproval tests us all. We want to be respected, appreciated, and given the benefit of the doubt. We want to be liked — by everyone. But, we won't be. Our support will never be unanimous. To the contrary, people have a remarkable capacity to be fickle. It could be our own kids, who ridicule and disrespect us. It could be our best friend, who stabs us in the back. It could be a co-worker, who uses us as a stepping stone to get ahead. It could even be someone we've led to Christ, who now acts like they owe us nothing. It could be a church member, challenging our authority. Or lots of them. Whatever the case, rejection stings. It throbs. It creates chronic pain. How do we stay strong in the midst of such mistreatment?

REALITY

Typically, trouble starts with words. We have to cope with the condemnation of rude verbal potshots and whispered suspicions. Sure, some people welcome criticism. Or, so they say. And yes, criticism can be constructive. Some of us are blind to our own faults; we could benefit from the observations and suggestions of others. But though the results of criticism may be positive, the intentions of those who offer it often aren't. Instead of wanting to help us stand, they attempt to knock us down.

When someone criticizes us they pass judgment on what we've said or done. Or, even who we are. They analyze and evaluate us. Sometimes our critics are right. We deserve their dissatisfaction. Still, it's discouraging to be weighed in the balances and found wanting. It can rob us of motivation. It can make us anxious or leave us depressed. It can goad us to fight or force us to run away and hide. I was friends with a pastor once who was so much under fire that Sundays were his least favorite day of the week. He didn't even want to be in church, much less preach a sermon. What he wanted to do was quit, but he needed the job.

RESPONSE

Criticism is tough to take when it's fair. But, what if it's not? The Apostle Paul had a confident defense against the unkind and unfair things being said about him in Corinth—he was sincere. To be sincere is to be free from deceit, hypocrisy, or falseness. It is to be genuine, real, and pure. Sincerity is a powerful antidote to poisonous disapproval. It's even something we can be proud of. Paul was. *"Now this is our boast: our conscience[24] testifies that we have conducted*

---

[24] Greek: "suneidēsis" (συνείδησις). This word literally means "a knowing with." It describes the human conscience; the internal measure of right and wrong everyone has. Conscience is a wonderful gift from God—private, personal, and persistent. A biblically informed conscience is a priceless possession.

ourselves in the world, and especially in our relations with you, with integrity and godly sincerity" (2 Corinthians 1:12).

This is our introduction to the term *"boast"* in Second Corinthians. Paul will repeat it a total of sixteen times.[25] It sounds strange. After all, spiritual leaders are supposed to be humble. Braggarts are universally scorned. But reluctantly, Paul chooses this form of self-defense — and for good reason.

Itinerant and self-righteous Jewish Christian preachers, perhaps from Jerusalem, have infiltrated the congregation at Corinth. They have stirred up some already disgruntled members of the church. Together, this defiant minority has launched a hostile attack on the credibility of the now-absent founder of the church, the Apostle Paul himself. They are demanding proof of his authenticity, making baseless accusations against him.

One of his opponents' nastiest attacks was the allegation of duplicity, i.e., speaking or acting in different ways to different people concerning the same matter. If someone suggests that you are duplicitous, they are charging you with not meaning what you say or saying what you mean. You are not what you claim to be. You are a double-dealer. To be accused of duplicity is to take a direct hit to your integrity. You've been torpedoed.

Some Christians are inclined to be cynical. They subscribe to all kinds of conspiracy theories, such as the notion that the moon landing in 1969 was filmed at a secret military facility somewhere in Nevada. Neil Armstrong was a big liar.

People like this presume that others cannot always be trusted. Sometimes in the most incidental things they see big cover-ups. In Paul's case, it was a simple change of travel plans that triggered their suspicions. He'd told the Corinthians that he planned to come see them, and then later modified those intentions (1 Corinthians 16:5-8).

---

[25] See 2 Corinthians 10:8, 13-17; 11:12, 16-18, 21, 30; 12:1, 5-6.

Instead of coming for two short stop-overs on his way to and from Macedonia, he would stay for a single extended visit. No big deal, right? But Paul's adversaries jumped on this as a serious lapse in fidelity. He had no choice but to explain himself. Underlying the entire interchange were the serious unresolved tensions between Paul and the church as a whole.[26]

---

[26] Another brief summary of Paul's relations with the Corinthians is in order here. It is a tentative reconstruction of his visits, letters, and the dispatch of envoys to the congregation: Paul arrives in Corinth for the first time from northern Greece and most directly, from Athens (Acts 18:1-18) around 51 AD (dates are approximate). He stays for a year and a half, planting the church and then departs in 53 or 54 AD to visit Jerusalem and return to his home-base church in Antioch, Syria. Sometime later, he goes to Ephesus in the Roman province of Asia for three years of evangelizing and teaching (Acts 19:1-41). During this time he hears rumors of sexual immorality in the Corinthian church, some 250 miles to the west, across the Aegean Sea. He writes them a letter about it (1 Corinthians 5:9). Sometime later, he hears more rumors about misconduct in Corinth. Then, some concerned congregants write him a letter asking for counsel on an extended range of serious troubles (1 Corinthians 7:1). The letter is hand-delivered by three members of the church (1 Corinthians 16:17). Paul writes First Corinthians in answer to their questions. But, the response of the church to his counsel was less than enthusiastic. Some had become arrogant and rebellious towards him, evidently stirred up by intruders seeking to usurp his authority and establish their own (1 Corinthians 4:18). This alliance became a vocally defiant minority of the congregation's members. News of a growing revolt reaches Paul. In response, he makes an emergency trip to Corinth (2 Corinthians 2:1; 12:14, 21; 13:1-2). While there, an individual in the congregation publicly insulted him and challenged his spiritual authority. All the while, the rest of the church members just sat and watched, doing nothing to stand up for the man who had led them to Christ. Paul subsequently refers to the experience as a *"painful visit"* (2 Corinthians 2:1). In defeat, he returns to Ephesus, abandoning his original plan to see them on the way to and from churches in northern Greece (2 Corinthians 1:16). He writes a stinging rebuke for their failure to defend him against his critics. This is the so-called "stern letter" that some scholars have equated with 2 Corinthians 10-13. It was delivered by Titus probably sometime in 55 AD. Later that same year, Paul leaves Ephesus for Troas, 100 miles to the north, where great evangelistic opportunities presented themselves (2 Corinthians 2:12). But, Titus, expected to meet Paul there with news from Corinth, doesn't arrive. Overcome with anxiety about the impact of his

Criticism is the noxious result of suspicion. As leaders, our worst critics are the individuals who don't know us well. That's why they don't trust us. And that's why they talk negatively about us. One of the best ways to prevent unfair disapproval in the first place is to build trusting relationships.

When people we lead start to question our motives, and talk about it, this is an indication of a serious lapse in rapport. At this stage of distrust none of us can ignore the gossip. If confidence is to be restored, we must clear the air.

Fundamental to successfully standing up for ourselves is the conviction that our conscience is clear. While a clear conscience in itself is not evidence of innocence; it is essential to personal credibility (1 Corinthians 4:4).

A clear conscience is a valuable asset when it comes to conflict and accusations of misconduct. It happened to me once. I pledged to the small church I was pastoring that if any of them was ever in the hospital, they could expect a personal visit from me. On one occasion a church member was in the hospital and I didn't go see her. She was disappointed and hurt at my absence. She didn't hesitate to share her frustration with some of her friends in the congregation. They were shocked to hear that I'd broken my promise. But, I didn't break my promise. No one told me she was in the hospital. Still, I was accused of not meaning what I said. But, my conscience was clear. I had done

---

"stern letter," Paul makes his way to Macedonia in hopes of finding Titus or at least hearing news of his mission. Finally, they reconnect. It was a mixed report. The compliant majority of the Corinthian congregation had disciplined Paul's "offender" (2 Corinthians 2:5-11; 7:6-16), belatedly demonstrating their loyalty to him. Still, staunch opposition to his leadership was perpetuated by the interlopers seeking to usurp him. Second Corinthians is Paul's response to this on-going assault on his methods and motives. It was sometime between 55 and 56 AD. He tells the church that he will soon arrive for a third visit and set matters straight, whatever it takes (2 Corinthians 13:1-4). This visit did happen as recorded by Luke in Acts 20:2-3. Paul stayed three months, suggesting that the letter and the visit were successful.

no wrong. Once I had explained myself, all was forgiven. But, what if I hadn't kept my promise? My conscience would have been nagging me, my integrity compromised, and my self-defense weakened.

Paul treasured his clear conscience. It had always served him well. One time, when he was falsely accused and arrested in Jerusalem for allegedly bringing a gentile into the inner court of the Temple, Luke records his defense against the accusation. *"Paul looked straight at the Sanhedrin and said, 'My brothers, I have fulfilled my duty to God in all good[27] conscience to this day'"* (Acts 23:1). Later, he couples a clear conscience with the capacity to love others. *"The goal of this command is love, which comes from a pure heart and a good conscience and a sincere faith"* (1 Timothy 1:5).

The apostle warns that catastrophic consequences are in store for those who don't keep their consciences clear. He encouraged Timothy to hold on to faith and a good conscience, and warns, *"Some have rejected these and so have suffered shipwreck in regard to the faith"* (1 Timothy 1:19). Peter links a clear conscience to an effective witness. *"Keeping a clear conscience, so that those who speak maliciously against your good behavior in Christ may be ashamed of their slander"* (1 Peter 3:16).

A clear conscience is inextricably connected with sincerity. Something is sincere if it passes the test of close examination. Look at yourself in the bright lights of your bathroom mirror—what you get is what you see. The proof of sincerity is conduct.

Paul extends his own integrity to include Silas, Timothy, Titus, Luke, and his entire apostolic team. *"Now this is our boast. Our conscience testifies that we have conducted ourselves in the world, and in*

---

[27] Typically, while we refer mostly to a "clear" conscience, biblical writers sometimes speak of a "good" conscience. There is probably not a significant difference between the two terms. A clear conscience *is* a good conscience.

our relations with you, with integrity and godly sincerity" (2 Corinthians 1:12).

I've observed that sometimes the reputations of lead pastors in a local church have been tainted by the misbehavior of various members of their staffs. If those around us are deficient in integrity, sooner or later, ours will come under fire too. We can't afford to surround ourselves with individuals whose life style does not verify their holiness. Guilt by association can, and must be, avoided. Paul's record stands for itself. He will later confidently say, "*Unlike so many, we do not peddle the word of God for profit. On the contrary, in Christ we speak before God with sincerity, as those sent from God"* (2 Corinthians 2:17).

If you can call God himself as witness to your conduct, you've got integrity. This kind of a clear conscience is attributable to our earnest response to his enabling grace. *"We have done so, not relying on worldly wisdom*[28] *but on God's grace"* (2 Corinthians 1:12). It is this virtue that Paul boasts about throughout Second Corinthians. He says, "*For I am the least of the apostles and do not even deserve to be called an apostle, because I persecuted the church of God. But by the grace of God I am what I am, and his grace to me was not without effect"* (1 Corinthians 15:9-10).

---

[28] Greek: "sophia sarkikē" (σοφία σαρκικῇ). This phrase is literally translated "fleshly wisdom." Here we find a fundamental flaw in the Corinthian congregation. For some reason, they considered themselves wise. But it was wisdom characterized by the values and standards of the pagan culture around them. "Sarkikē" is the polar opposite of "pneumatikē"; i.e., spiritual wisdom from the Holy Spirit himself. Paul confronts the Corinthians with this serious deficiency early in his correspondence with them. "*Brothers and sisters, I could not address you as people who live by the Spirit but as people who are still worldly—mere infants in Christ"* (1 Corinthians 3:1). Their worldliness was the root of all their problems and spiritual immaturity. Worldly wisdom is self-serving shrewdness, motivated by the desire for personal gain. There is nothing of God's grace in it; what he has done and his continuing enablement is no factor in such a disposition and its resultant conduct. Paul labels it foolishness. *"Has not God made foolish the wisdom of the world?"* (1 Corinthians 1:20)

It is permissible, and important, that each of us take pride in having a clear conscience and being exemplary in our conduct. It's only under the pressure of disapproval that we may have to mention it. But, when necessary, we will draw attention to what God has been doing in our lives. After all, we are his workmanship (Ephesians 2:10).

Having attempted to re-establish his credibility with the Corinthians, Paul now addresses the specific charges against him. Richard Nixon's deceit regarding the Watergate scandal in 1972 introduced "credibility gap" into our national vocabulary. But for us, there should be no discontinuity between what we say and what we do. Paul will not let such insinuations against him remain unanswered. *"For we do not write you anything you cannot read or understand"* (2 Corinthians 1:13).

Reading between the lines is typically risky business. Suspicious people do it as a matter of course. They assume that there must be something being said besides what's being said. While words serve to reveal what we are thinking, they can also be used to conceal what we are thinking. We sometimes say what is sociably acceptable, leaving things not so agreeable unsaid. Doing that for self-serving purposes is a bad habit to get into. Paul doesn't go there. He is a truth-teller and a promise-keeper. Of course, his critics claim he is anything but forthright.

Spiritual anarchists are unscrupulous; they attack your character. Paul is accused by his competitors of being two-faced, like Batman's nemesis Harvey Dent, Gotham City's clean-cut district attorney who is not what he appears to be. Paul is charged with saying one thing and meaning another, of being one thing in one situation and something else in another. But, he's not the villain he's alleged to be. In the face of such allegations, he doesn't hesitate to testify in his own defense.

The apostle's detractors are claiming that his letters and his personal presence are contradictory. Paul assures the Corinthians that there is no credibility gap in either who he is, or what he says — in letter or in person. It is, in fact, his accusers who are duplicitous.

I have known church members so jaded in their perception of me that they misconstrued virtually everything I said. It got so bad once that we had to hire a professional mediator to come in to assist the elders and me to be reconciled to our distrustful brothers and sisters. When we satisfactorily defended ourselves against their charges, the mediator asked if they accepted what we had to say. Did they believe we were innocent? They sheepishly replied, "Yes, but they *could* have done it."

Paul insists that he didn't, and couldn't have done, what he was being accused of doing. Again, he says *"we"* (2 Corinthians 2:17), because he and his coworkers share the same integrity. We can stand tall when we are able to speak truthfully for ourselves and those who are partners in leadership with us.

Despite the hostile temperament of his adversaries, Paul never stops hoping for reconciliation with them and the entire congregation. *"And I hope that, as you have understood us in part, you will come to understand fully that you can boast of us just as we will boast of you in the day of the Lord Jesus"*[29] (2 Corinthians 1:13-14).

Keep in mind, this controversy over leadership credibility has divided the Corinthian church. There was a defiant minority, egged on by newly arrived, self-serving Jewish Christian preachers. And then, there was the majority of the membership who were vacillating

---

[29] First century Christians were incurably eschatological. They lived each day as if were their last, ever cognizant of the fact that the old world order was on its way out and the new one was at the door. Such a mentality became a part of their daily talk. This is an example. There was anticipated joy, and sobering recognition of final accountability. *"For we must all appear before the judgment seat of Christ, so that each of us may receive what is due us for the things done in the body, whether good or bad"* (2 Corinthians 5:10). Both attitudes were a settled part of their way of thinking and conversation.

between believing the accusations of Paul's critics and what they knew to be true of him from years of personal experience. Regrettably, this was typical behavior for a congregation infamous for quarreling over which of their leaders was the best (1 Corinthians 1:11-12).

The Corinthian Christians were easily impressed with superficial credentials, like pedigree, education, speaking skills, and even physical appearance. This characteristic exposed their spiritual immaturity. Paul has confronted them about it before. *"You are still worldly. For since there is jealousy and quarreling among you, are you not worldly? Are you not acting like mere humans? For when one says, 'I follow Paul,' and another, 'I follow Apollos,' are you not mere human beings?"* (1 Corinthians 3:3-4)

Had they outgrown such childishness, the conflict between Paul and the recently arrived intruders could have been avoided altogether. They would have backed their apostle and set his adversaries straight—from the start. Paul is still hoping that they will recover their confidence in him and become his staunch advocates once again.

Unresolved tension notwithstanding, the apostle takes every opportunity he can to assure the congregation of how much he values the relationship they already have and to express his desire that it will one day be restored to full harmony. For now, he urges the teetering congregants to give him the benefit of the doubt. He acknowledges that they have only partially understood each other. But, there's hope for renewed understanding and devotion—if they'll give him the chance. It is this restoration of the congregation's unified confidence in him that is the essential purpose of this entire letter.

I've noticed that once church members are disappointed, offended, or hurt by their spiritual leaders, they often calcify in their resistance towards them. From then on, everything the leaders say or do is viewed as further confirmation of their untrustworthiness. No benefit of the doubt is extended. They are ready to file for divorce.

Relationships depend on trust. How joyful it is when grace is extended, forgiveness is granted, and impasses are overcome. Then leaders and followers alike can genuinely boast about one another. So, if you are a follower, verbalize your approval of your leaders. If you are a leader express your appreciation of your followers. Let's join Paul in calling our church members *"My joy and crown"* (Philippians 4:1). Done right, boasting is good. We boast about them; they boast about us. Win-win!

It is always tragic when Christians part company never to be reconciled again. Pretty silly really, since someday we will be living together for eternity. So, why are we waiting until we get to Heaven to work things out? What our stubborn pride needs is an injection of undiluted grace. The alternatives are scary. *"God opposes the proud but shows favor to the humble"* (James 4:6; 1 Peter 5:5). And make no mistake, the Day of the Lord will expose every instance of misconduct and every misguided motivation of our hearts. Paul's mention of it here (2 Corinthians 1:14) is an inferential warning to both his critics and those who are entertaining their accusations.

Not one to tip-toe around conflict, Paul addresses the specifics of the allegations against him. He is not a liar. *"Because I was confident of this, I planned to visit you first so that you might benefit[30] twice"* (2 Corinthians 1:15). His original itinerary included a stopover in Corinth on his way to Macedonia and once again on his return. Paul acknowledges that he postponed that planned visit. His reasons, though, were motivated by pastoral concern not personal convenience. *"I call God as my witness – and I stake my life on it – that it was in order to spare you that I did not return to Corinth"* (2 Corinthians

---

[30] Greek: "charis" (χάρις). This term is typically translated as "grace." It is anything that affords pleasure or delight. Here, Paul uses it to describe the sweetness of Christian fellowship.

1:23). The Corinthians needed to make some decisions – were they going to be loyal to him or take up with his antagonists? They needed some time to think it over. Paul accommodated them. Predictably though, his enemies twisted this polite concession so that it appeared to be inconsiderate and self-serving.

Paul further explains. *"I wanted to visit you on my way to Macedonia and to come back to you from Macedonia, and then to have you send me on my way to Judea"* (2 Corinthians 1:16). His initial plan was to go directly from Ephesus to the cities of northern Greece; Philippi and Thessalonica in particular. For the reasons stated above, he opted instead for a single extended visit to Corinth, rather than two short ones. *"After I go through Macedonia, I will come to you...Perhaps I will stay with you a while, or even spend the winter, so that you can help me on my journey, wherever I go"* (1 Corinthians 16:5-6).

The apostle appeals to those whose ears are being bent by his adversaries. *"Was I fickle when I intended to do this? Or do I make my plans in a worldly manner so that in the same breath I say, 'Yes, yes' and 'No, no?'"* (2 Corinthians 1:17). He repudiates indictments of flip-flopping. If a simple change of plans means a person is duplicitous, then any chance of trusting rapport goes up in smoke. Paul says what he means and means what he says. He does not need to cross his heart and hope to die. Or stick a needle in his mother's eye. Authentic spiritual leaders do not tell people what they want to hear, or manipulate them with half-truths and flattery. We speak the truth in love (Ephesians 4:15). That's what integrity does.

RATIONALE

The charge of duplicity is especially repugnant to the apostle because it is so out of character with God himself. *"But as surely as*

God is faithful,[31] *our message to you is not 'Yes' and 'No'"* (2 Corinthians 1:18). As God is faithful, Paul is faithful.

Leaders with integrity actualize[32] the character of God; they embody and personify it. It will take more than contrived charges about insignificant decisions to detract from the reputation of one whose character is modeled after God himself. The testimony of Paul's life is credible because God is its source. There is no credibility gap.

Periodically with Paul, the turn of a phrase catapults him into a spontaneous doxology. That happens here. He gets Christological. It is a fitting amen to everything he's been saying. *"For the Son of God, Jesus Christ, who was preached among you by us – by me and Silas and Timothy – was not 'Yes' and 'No,' but in him it has always been 'Yes'"* (2 Corinthians 1:19). Jesus sends no mixed message to the world. He is the unequivocal affirmation of every promise God has ever made. *"For no matter how many promises God has made, they are 'Yes' in Christ. And so through him the 'Amen'*[33] *is spoken by us to the glory of God"* (2 Corinthians 1:20). Like D.L. Moody is famous for saying, "God never made a promise too good to be true."[34] Jesus guarantees that. Christ

---

[31] Unlike English, sentence syntax in Koiné Greek is flexible. This is especially helpful in making your point more powerfully. In the original text Paul says, "faithful is God." The first word in the sentence is the one that gets the stress. It's kind of like Yoda saying to Luke Skywalker, "Afraid you are."

[32] This term is used by Michael J. Gorman in his book, *Elements of Biblical Exegesis,* in reference to the intended result of biblical research. The exegete lives out the text being interpreted; we become a walking, talking exegesis of God's Word for all to read.

[33] This universal exclamation is transliterated into multiple languages from the Hebrew and Greek "amen" which means "let it be." Christ is the Amen of God. *"These are the words of the Amen, the faithful and true witness, the ruler of God's creation"* (Revelation 3:14).

[34] brainyquote.com/quotes/quotes/d/dwightlmo157634ht-ml. Accessed November 24, 2015.

is living proof that God can be trusted. That should cause us all to burst into praise.

RESOURCES

For Paul, theology is always applied theology. Doxology translates into reality. *"Now it is God who makes both us and you stand firm in Christ"* (2 Corinthians 1:21). The character of God can be relied upon. In fact, everything depends on it. Together, Christian followers and their leaders are established in their faith; they stand firm. Not tentative. Not tottering.

In his short but insightful commentary on Ephesians, Watchman Nee divides the six chapters of that letter into three categories, which becomes the title of his book, *Sit, Walk, Stand.*[35] The Christian life begins with what God has done. Nee says the first half of Ephesians outlines what it means to be seated in heavenly places with Christ (Ephesians 2:6). Before we do anything for God, we should rest in what he has done for us. We should sit. Once our mental assurance is fully established — that by grace we are saved through faith, not of ourselves — then it is time for us to get up and walk; living our lives for Christ. But, there's one more thing to consider; we sit, we walk, and then, we stand.

> *Finally, be strong in the Lord and in his mighty power. Put on the full armor of God so that you can take your stand against the devil's schemes...so that when the day of evil comes, you may be able to stand your ground, and after you have done everything, to stand.* (Ephesians 6:10-11, 13)

The conflict between flesh and blood and unseen spiritual powers has been raging in Corinth. Paul's earnest concern is that when the dust settles, both he and the Corinthians will be on their

---

[35] Nee, Watchman. *Sit, Walk, Stand.* Carol Stream, IL: Tyndale House Publishers, 1977.

feet, firmly established in their faith. He has admonished them along these lines before. *"Therefore, my dear brothers and sisters, stand firm. Let nothing move you"* (1 Corinthians 15:58).

Spiritual stability is accomplished by a synergy between us and God. We *"work out"* our salvation with fear and trembling, and he brings to completion the *"good work"* he has begun in us (Philippians 2:12; 1:6). We can be confident of this because, as Paul points out here, *"He anointed us"*[36] (2 Corinthians 1:21). Like Christ, we are chosen and we are empowered. We are anointed ones.

Not only are we empowered by God, we have been authenticated by him. He has *"Set his seal of ownership on us, and put his Spirit in our hearts as a deposit, guaranteeing what is to come"* (2 Corinthians 1:22). Paul loves to talk of such assurance.

> *And you also were included in Christ when you heard the message of truth, the gospel of your salvation. When you believed, you were marked in him with a seal, the promised Holy Spirit, who is a deposit guaranteeing our inheritance until the redemption of those who are God's possession – to the praise of his glory.* (Ephesians 1:13-14)

I'm a long time client of my auto insurance company. I won't mention it by name, but let's just say they've been like a good neighbor to me for a long time. Because of the length of my loyalty to them and my good driving record, I received a letter a while back assuring me that they would never deny me insurance coverage. The Holy Spirit is like that for us. God will keep his promises; it's guaranteed. Paul calls this assurance a *"deposit."*[37] The indwelling

---

[36] Greek: "chriō" (χρίω). The verb *"anointed"* describes the consecration of Jesus to his messianic office. "The Christ" means "the anointed one."

[37] Greek: "arrabōn" (ἀρραβῶν). This legal term was common in first century documents. It describes the initial installment payment, guaranteeing that the balance is sure to follow. It is used in modern-day Greek for an engagement ring.

presence of the Holy Spirit is a mark of ownership and authenticity resonating *"in our hearts"* (2 Corinthians 1:22).

I was privileged to pastor the same church for twenty years. For the second half of those two decades I was loved and appreciated by virtually everyone in the congregation. But that wasn't always the case. Twenty years earlier the pastor of our church had resigned. My wife and I were members. Our kids were in the youth group. I was one of the elders. When it was suggested that I take the pastor's place, I politely declined. Then one Sunday when we came to church, everyone was wearing big green buttons with bold black type that read "Jim Crain for Pastor." I was flattered, but shrugged it off. But the groundswell for the prospect of my becoming the church's next pastor kept growing, championed by one of the deacons. Finally, I accepted their confidence in me and took the job. Less than two years later, though, that same deacon instigated a campaign to get rid of me. He wasn't as happy with my leadership as he thought he'd be. It got nasty. False accusations about me were flying. Phone lines were buzzing. Anonymous letters were being sent to the members of the congregation suggesting that I was destroying the church. Finally, a congregational vote was taken and despite all the charges against me, I was confirmed by a vast majority of the membership to continue on as their pastor, worthy of their love and respect. My integrity was verified. My ministry, endorsed. My sincerity, substantiated. In time, all of my disgruntled opponents were gone.

THINK

1. What are your chances of being approved and appreciated by 100% of the people you lead and serve?

2. How do you respond to disapproval? Does it make a difference if the criticism you get is deserved? What if it's unfair?

3. Do you function well under the watchful eye of critical people?

4. Are you a critical person yourself?

5. What is the secret to standing up to unkind criticism?

6. Everybody has critics. True or false?

7. What preventive measure can we take to minimize criticism from people we live and work with?

8. When confronted with unfair disapproval, what should we always do?

9. What role does a clear conscience play in withstanding unfair criticism?

10. What three resources has God provided to enable us to maintain our sincerity despite unfair criticism?

ACT

1. If you are overly dependent on the approval of others, find a trusted friend and confess your sin. Ask the person to hold you accountable, agreeing to meet with them once a month for a check-up.

2.   Examine your conscience on a daily basis; if it is not clear, confess your sins to God (1 John 1:9). Determine to listen to, and follow, the voice of the Holy Spirit.

3.   Make a list of your known, or suspected, critics. Commit yourself to pray for them every day. Then set up an appointment with each of them to have lunch or coffee, just to get to know each other better.

4.   Tolerate no credibility gap between what you say and do. Say what you mean, mean what say. Ask your colleagues to point out any perceived discrepancies they observe.

5.   On a daily basis, humbly repeat to yourself, "I am God's anointed servant."

Chapter 3

Courageous Confrontation

2 Corinthians 1:23-2:11

As an adolescent, my middle daughter was a wisp of a thing. At one hundred pounds dripping wet and wearing size two clothes, she was petite. But, there was a brave soul in that diminutive body. One day she shocked us all when she confronted a total stranger, double her body weight and a good foot taller.

The family was in San Francisco for the day. We were standing in a long line waiting for a cable car to take us from Market Street to Fisherman's Wharf. Out of nowhere, a big burly bruiser and his girlfriend walked right past us and cut into the front of the queue. Everyone saw it. No one did anything about it. My daughter asked, "Dad, did you see that?!" I did, but I wasn't going to risk life and limb confronting the tattooed trespasser. I just stood there and fumed. Before any of us knew it, off my daughter went, striding up to this guy and confronting him with his rude selfishness. He was stunned. We were stunned.

Two things happen when we are courageous enough to confront people with their bad behavior. First, it proves that we care about those being mistreated and those doing the mistreating. Second, we make it clear that justice is important. If the occasion demands it, we are not willing to look the other way. We take the risk of doing something. This doesn't imply that we are free to start minding other people's business. It doesn't give us license to evaluate the conduct of everyone we know. We are not vigilantes. We are not probation officers. But we are concerned citizens. When someone we love is hurting someone else we love, or themselves, we act. We know what kinds of behavior to confront, and when and how to do it.

WHEN TO CONFRONT

The first test in the confrontation process is to ascertain when confrontation is called for. Not all conduct requires intervention. For starters, the observed behavior needs to be sinful. Is someone's misconduct a clear-cut violation of Scripture?

When God has not prohibited or commanded certain behavior, we are all free to follow our conscience. You may have valid reasons to be alarmed about choices your Christ-following friends make when it comes to such decisions, but those things are between them and their own sense of right and wrong. Matters of conscience don't call for confrontation. Note too, that we are talking about the conduct of professed Christians. While the sinful behavior of nonbelievers may give us due cause for concern, their lifestyle decisions are not our responsibility. Paul asks, *"What business is it of mine to judge those outside the church? Are you not to judge those inside? God will judge those outside"* (1 Corinthians 5:12-13). But, let's be clear about it; we are to judge those on the inside, if and when they need it.

A collateral stipulation in identifying behavior requiring confrontation is to confirm that the transgression is ongoing and the person doing it is unrepentant about it. Paul encountered precisely such a situation in Corinth. One of the members of the church was having sex with his stepmother. He was not making any effort to hide it. Or repent of it. By all appearances, the two of them were flaunting it. It was a conspicuous parade of contempt for God's will. Paul says, *"It is actually reported that there is sexual immorality among you, and of a kind that even pagans do not tolerate: a man is sleeping with his father's wife"* (1 Corinthians 5:1). Exasperated, he protests. *"And you are proud! Shouldn't you rather have gone into mourning?"* (1 Corinthians 5:2)

Indisputable, continuous, unrepentant violations of Scripture do not call for tolerance; they call for intervention. Contemporary Christians often seem to be complacent about things that God condemns. Paul challenges that mentality. *"Your boasting is not good. Don't you know that a little yeast works through the whole batch of dough?"* (1 Corinthians 5:6) Serious sins require severe consequences. *"Expel the wicked person from among you"* (1 Corinthians 5:13).

It is just this type of disciplinary shock treatment; i.e., excommunication, that we are trying to forestall when we confront people with their sinful misconduct. That's why we are confronting them — for their own well-being and for the health of the whole church. We start by asking the right questions. Is the behavior an undeniable violation of Scripture? Is the sinful conduct ongoing and unrepentant?

I met with a man every week for nearly two years to help him save his marriage. He didn't love his wife, but he knew he should. He wanted to love her, but he didn't. He was trying. Then he fell in love with a woman at work — and stopped trying. One day he told me that he was going to divorce his wife and marry his co-worker. I said, "You can't do that!" He had no biblical cause to end his marriage.[38] He said, "I don't care. God will have to forgive me or kill me, but I'm going to do it anyway." He did. He was through with doing what was right.

Who doesn't struggle with sin? Sometimes it's the same sins, for years. That doesn't call for confrontation. It calls for compassion, encouragement, and commitment from those who love us. It's when we have become hardened to transformation and resistant to assistance that we are candidates for church discipline.

---

[38] *"I tell you that anyone who divorces his wife, except for marital unfaithfulness, and marries another woman, commits adultery."* (Matthew 19:9)

The school where I teach is a Christian university. We have a Student Handbook that spells out the behavioral standards expected of every student enrolled. It constrains them from things like using tobacco, alcohol or drugs. Sexual promiscuity is prohibited, on campus or off. Homosexual conduct is not condoned.

It's not as though students don't wrestle with these temptations; they do. But, those who are working to overcome admitted weaknesses are not expelled from school. They acknowledge their problem, pledge to keep working on it, and are willing to commit themselves to counsel and accountability. We work with them, even when they periodically slip up. They are repentant. If they are not, then it's time for discipline.

The sexual impropriety going on in Corinth qualified for confrontation. It was scandalous and flagrant. The sinners' impudence, like leaven, had the potential of spreading throughout the entire church. It was time for resolute intervention. But the followers and their leaders weren't up to the task. Paul, at his apostolic best, steps in. He declares,

> *For my part, even though I am not physically present, I am with you in spirit. As one who is present with you in this way, I have already passed judgment in the name of our Lord Jesus on the one who has been doing this. So when you are assembled and I am with you in spirit, and the power of our Lord Jesus is present, hand this man over to Satan for the destruction of the flesh, so that his spirit may be saved on the day of the Lord.* (1 Corinthians 5:3-5)

HOW TO CONFRONT: DISCREETLY

Spiritual leaders with integrity know when to confront—and how to confront. From the start, Corinth was an unruly congregation. On more than one occasion, and concerning multiple issues, confrontation was called for. Paul had the wisdom to know what to do. Or to refrain from doing it. *"I call God as my witness—and I stake my life on it— that it was in order to spare you that I did not return to*

Corinth" (2 Corinthians 1:23). The apostle puts himself under oath.[39] It would be flippant for him to say, "So help me, God!" But that's the spirit of it.

Timing is everything when it comes to the disciplinary exercise of spiritual authority. The right discipline at the wrong time will not work. As their father in the faith, Paul knows the Corinthians all too well. He knows they are quite capable of being rebellious and obstinate. In his first letter he faced them with their recalcitrance. *"What do you prefer? Shall I come to you with a rod of discipline, or shall I come in love and with a gentle spirit?"* (1 Corinthians 4:21).

If a situation calls for action, we must be determined enough to implement it. Paul's motivation is to be helpful, not harmful. The apostle has delayed his return to Corinth to give the church a chance to change their attitude. Later, he will be less congenial. *"I already gave you a warning when I was with you the second time. I now repeat it while absent: On my return I will not spare those who sinned earlier or any of the others, since you are demanding proof that Christ is speaking through me"* (2 Corinthians 13:2-3).

HOW TO CONFRONT: HUMBLY

Abuse of spiritual authority cannot be condoned. The exercise of it is no excuse to be domineering. Paul knows that. *"Not that we lord it over your faith, but we work with you for your joy"* (2 Corinthians 1:24).

Leaders with integrity have no inordinate desire to dominate people. It is never a matter of "my way or the highway." Spiritual authority is not about tearing people down; it's about building them up. Paul later says, *"This is why I write these things when I am absent, that when I come I may not have to be harsh in my use of authority – the*

---

[39] There's a subtle bravado to Paul's statement here. He implies that he is willing to *"call God"* to testify against him if he's not telling the truth. Interestingly, the verb he chooses here is the same one he used when he appealed to Caesar for justice in Acts 25:11.

authority the Lord gave me for building you up, not for tearing you down" (2 Corinthians 13:10).

We don't lord it over people, we work with them. *"But we work with you for your joy, because it is by faith that you stand firm"* (2 Corinthians 1:24). Good leaders walk alongside their followers; they don't drag them from the front, or prod them from behind. Faith is not demanded; it's encouraged.

After all, Christian followers and their leaders alike, live in the freedom of God's grace. That liberty presumes autonomy. At the same time, it is not an independent latitude, but rather, an interdependent one. Paul says *"we work with[40] you"* (2 Corinthians 1:24). Such synergy presumes that two things put together are stronger than either of them can be separately. Ask any carpenter, two 2x4s nailed together are stronger than one 4x4. Christian community is synergistic. Leaders with integrity work with the people under their influence until they can *"stand firm"* (2 Corinthians 1:24). We are strong—together. The result is *"joy"*[41] (2 Corinthians 1:24). Nonetheless, working with people sometimes demands that we confront them.

HOW TO CONFRONT: CAREFULLY

Confrontation means to stand in front of, to meet face to face; to encounter someone or something to be dealt with. The word itself is derived from the Latin *confrontāri* which literally means "with foreheads." Hence, we talk about getting in someone's face. Sometimes, it just needs to be done. But, when we butt heads with people whose behavior is sinfully destructive to themselves and to others, we do so carefully. Confrontation is all about discretion. It's

---

[40] Greek: "sunergos" (συνεργός). This word transliterates into English as "synergy," i.e., the interaction of elements that when combined produce an effect that is greater than the sum of the individual parts.

[41] Greek: "chara" (χαρά). This word is a cognate of "charis," the Greek word for "grace."

not something we clumsily rush into. We practice restraint. Paul did. *"So I made up my mind that I would not make another painful visit to you"* (2 Corinthians 2:1). True spiritual leaders do not inflict pain on the people under their care. They do not agitate or aggravate. Confrontation is delicate. It is, therefore, deliberate, carefully considered, and intentional.

When I was a kid, my Aunt Pat had a green parakeet she called "Budgie." One day while she was out shopping, my cousins and I let Budgie get out of his cage. Immediately, he started flying all over the house, banging himself into everything. We panicked, chasing him from room to room. Things were getting worse. We were tense. The parakeet was tense. Finally though, when Aunt Pat got back, she calmly told us that we were going about it all wrong. She said, "Watch!" Getting down on her hands and knees near Budgie, she slowly extended her index finger, talking to him gently. In less than a minute, the frantic little bird hopped on to her finger and she calmly put him back in his cage. Everyone was relieved.

If you rush a sinning Christian, you will probably make the situation worse. Paul had tried that with the Corinthians, with both his emergency visit and the stern letter he wrote to them. It was a mistake—one he was determined not to repeat. No more clutch visits. No more emergency memos. In tense negotiations, seasoned spiritual leaders stay calm and collected.

I knew a pastor once who was quick to fire off emails to people he was frustrated with. Almost always, it was a mistake. Inevitably, he regretted pushing the "send" button too soon. What he said, and how he said it, was not carefully considered. I've tried to learn from his blunders. Every tense email I'm inclined to write has to wait three days. As you can guess, most of the time it doesn't get sent at all. Or, it is carefully revised.

Leaders with integrity take no satisfaction in putting people in their place. Instead, we pray first. We think first. With Paul we calmly say, *"I made up my mind"* (2 Corinthians 2:1). We weigh our options. We consider our tactics. We concern ourselves with the feelings of others and how to evoke the most positive response from them. What we want to accomplish is increased relief, not intensified grief.

Children need discipline. If we love them we will do it. And, we will do it right. When our kids were little and one of them had a spanking coming, we never disciplined them in front of their brothers and sisters. It was always "Come with me to your room." Once alone, we looked the child in the eye, asked them what they'd done wrong, and if they recognized that they needed to be punished. Then discipline was administered. After that, we hugged them and then rejoined the family. Everyone knew the issue was resolved. It was deliberate. It was calm. It was careful.

HOW TO CONFRONT: EMOTIVELY

When I was a rookie youth pastor, I watched the elders of our church make a mistake. Circumstances had forced them to publicly discipline one of the parishioners. The decision was right. But I questioned their strategy in carrying it out. In a misguided effort to appear authoritative, they decided to show no emotion when they announced their disciplinary action to the congregation. Well, it didn't work. The people concluded that they were coldhearted and insensitive to the offender and his family. It was sad, because they really did care. Their misstep was that they didn't show the people their hearts.

Paul is a welcome contrast to that kind of miscalculation. He openly displays tender vulnerability. *"For if I grieve you, who is left to make me glad but you whom I have grieved?"*[42] (2 Corinthians 2:2). He

---

[42] Scholars debate the specifics of Paul's grief. A common reconstruction of the particulars of this circumstance centers on the immoral man of 1 Corinthians 5. He was having sex with his stepmother and openly flaunting

60

further explains. *"I wrote as I did, so that when I came I would not be distressed by those who ought to make me rejoice. I had confidence in all of you, that you would all share my joy"* (2 Corinthians 2:3). The apostle tells them plainly that his own well-being is bound up with theirs.

Paul's emotional attachment to the Corinthians runs deep. He does not camouflage it. *"For I wrote to you out of great distress and anguish[43] of heart and with many tears, not to grieve you but to let you know of the depth of my love for you"[44]* (2 Corinthians 2:4). Love expresses itself. It wouldn't hurt for us to discreetly tell people of the distress that we are feeling in hopes of reconciliation with them. Authentic confrontation is always an expression of grief. When we face people with their sins, we are ready to let our anguish show — and our tears flow. Paul's words do not indicate wounded pride, but a breaking heart.

The man I mentioned earlier, who was stubbornly divorcing his wife even though he knew it was wrong, left the leadership of the church with no choice but to discipline him. The announcement of his excommunication was to be made to the whole congregation on a Sunday morning. And, even though he had been advised of what was going to happen, in a final display of defiance, there he was that day, sitting in the third row of the auditorium. It was my duty to verbalize the decision that nearly thirty congregational leaders had made to expel him from the church. It was a sad day. The truth was

---

it. The congregation was complicit in the illicit situation by not doing anything about it. Paul took action, insisting that they expel him from the church (1 Corinthians 5:13). In retaliation the man became the leader of the opposition to Paul's authority — doing his best to make his life miserable. This is a possible scenario, but it can't be conclusively verified.

[43] Greek: "sunochē" (συνοχῇ). This term connotes being "choked up." The word comes into Latin as *angere*, meaning to choke; which is the origin of our word anguish.

[44] Just what letter Paul is referencing here is a matter of discussion. Some conclude that it is First Corinthians. Others remain convinced that it is the "stern" letter that is no longer in existence. There are reasonable arguments for both views.

spoken in love. We were grief stricken as he strode angrily out the side door of the sanctuary. For the next several months we found ourselves experiencing what Paul meant when he said, *"If anyone has caused grief, he has not so much grieved me as he has grieved all of you, to some extent — not to put it too severely"* (2 Corinthians 2:5). Sinful, unrepentant Christians hurt themselves and the believing community of which they are a part.

At Corinth Paul was the target of one man's vitriol. The culprit is not identified, but everyone knew who he was. The apostle tries not take the offenses personally. The truth is, everyone is offended by an unrepentant sinner in their midst. Paul pinpoints the problem, but he refrains from overstating it. In almost a footnote, he says *"not to put it too severely"*[45] (2 Corinthians 2:5). He doesn't want to increase the tension of the situation, for the Corinthians or himself. It is a reliable rule of thumb that when we find ourselves reacting to people we lead, instead of responding to the problems they present, we should recuse ourselves from the process of confronting them until we can practice better self-control.

Unrepentant Christians are an affront to the entire church. But, sin in the camp is not seen for what it is by everyone. That's why Paul assesses the grief of the Corinthians with the phrase *"to some extent"* (2 Corinthians 2:5). But, whether everyone recognizes the danger or not, the consequences of un-remedied misconduct will surely be suffered by all. It is the leaders' task to identify the severity of the impropriety and respond appropriately.

HOW TO CONFRONT: COURAGEOUSLY
There are times when minding our own business is wrong. Some Christians purposefully look the other way while foolhardy individuals destroy themselves — and others. This is loveless

---

[45] Greek: "epibareō" (ἐπιβαρέω). The verb which Paul chooses here connotes putting too heavy a load on something or someone.

conduct. Love always does what is in the best interests of another person. We take a risk when we commit ourselves to love someone. There is no guarantee that they will appreciate the intervention they so desperately need. Our efforts may not pay off. Still, we try.

It would have been a temptation for our church to let one of its members divorce the wife he didn't love and marry the woman he did. Sadly, it happens all the time. We want people to be happy, even when we are rightly worried that they won't be. But, if their actions are contrary to the clearly stated obligations of God's Word, any happiness found will be short-lived at best. We lose sight of that sometimes. Or, maybe, we've watched too many movies where sinful people live happily ever after. In that kind of a moral fog, we lose our bearings. And, our nerve. So, we don't do anything while our self-destructive friends walk head-on into irreparable heartache and pain. The wages of sin is death. A church that doesn't discipline errant members doesn't love them. And, the entire congregation will pay the price of such faintheartedness.

In the case of the incestuous sinner at Corinth, Paul stepped in with apostolic authority and insisted that the church expel him (1 Corinthians 5:13). For once, they did what they were told—to *"hand him over to Satan"* (1 Corinthians 5:5). It was a last-ditch effort to save his soul. And, the health of the entire congregation.

A little leaven leavens the whole lump (1 Corinthians 5:6). Paul's insistence that they excommunicate the offender was a test of their compliance. *"Another reason I wrote you was to see if you would stand the test and be obedient in everything"* (2 Corinthians 2:9). This time, they passed. *"The punishment inflicted on him by the majority[46] is sufficient"* (2 Corinthians 2:6). The courage of authentic love often-

---

[46] Some of the church members, perhaps, did not think the discipline was severe enough. Paul assures them that it was. Remarkably, he steps in to defend the guilty party, who may have even been the ringleader of the coup being plotted against his leadership.

times has a happy ending. The risk of resistance, rejection, or increased hostility is taken and the confronted sinner repents. *"Godly sorrow brings repentance that leads to salvation and leaves no regret"* (2 Corinthians 7:10). The punishment was inflicted; the intended result was achieved. Time to celebrate!

HOW TO CONFRONT: LOVINGLY

Authentic love is effortful. And purposeful. We don't just feel something; we do something. Love is the essence and energy of being a Christian; without it, everything else is hollow. *"If I speak in the tongues of men and angels, but have not love, I am only a resounding gong or a clanging cymbal"* (1 Corinthians 13:1). Without love, we gain nothing. *"If I give all I possess to the poor and surrender my body to hardship that I may boast, but do not have love, I gain nothing"* (1 Corinthians 13:3). Without love, we lose our very identity. *"If I have faith that can move mountains, but do not have love, I am nothing"* (1 Corinthians 13:2).

If love isn't our motive and manner when we confront people with their sins, any intervention we try will most likely backfire. Again, we are not seeking the satisfaction of setting someone straight. Our purpose is to restore them. Our intention is to renew their fellowship with God and the church. Prerequisite to reconciliation, though, is repentance. Only then can restoration begin.

The Corinthian offender, whether he was the incestuous man of 1 Corinthians 5, or the ringleader of the defiant minority in the church—or both—has been brought to his knees by disciplinary action. Repentance sufficient for forgiveness is the first step in the restoration process. And, sometimes it's a lengthy one. Love initiates and sustains the energy necessary to complete it.

Once forgiveness is sought and granted, it is time to be gracious. *"Now instead, you ought to forgive[47] and comfort[48] him, so that he will not be overwhelmed by excessive sorrow"* (2 Corinthians 2:7). Too much discipline breaks the sinner's spirit. The appropriate amount breaks their will. Love drives no sinner to despair. Once forgiven, the sins can be forgotten. That takes comfort and encouragement. Love is there to give it — to walk alongside, arm in arm, until the restored ones are once again steady on their feet. This is the essence of Christianity. The one who broke the fellowship is restored to it.

There is such a thing as excessive sorrow. That's what the vengeful citizens of Boston vainly hoped would be Hester Prynne's fate when they sentenced her to wear a scarlet letter as evidence of her sins.[49]

Church discipline is restorative not merely punitive. In the case of the Corinthian offender, the forfeited fellowship was renewed. The prodigal son was out of the pig pen. He's home now. It's time to celebrate. Slaughter the fatted calf. Find an elegant robe and an expensive ring. Come on, big brother, join the fun!

Love has the courage to confront, and to forgive. *"I urge you, therefore, to reaffirm[50] your love for him"* (2 Corinthians 2:8). There are some important principles implied here: if the sin is private, the confrontation and reaffirmation, should be private. If the sin is public, the confrontation should be public. The reaffirmation should be too. And joyful!

---

[47] Greek: "charidzomai" (χαρίζομαι). This verb has the term grace as its root. It is pardon freely given.

[48] Greek: "parakaleō" (παρακαλέω). The noun form of this verb was used by Jesus to describe the Holy Spirit as the one called alongside to comfort and encourage us (John 14:16).

[49] Hawthorne, Nathaniel. *The Scarlet Letter*. Boston: Tricknor, Reed & Fields, 1850.

[50] Greek: "kuroō" (κυρόω). The root of this word means to ratify or confirm publically. The implication is that the Corinthians should make a judicial resolution to treat the repentant sinner with mercy and love.

It should not escape our attention that in this situation Paul has become an advocate for his worst adversary. And that's the point. He has disciplined himself not to take the offense personally, though the pain of the attacks had certainly been real. Like every authentic spiritual leader, he knows the primary bearer of all sin is God himself. The apostle emulates Moses, who said to his stubborn followers, *"You are not grumbling against us, but against the LORD"* (Exodus 16:8).

HOW TO CONFRONT: INTELLIGENTLY

Finally, let's never lose sight of the invisible. The people of God have a powerful and unscrupulous enemy — Lucifer himself. One of Satan's strategies is as time-tested as warfare itself: divide and conquer. The devil knows that if he can get an individual Christian caught up in a web of bad behavior, and at the same time sway the church to do nothing about it, he can claim some new territory. But, if we recognize that tactic and are united in confronting our wayward brothers and sisters — forgiving and restoring them once they come to their senses — then the enemy is repelled. This is military intelligence. Like the war on terrorism; you can't defeat a determined foe unless you know in advance what they are up to. Victory depends on the intelligence that precedes it. Uncover a plot and you prevent a catastrophe.

Paul is an experienced strategist in the incessant conflict between good and evil. He writes, *"In order that Satan might not outwit us. For we are not unaware of his schemes"* (2 Corinthians 2:11). It is crucial that we know what our enemy is up to. His tactics are as simple as they are sinister. His diabolical intention is to defeat Christ by destroying his followers. What the evil one apparently doesn't realize is that he has already lost the war. Still, we can't concede even a single battle.

When it comes to church discipline, it is crucial that we confront sinners when it is called for. We have a strategy too. The sequence to decisive victory entails confrontation that leads to repentance that, in turn, calls for forgiveness. When granted, forgiveness results in restoration.

So far in this particular conflict, the troops on the ground in first century Corinth have been following their field commander's orders. Repentance has been achieved, now the restoration process must be completed. *"Anyone you forgive, I also forgive. And what I have forgiven — if there was anything to forgive — I have forgiven in the sight of Christ for your sake"* (2 Corinthians 2:10).

The forgiveness Paul calls for from the Corinthians, he extends himself. Leading by example, he graciously minimizes the offenses committed against him, though they were anything but minimal. Now, a united clemency must be granted. The apostle makes the process easier by acting like he's unclear about the nature of the offenses against himself and the congregation—but everyone was perfectly aware of what had happened. Still, once someone repents, it's time for amnesty. If he can forgive, they can forgive. They must forgive. In the end, the conflict created by sin is relieved. When it comes to combat with the devil, we do like the contestants on the reality TV show *Survivor*; we "outwit, outlast and outplay."

THINK

1. Is it ever appropriate to involve ourselves in someone else's business?

2. Under what conditions would you assume responsibility to confront an individual about their sinful behavior?

3. What does it mean to confront someone?

4. What two questions must we answer before we confront someone about their sins?

5. List some examples of behavior that could be classified as clear-cut violations of Scripture.

6. What did Paul urge the church to do about the sinner in their midst? Have you ever observed or participated in church discipline? What were the results?

7. Why is it important to confront people carefully?

8. Why is it important to confront people humbly?

9. Why is important to confront people emotively?

10. Why is important to confront people intelligently?

ACT

1. Is there someone within your sphere of influence who is living in conspicuous violation of Scripture and is unrepentant about it? Now, ask God if he wants you to intervene.

2. Meet with the leaders of your church to plan a detailed procedure to follow in the event that you need to excommunicate an errant member of your congregation.

3. Ask a coworker to read this chapter and then give them permission to offer you a candid evaluation of how your leadership style measures up to these biblical standards.

4. How difficult is it for you to express your emotions? Ask someone you know well for feed-back.

5. List the names of people you have not forgiven for sinning against you. Now, take those names to God and grant them absolution for their sins.

Chapter 4

Maximized Competence

2 Corinthians 2:12-3:5

Every four years the premier athletes of the world compete in the Olympics. Those of us glued to the televised   coverage of the Summer and Winter Games are vividly reminded that we are watching the best of the best. In professional athletics, the winners are determined by one-time events, like the Super Bowl. Or by a series of final contests, as in the NBA playoffs, the World Series, the Stanley Cup, or Wimbledon. "March Madness" showcases collegiate basketball excellence. Once a year, music lovers watch the Grammys. The singers, songwriters, musicians, and producers granted the golden gramophone are unsurpassed at what they do. When Hollywood hosts the Academy Awards, the most skillful actors and movie makers in the world are honored with an Oscar.

In every competitive venue or field of artistry, there are people so undeniably talented that they become the standard of excellence for what they do. For example, an aspiring actress may be bluntly told that she's "no Meryl Streep." Steve Jobs was a legend soon after his death. Some individuals are so iconic, a single name is all that's necessary — Leonardo, Michelangelo, Beethoven, Mozart, Edison, and Einstein. They are the epitome of talent, intelligence, discipline, and excellence. They are indisputably competent.

When people are competent they have sufficient knowledge, skill, or experience for some specified purpose; they are properly qualified. Everyone appreciates and respects competence. We know competence when we see it. We long for it ourselves. After all, who wants to be deficient? Or to be thought of as inept? Each of us wants to be capable of doing what is expected of us.

I have a friend who designs computer chips at a Silicon Valley company. Using his influence with management, he landed a job for a mutual friend of ours, doing the same thing. The trouble was that our pal was far from adequate for the task he was hired to do. He used to phone me from his cubicle to say just how petrified he was that someone would figure out that he didn't know what he was doing. But, with some continued coaching, my terrified buddy worked hard and learned fast. Today, he is one of the principal engineers at the same company where he got his tentative start. When it comes to designing computer chips, he's as confident as you can get. He is competent. He is equal to the task.

REMEMBERING OUR PURPOSE

Competency starts with an intended reason for doing something. Every competent person begins with a purpose—including the Apostle Paul. He tells the Corinthians, *"Now when I went to Troas*[51] *to preach the gospel of Christ..."* (2 Corinthians 2:12).

Troas was a beachfront town on the west coast of what is Turkey today. But Paul wasn't going there for R&R. He had more important things in mind. As an evangelist, he had a singular concern—to win people to Christ. We do too. We know the answer to the question Rick Warren asked in the subtitle of his book, *The Purpose Driven Life,* "What on earth are you here for?"[52] In Troas, Paul was at the beach, but for him it was more like a beachhead for the advancement of the gospel. He was a tentmaker by occupation, but a preacher by vocation. He wasn't on the coast to wiggle his toes in the

---

[51] Troas was Luke's hometown. It was the point of departure for the gospel's initial foray into Europe (Acts 16:8-11). It was there that Luke joined Paul's evangelistic team that already included Silas and Timothy.

[52] Warren, Rick. *The Purpose-Driven Life.* Grand Rapids, MI: Zondervan, 2002.

Mediterranean or soak up some summer sun. He was there to preach. That's what excites and rejuvenates him.

In his book, *Conformed to His Image*, Kenneth Boa says that "purpose shapes priorities."[53] When it is our purpose to preach Christ, everything else is secondary. Not that it's wrong to relax at the beach; but, when our mission is evangelism, splashing in the surf just isn't enough fun.

An acquaintance of mine is a successful contractor who has made more than enough money over the years. Every summer he used to treat himself and his wife to an extravagant vacation — cruises and resorts all around the world. He admits it was self-indulgent and expensive. And boring. These days he does his vacations differently; he spends a week or two on some mission field, lending his energy and expertise to help expand God's Kingdom.

Athletes, musicians, actors, entertainers, and entrepreneurs sacrifice everything else to train, practice, plan, study, and rehearse what they are devoted to. It's their purpose that drives them to pay the price to succeed. Spiritual leaders with integrity do the same thing.

But, while it is our focused concern to enlarge the Kingdom of God, our lives should never be out of balance. I heard a high-tech tycoon admit once that though he was enviably successful, he'd lost his family in the process. He was asked if a person could be devoted to their family and devoted to their work too. He said, "No, it's one or the other." But Jesus doesn't ask us to sacrifice our families to preach his gospel. Equilibrium is good. We balance our God-given responsibilities. Still, wherever we go and whatever we do, making disciples of Christ is our highest obligation; spouse and children at our side. Purpose shapes priorities.

---

[53] Boa, Kenneth. *Conformed to His image: Biblical and Practical Approaches to Spiritual Formation*. Grand Rapids, MI: Zondervan, 2001.

My wife and I have some long-time friends who are missionaries in Santiago, Chile. From the start, they have found almost nothing but open doors for the gospel. Not only have hundreds of Chileans been converted to Christ, they are now being commissioned as missionaries themselves, to other countries in South America, Africa, and the Middle East. Every time our friends see a door, they push on it. Most often, it opens. And, through it they go.

When the Apostle Paul arrived in Troas he was convinced that opportunity was knocking. Everything looked ripe for soul-winning success. He testifies that *"The Lord had opened a door for me"* (2 Corinthians 2:12).

God-ordained opportunity is the essential story line of the Book of Acts. As Gordon Fee and Douglas Stuart point out in, *How to Read the Bible for All Its Worth,* Acts is the record of the exciting, joyful, Holy Spirit-empowered advance of the gospel from Jerusalem to Rome.[54] The apostles had a weather eye for evangelistic opportunities. And, they took advantage of them. Inevitably, success followed. Troas was no exception. Once again, God was opening the door. But brace yourself—this time, Paul didn't go through it.

In his best-seller, *The 7 Habits of Highly Effective People,*[55] time-management guru, Steven Covey, has a chapter entitled "First Things First." He talks about four kinds of situations that typically compete for our attention, time, and energy: urgent things, important things, urgent and important things and unimportant things. That observation resonates with most of us because we often find ourselves wasting time and energy on what isn't important at all. One of the biggest challenges we all face is attending to what is

---

[54] Fee, Gordon and Douglas Stuart. *How to Read the Bible for All Its Worth.* Grand Rapids, MI: Zondervan, 1982.

[55] Covey, Steven. *The 7 Habits of Highly Effective People.* Provo, UT: Franklin Covey, 1998.

urgent and important. Preaching the gospel is the ultimate example of that.

In Troas Paul found himself facing responsibilities that were both important and urgent. An open door for evangelism was right in front of him — with virtually guaranteed success. But, at the same time, there was something equally important and urgent he had to deal with. Transparently, the apostle admits that despite the promising opportunity right in front of him, he *"still had no peace of mind"* (2 Corinthians 2:13). He explains why. *"Because I did not find my brother Titus there"* (2 Corinthians 2:13).

We've been surprised to realize that Paul wasn't admired or appreciated by all the Christians at Corinth. Many of them were critical of him. And vocal about it. The rest of the church was wobbling in their commitment to him, even though he'd led most of them to Christ some five years earlier. To address these issues, the apostle had written them a confrontational letter, *"out of great distress and anguish of heart and with many tears"* (2 Corinthians 2:4). But, he'd yet to hear how they were responding to his concerns. Weeks, maybe months, had gone by. No news. So, he dispatched one of his young assistants, Titus, to see what was going on. They had agreed to meet up in Troas. So far though, Titus was a no-show. Paul couldn't wait. Too anxious to sit still, he made a move. *"So I said good-bye to them and went to Macedonia"*[56] (2 Corinthians 2:13).

Paul felt forced to realign his priorities. It wouldn't be implausible to conclude, that to his way of thinking, there was no sense in leading more people to Christ, when the people you've already converted are at risk. But, how can you walk away from a

---

[56] Paul will mention this distress again in 2 Corinthians 7:5 where he reports: *"For when we came into Macedonia, this body of ours had no rest, but we were harassed at every turn — conflicts on the outside, fears within."* In 2 Corinthians 7:6 he calls himself *"downcast"*; i.e., discouraged to the point of depression.

God-given opportunity? Isn't that a higher priority? But then, that's the trouble with priorities; they aren't always easy to line up.

Once the decision was made though, Paul didn't sit around second-guessing himself. Sometimes, doing something is better than doing nothing. So, off he went to complete a prior urgent and important obligation.

REALIZING OUR RESPONSIBILITY

Paul left Troas and headed for Macedonia in northern Greece. Corinth was in southern Greece, but at least he was closer. Finally, he meets up with Titus, who had good news to report. Paul's discouragement was quickly transformed into triumph. *"But thanks be to God, who always leads us in triumphal procession in Christ"* (2 Corinthians 2:14, NIV 1984). As Christian leaders, most of us know that there's always an end to periods of distress and discouragement. Victory is assured — sooner or later. The picture Paul paints to describe his relief is vivid. He calls to mind the Roman Triumph.

In the first century, Rome ruled the world. By brute force they established the *Pax Romana* – the Roman peace. From Spain to India, the empire was kept in order by military might. They expanded and defended their territorial domination with legions of soldiers commanded by courageous and battled-tested generals. When one of those generals returned from a victorious campaign, his reception in the capital was nothing less than jubilant. There was a grand parade through the streets of the city. Leading the way were government officials and members of the senate. Next were musicians. Then came the priests, waving censers of fragrant smoke, followed by the general himself, riding in a chariot, drawn by four white horses. He wore a purple tunic, embroidered with golden palm leaves. In his hand was a scepter with a Roman eagle on the top. After him, came his family. His officers followed next, shouting "Triumph! Triumph!" At the end of the procession, in chains, were the vanquished troops of their conquered opponents. The destination was the Colosseum, where in a few hours they would meet their deaths—all to the cheering of thousands of elated revelers. That's the kind of exuberance Paul was feeling as he gives God the glory for the triumph in his own heart over anxiety and discouragement.

With the imagery of the Roman Triumph still in mind, Paul says that God, *"uses us to spread the aroma of the knowledge of him everywhere"* (2 Corinthians 2:14). Every day, everywhere Christians go, the scent of Christ goes with us. It also ascends to God. *"For we are to God the pleasing aroma of Christ"* (2 Corinthians 2:15). This fragrance emanates from us and among us. But, it is a bittersweet smell. When the pagan priests in the Roman Triumph wafted the smoking incense as the parade marched through the main boulevards of the capital city, the fragrance of triumph was in the air. But, at the same time, it was the odor of death to the defeated enemy soldiers. Each step brought them closer to their certain demise in the arena. The same fragrance indicated both the thrill of victory and the agony of defeat, *"among those who are being saved and those who are perishing"* (2 Corinthians 2:15).[57] The gospel is personified in those of us who live it, and preach it.

Ultimately, there are just two categories of individuals in this world: those who are being saved, and those who are perishing. As Bob Dylan used to sing, "He who is not busy being born is busy dying."[58] Just by being in our presence, non-Christians are confirmed in their spiritual condemnation. *"To the one we are an aroma that brings death"* (2 Corinthians 2:16). When the gospel is

---

[57] The dynamic states of both the lost and the saved are described with present tense participles in the original Greek. But there is one significant distinction. Those who are *"being saved"* are described with a passive participle; i.e., the condition and experience is happening to them. They are receiving it. By contrast, in the case of those who *"are perishing,"* the voice of the participle is active; they are destroying themselves.

[58] Dylan, Bob. "It's Alright, Ma (I'm Only Bleeding)." *Bringing It All Back Home.* Columbia, 1965.

rejected there is a deadly stench, because people are perishing. But, thankfully, what is bitter is also sweet. *"To the other, an aroma that brings life"* (2 Corinthians 2:16).

The responsibility of being the aroma of Christ is sobering. Paul asks, *"And who is equal to such a task?"* (2 Corinthians 2:16). That brings us back to competence. Who is adequate for such an obligation? Who is qualified to play such a role? Who has the sufficient skill, knowledge, and experience for something like that? We are a life-and-death message to everyone we meet. This is our God-ordained destiny. Are we equal to the task?

Some people are clearly incompetent to represent Christ in this world. Paul has a few of them in mind. *"Unlike so many, we do not peddle the word of God for profit"* (2 Corinthians 2:17). Peddlers in the first century were oftentimes fast-talking sellers of cheap merchandise. The intruders at Corinth, stirring up trouble and drawing attention to themselves, fit that description. Paul contrasts himself to them. *"On the contrary, in Christ we speak before God with sincerity,*[59] *as those sent from God"* (2 Corinthians 2:17). Foundational to being leaders with integrity is the fact that we are *"in Christ."* And, that we are *"sent from God."* These are our credentials. This is what commends us to others.

RELYING ON OUR RESOURCES

As a college professor I've written many recommendations for students seeking admission to graduate school or trying to land their first job. I'm glad to do it. A recommendation is an initial kind of credential.

Credentials are evidence of authority, status, and competency. In most professional fields of employment, credentials are crucial.

---

[59] Greek: "eilikrineias" (εἰλικρινείας). This term describes anything that can be held up to bright sunlight and shown to be flawless. It is the essence of spiritual integrity.

When a person's credentials are challenged, it's usually a sign of trouble. Someone has lost confidence in them.

You'd think that Paul would have nothing to prove when it came to his credibility with the Corinthians. After all, he was hand-picked and commissioned by Christ himself. He was an apostle, evangelist, and church planting pastor-teacher par excellence. And yet, they were asking for a letter of recommendation from him. What?! Like us, he's flabbergasted. And indignant. *"Are we beginning to commend ourselves again? Or do we need, like some people, letters of recommendation to you or from you?"* (2 Corinthians 3:1). How could they have forgotten his impact in their lives? *"You yourselves are our letter, written on our hearts, known and read by everybody"* (2 Corinthians 3:2).

I don't know how you prove your competency on your job. Or, what testimonials you would need to convince your employer or your customers, patients, or clients that you are good at what you do. But in the Kingdom of God, the best credentials we can have are the changed lives of the people we've influenced.

My missionary friend in Chile calls me his spiritual father. He came to Christ through my influence (along with many others) when he was a teenager. After decades of service in South America and other parts of the world, he has spiritual children of his own now. Grandchildren too. Once when I was visiting him, we took a quick trip to see some new Christians in the isolated town of Tacna, Peru. After one of the church services, a young Peruvian teenager got the two of us aside. In Spanish she said to me, "If it wasn't for you, he wouldn't be here. And, if it wasn't for him, I wouldn't be here!" After that experience I told God, "Okay, I can die now."

Paul challenges the Corinthians to realize that they themselves are the only recommendation he needs. As childish as they could be, their lives had been changed. He reminds them, *"You yourselves are our letter, written on our hearts, known and read by everyone. You show that you are a letter from Christ, the result of our ministry, written not with ink but with the Spirit of the living God, not on tablets of stone but on tablets of human hearts"* (2 Corinthians 3:2-3). They were the living fulfillment of Jeremiah's ancient prophecy. *"This is the covenant I will make with the people of Israel after that time, declares the LORD. I will put my law in their minds and write it on their hearts"* (Jeremiah 31:33). The apostle tacitly suggests that the imposters in Corinth have no such testimonial.

Paul seldom acts triumphantly, but he does so here. *"Such confidence we have through Christ before God"* (2 Corinthians 3:4). There is no higher letter of recommendation than one written by Christ and co-signed by God. That being said, the apostle quickly resumes his characteristic humility. He knows where his competency comes from. He knows why he is equal to the task to which he has been assigned. *"Not that we are competent in ourselves to claim anything for ourselves, but our competence comes from God"* (2 Corinthians 3:5). And, there you have it. The simple explanation of our success as spiritual leaders is that we are sincere men and women, sent from God.

Perhaps, you've heard of *The Peter Principle*.[60] It's a classic book on leadership by Lawrence J. Peter, based on the premise that something that works will be used in progressively more challenging applications until it fails. In terms of people, in any organization there are individuals who keep getting promoted until they reach their maximum level of incompetence. Sadly, in the process, the organization's hierarchy tends to perpetuate itself, with junior employees being expected to do their work until they reach their own level of incompetence. The disconcerting thing about the Peter Principle is that in time, every post tends to be occupied by someone who isn't up to the job. Ultimately, this incompetency is due to a mismatch of task and talent.

---

[60] Peter, Lawrence J. and Raymond Hull. *The Peter Principle: Why Things Always Go Wrong*. New York: Collins Business, 2009.

Corporate practices have limited application in the Kingdom of God. Presuming that the work of the church, or any Christian enterprise, is ultimately under the supervision of the Holy Spirit himself, the best thing any of us can hope for is that we are equal to the task he has assigned for us to do. Let's take heart. If God has appointed us to something, he will enable us to do it.

I take consolation in the fact that though there are certainly more skilled teachers and preachers than myself, I still have the gifts, knowledge, wisdom, and experience for the tasks to which I have been commissioned. Together with Paul, we can all confidently confirm that *"our competence comes from God"* (2 Corinthians 3:5).

THINK

1. What does it mean to be competent?

2. Make a list of people you consider competent at what they do.

3. Do you consider yourself competent?

4. How important is purpose in becoming competent?

5. What role do priorities play in becoming a competent person?

6. What does Paul mean by calling us *"the aroma of Christ"*?

7. Are you *"the smell of death"* to the non-Christians around you?

8. What enables you to be *"equal to such a task"*?

9. Paul describes some people who were woefully incompetent in representing Christ. How can we avoid their mistakes?

10. What is the best recommendation any of us can have regarding our personal competence?

ACT

1. Ask someone who knows you well to itemize the ways in which you are competent as a spiritual leader. Then ask them to list the areas in which you seem to be incompetent.

2. What evidence can you give to indicate that communicating the gospel is the highest priority in your life?

3. Review the way you have spent your time over the last week. Put each activity into one of Steven Covey's categories: Urgent but Unimportant/Important but not Urgent/Urgent and Important/Unimportant and not Urgent.

4. Plan your next vacation to be one of service on some mission field at home or abroad.

5. Make a list of the individuals who are living credentials of the effectiveness of your ministry. Your life matters!

Chapter 5

The Indispensable Impact of a Godly Face

2 Corinthians 3:6-18

In the first few weeks after 9/11, Americans added a new word to their vocabularies. Before long, we all knew that a "burqa" is the covering Muslim women in some parts of the world wear when they are in public. The garment covers their entire bodies from head to toe; there is only a slit for their eyes. And sometimes not even that, but a mesh-screened veil for them to see through. The woman's identity is concealed from everyone but her family, especially her face.

More than any other aspect of the human anatomy, our faces identify who we are. The rest of our body parts all look more or less the same. But, our faces single us out. They speak volumes about the kind of person we are, revealing our character and the presence or absence of gentleness, sensitivity, honesty, and kindness—all accented by our eyes, "the windows of the soul."[61] Some experts claim that it takes about seven seconds for a perceptive person to see just who it is who lives inside of us.

Spiritual leaders with integrity influence others with their faces; in specific, a godly face. Who wouldn't want a godly face? The question is how to get it. And, keep it. That's one of the intended lessons in this section of Second Corinthians. To make his point, the

---

[61] While the origin of this saying is uncertain, it has become proverbial in many cultures. Jesus said something similar. *"The eye is the lamp of the body. If your eyes are healthy, your whole body will be full of light. But if your eyes are unhealthy, your whole body will be full of darkness. If then the light within you is darkness, how great is that darkness!"* (Matthew 6:22-23)

Apostle Paul takes us back to Exodus. It's the story of Moses at Mount Sinai. Let's review this familiar biblical narrative.

While the ancient Israelites were camped at the foot of the mountain, *"Moses went up to God"* (Exodus 19:3) where he was instructed to establish a covenant between Yahweh and his people. Moses returns to the camp, assembles the elders, *"and set before them all the words the LORD had commanded him to speak. The people all responded together, 'We will do everything the LORD has said'"* (Exodus 19:7-8).

In time, the covenant was confirmed and the Ten Commandments etched in stone (Exodus 24:3-12). For Moses the entire process entailed several trips up and down the mountainside, into and out of the presence of God. It was his exclusive privilege. Yahweh made it clear. *"Moses alone is to approach the LORD; the others may not come near"* (Exodus 24:2).

There follows several chapters in Exodus describing the Tabernacle, its furnishings, the ark of the covenant, the altar and courtyard, the priests' garments, the sacred utensils, and more. In this elaborate "Tent of Meeting," Moses' intimacy with Yahweh continued to be his daily experience. *"The LORD would speak with Moses face to face, as one speaks with a friend"* (Exodus 33:11). In these multiplied encounters, Moses grows comfortable with his unique confidentiality with God — emboldened even.

> *Moses said to the LORD, "You have been telling me, 'Lead these people', but you have not let me know whom you will send with me. You have said, 'I know you by name and you have found favor with me.' If you are pleased with me, teach me your ways so I may know you and continue to find favor with you. Remember that this nation is your people."* (Exodus 33:12-13)

Yahweh responds, *"My Presence will go with you, and I will give you rest...I will do the very thing you have asked, because I am pleased with you and I know you by name"* (Exodus 33:14, 17).

Moses daringly demands, *"Now show me your glory"* (Exodus 33:18). Yahweh complies. What follows is the ultimate of epiphanies.

> *Then the LORD came down in the cloud and stood there with him and proclaimed his name, the LORD. And he passed in front of Moses, proclaiming, "The LORD, the LORD, the compassionate and gracious God, slow to anger, abounding in love and faithfulness, maintaining love to thousands, and forgiving wickedness, rebellion and sin."* (Exodus 34:5-7)

These repeated personal rendezvous Moses had with Yahweh had a dramatic effect in his life. It even changed the way he looked. The Moses who went up the mountain was not the same man who came down. Something about him was different. Noticeably different. Moses' intimate time alone with God had changed his face — it was glowing! *"When Moses came down from Mount Sinai with the two tablets of the covenant law in his hands, he was not aware that his face was radiant because he had spoken with the LORD"* (Exodus 34:29).

In Cecil B. DeMille's film classic, *The Ten Commandments*, the best special effect they could come up with in 1955 to portray this dramatic change in appearance was as simple as it was ingenious. When actor Charlton Heston went up the mountain, his hair and beard were brown. When he came down, they were white. He wasn't the same man. And, it showed. In the real story, it wasn't Moses' hair that had been transformed, but his countenance.

PRIVILEGED STATUS

Now that we've rehearsed Moses' intimate experiences with God, let's get back to Second Corinthians and the lesson Paul draws from it. It's a given, Moses is the greatest hero of the Old Testament. He's the personal symbol of the Old Covenant itself. He's more prestigious than any other Old Testament character. As God himself said, *"When there is a prophet among you, I, the LORD, reveal myself to them in visions, I speak to them in dreams. But this is not true of my servant Moses...with him I speak face to face"* (Numbers 12:6-8).

That's status. But, get ready for this—Paul is about to say that Christian leaders of every era, including today, have an even greater spiritual prestige than Moses. It's sort of like what Jesus said about John the Baptist.

> *What did you go out into the wilderness to see? A reed swayed by the wind?... A man dressed in fine clothes?... Then what did you go out to see? A prophet? Yes, I tell you, and more than a prophet... Truly I tell you, among those born of women there has not risen anyone greater than John the Baptist; yet whoever is least in the kingdom of God is greater than he.* (Matthew 11:7-11)

Using similar superlatives, Paul speaks of us in contrast to Moses. Moses, mind you! We have an even more privileged place in the sovereign economy of God. And, it is all due to the Covenant under which we have been destined to serve him. Paul defends this thesis by contrasting the covenants, Old and New.

A covenant is an agreement. It is a sacred contract. From the start, God has been gracious enough to enter into several covenants with human beings. The two most important ones divide our Bibles; the Old and New Testaments.

Covenants have some common characteristics. First, they are drawn up by God, not by us. Nor are the terms negotiable. We can accept or reject the stipulations, but we can't haggle over them. God offers us a relationship with himself. If we are willing to abide by the terms of the agreement, then God binds himself to fulfill his side of the bargain too.

The contract we call the Old Covenant was originally established between God and Abraham, some 430 years before Moses (Galatians 3:17). The laws themselves were added later to fully delineate the terms of the agreement. At the foot of Mount Sinai, the Israelite nation gave united verbal consent to the contract, pledging their loyalty to Yahweh (Exodus 19:8). They were to demonstrate their devotion to him by obeying the Ten Commandments and a long list of additional rules and regulations. Through Moses, God said to them,

> *You yourselves have seen what I did to Egypt, and how I carried you on eagles' wings and brought you to myself. Now if you obey me fully and keep my covenant, then out of all nations you will be my treasured possession…you will be for me a kingdom of priests and a holy nation.* (Exodus 19: 4-7)

God would protect and bless his people, if they would obey him.

> *Now, Israel, hear the decrees and laws I am about to teach you. Follow them so that you may live and may go in and take possession of the land the LORD, the God of your ancestors, is giving you. Do not add to what I command you and do not subtract from it, but keep the commands of the LORD your God that I give you.* (Deuteronomy 4:1-2)

Loyalty would be rewarded by multiplied blessings. Curses were the promised consequences of disloyalty.[62] The terms of the covenant were reiterated time and again by Moses and his successors, the prophets.

Tragically, the stated intentions of God's people at Sinai were followed by dismal failure. They violated the terms of the covenant. Repeatedly. The agreement was ineffectual because they couldn't keep it. Or, wouldn't keep it. For this reason, the writer of Hebrews argues that the Old Covenant had to be replaced. *"If there had been nothing wrong with that first covenant, no place would have been sought for another"* (Hebrews 8:7). A new contract was put into effect. We call it the New Testament. Like any other last will and testament, the

---

[62] See Deuteronomy 28 for the specifics.

new document cancels the old. *"By calling this covenant 'new' he has made the first one obsolete"* (Hebrews 8:13). The New Covenant was not just new in sequence; it was new in kind.

No longer would human relationship with God be dependent on conformity to rules, regulations, and rituals. Paul spells that out clearly when he says,

> *Therefore no one will be declared righteous in God's sight by the works of the law... But now apart from the law the righteousness of God has been made known, to which the Law and the Prophets testify. This righteousness is given through faith in Jesus Christ to all who believe.* (Romans 3:20-22)

Or, to put it more succinctly, *"Believe in the Lord Jesus, and you will be saved"* (Acts 16:31).

In contrasting the Old and New Covenants, Paul compares us to Moses, who was faithful in serving God under the Old Covenant — so much so, that Jesus sometimes referred to the entire body of the Law, and the covenant itself, as simply, *"Moses"* (Mark 7:10).

Moses was the personification of the Old Covenant. Now, a similar role is given us to play. We are *"ministers of a new covenant"* (2 Corinthians 3:6). Our prestige is inseparable from the covenant under which we serve; and therein lies our privileged status.

Paul describes the Old Covenant as an agreement *"of the letter"*[63] (2 Corinthians 3:6). By contrast, the New Covenant is designated as *"of the Spirit"* (2 Corinthians 3:6). This is a fundamental difference.

The fine print of the Old Covenant was put into writing. Those codified statutes totaled some 248 commands and 365 prohibitions.[64] Just thumbing through Deuteronomy and Leviticus, you feel the

---

[63] Greek: "gramma" (γράμμα). This term can refer to a single letter, or any writing, document, or record. It is the origin of our word "grammar."

[64] chabad.org › Jewish Practice › Mitzvahs & Traditions. Accessed January 7, 2016.

oppressive weight of its tedious detail. The covenantal obligations included everything from the transcendent duties of the Ten Commandments themselves to mundane minutia, like what to do about skin blemishes or mildew in your house. There were hundreds of 'i's to dot and 't's to cross. It was an impossible task. No wonder James concludes, *"For whoever keeps the whole law and yet stumbles at just one point is guilty of breaking all of it"* (James 2:10).

The astringency of the Law is underscored by remembering that it *"was engraved in letters on stone"* (2 Corinthians 3:7). The original Ten Commandments were laser-beamed into granite by the finger of God himself (Exodus 32:15-16). The replacement tablets were chiseled into stone by Moses (Exodus 34:1). Cold and hard are apt adjectives to describe the Old Covenant's inflexible demands.

Living under the Law was like living under a curse. *"All who rely on observing the law are under a curse, for it is written: 'Cursed is everyone who does not continue to do everything written in the Book of the Law'"* (Galatians 3:10). Paul draws this line of thought to its starkly simple conclusion: *"For the letter kills, but the Spirit[65] gives life"* (2 Corinthians 3:6).

Essentially, all laws are the same; they can only tell us what we have done wrong, or should have done better. Spiritual vitality must come from some other source. The operative power of the New Covenant is personal—the Holy Spirit himself. He alone can enable us to be spiritual; to live in moment by moment harmony with the stated will of God.

That said, it would be faulty exegesis to disparage the laws of God or the covenant they represented. Those rules and regulations, all 613 of them, were a gift from Yahweh to his people. They served two very practical purposes. First, they established boundaries between God's people and their pagan neighbors.

---

[65] Greek: "pneuma" (πνεῦμα). This word can refer to wind, breath or spirit. Here, it is the term used to designate the Holy Spirit.

> *The LORD said to Moses, "Speak to the Israelites and say to them: 'I am the LORD your God. You must not do as they do in Egypt, where you used to live, and you must not do as they do in the land of Canaan, where I am bringing you. Do not follow their practices.'"* (Leviticus 18:1-3)

Second, the laws were guidelines by which the people could have an amiable relationship with God and each other. The Law, then, was a service. Paul calls it a *"ministry."* And, it was a glorious ministry. He says that it *"came with glory"* (2 Corinthians 3:7).

The glory of God is a hard thing to define. It's sensory. Almost always there is light. Blinding light. You see it. It's auditory. You hear it. Often, it makes the ground shake. You feel it. You fear it. You want to run. You want to hide. And, rightly so. It's the presence of God.

It reminds me of the time some missionary friends and I scaled Mount Arenal in northern Costa Rica. Arenal is an active volcano. At the timberline that afternoon, with only the lava fields ahead of us — and humongous boulders being spewed down the mountain side in our direction — we were confronted with a sign in faulty but effective English: "Do not pass this point, in danger of dead."

The ancient Israelites were definitely feeling in danger of dead. Moses' face reminded them of their potential peril. Paul reiterates their terror. *"The Israelites could not look steadily at the face of Moses because of its glory..."* (2 Corinthians 3:7). A quick glimpse is all they could manage. *"When Aaron and all the Israelites saw Moses, his face was radiant, and they were afraid to come near him"* (Exodus 34:30).

God's glory is terrifying. It is also transforming. In Moses' case, it changed his looks. After experiencing the presence of Yahweh for forty days, his face was radiant. In fact, the glory of God was so blazingly bright in his countenance, the people recoiled. It was a kind of culmination to a month of dread, encamped at the foot of Mount Sinai. The fear was orchestrated by God himself. *"The LORD said to Moses, 'I am going to come to you in a dense cloud, so that the people will hear me speaking with you and will always put their trust in you'"* (Exodus 19:9).

God's glory came complete with thunder, lightning, thick clouds, and a crescendo of supernatural trumpet blasts. Everyone in the camp trembled (Exodus 19:16-17). Everything trembled. *"Mount Sinai was covered with smoke, because the LORD descended on it in fire. The smoke billowed up from it like smoke from a furnace, the whole mountain trembled violently"* (Exodus 19:18). Sinai was off limits. Everything and everyone faced potential execution (Exodus 19:12). Everyone, but Moses. He was welcomed into God's presence. His face was evidence of where he had been.

The Exodus account plainly tells us just why Moses's face was aglow, and how it happened. *"His face was radiant because he had spoken with the LORD"* (Exodus 34:29). Not to unduly spiritualize the historical record; there is a legitimate lesson here—time alone with God is what will give us the indispensable impact of a godly face. Mysteriously and mystically, the glory of God comes over us. It permeates us. It radiates from us. When we spend enough time in solitude with him, it will show. If the glory of the Old Covenant was so transforming, just think what the glory of the New Covenant can do.

Surprisingly, Moses himself wasn't aware of his visible transformation until the people reacted to it (Exodus 34:29-30). So, he took to covering his face with a veil to calm them down. But then, over time, the glow began to fade. Insecurity started to set in. Moses kept wearing the veil, but now it wasn't in deference to the people's fears but instead, to cover up what was disappearing. You don't get that impression from the narrative of Exodus, yet that's the application of the episode Paul makes in Second Corinthians.

The Old Testament account simply reads, *"He put a veil over his face"* (Exodus 34:33). But eventually, Moses knew what the people didn't; the glory was fading. Exodus doesn't document it, but Paul does. *"The Israelites could not look steadily at the face of Moses because of its glory, transitory though it was"* (2 Corinthians 3:7).

This is no discredit to Moses. Paul has nothing but respect for his luminous predecessor. His interpretation of Exodus though, is clear—Moses' facial glory was transitory because the covenant he represented was transitory. Moses personified the fact that the Old Covenant was destined to obsolescence. As beneficiaries of its eventual demise, we have a privileged status superior to that of even Moses.

In contrasting the covenants, Paul acknowledges that the Old Covenant served a valuable purpose, both for those who lived under it and for those of us who would represent its replacement. Paul tells the Galatians,

> *Before the coming of this faith, we were held in custody under the law, locked up until the faith that was to come would be revealed. So the law was our guardian until Christ came that we might be justified by faith. Now that this faith has come, we are no longer under a guardian.* (Galatians 3:23-25)

Contractually, the Law has been superseded by faith in Christ, who initiated a brand new—and final—covenant between God and his people. What had been coming to an end for centuries was permanently dispensed with at Pentecost. Moses' fading face was symbolic of that fact. Paul protracts the point in 2 Corinthians 3:7-18. Scholars call it a digression, but it's an important one. It is an argument from the lesser to the greater. The giving of the Law, and the establishment of the covenant it represented, was a glorious thing. Added to the thunder, lightning, smoke, and earthquakes; angels were present.[66] It was tremblingly glorious.

---

[66] See Acts 7:53; Galatians 3:19; Hebrews 2:2.

Yet, in contrast to the New Covenant, there is no comparison. Paul asks, *"Will not the ministry of the Spirit be even more glorious?"* (2 Corinthians 3:8) Law has been replaced by grace and truth. *"For the law was given through Moses; grace and truth came through Jesus Christ. No one has ever seen God, but the one and only Son, who is himself God and is in closest relationship with the Father, has made him known"* (John 1:17-18).

Paul continues to draw the contrast between the covenants. The Old Covenant was glorious. It was also a *"ministry"* (2 Corinthians 3:7, 9). Or, it was intended to be. But, disappointingly, because of the disloyalty of God's people, it became a ministry *"that brought condemnation"* (2 Corinthians 3:9). Violators of the law were convicted transgressors. And, apart from the temporary atonement of animal sacrifices, they were helpless to do anything about it.

> The law is only a shadow of the good things that are coming — not the realities themselves. For this reason it can never, by the same sacrifices repeated endlessly year after year, make perfect those who draw near to worship. Otherwise, would they not have stopped being offered? For the worshipers would have been cleansed once and for all, and would no longer have felt guilty for their sins. But those sacrifices are an annual reminder of sins. It is impossible for the blood of bulls and goats to take away sins. (Hebrews 10:1-4)

In the end, Law can do nothing but condemn. *"The letter kills"* (2 Corinthians 3:6). Paul concludes, *"How much more glorious is the ministry that brings righteousness!"* (2 Corinthians 3:9) It is incomparably more glorious than the ministry of the Law, because it actually saves us from the condemnation of our sins. *"For what was glorious has no glory now in comparison with the surpassing glory. And if what was transitory came with glory, how much greater is the glory of that which lasts!"* (2 Corinthians 3:10-11) As successors to the apostles themselves, this is the covenant we represent and proclaim.

SOBERING RESPONSIBILITY

Paul concludes, *"Therefore, since we have such a hope, we are very bold"*[67] (2 Corinthians 3:12). The prospect of having free access to God, and to speak with him intimately whenever we want to, serves as an ever increasing source of hope and self-assurance for all of us. *"Let us then approach the throne of grace with confidence, so that we may receive mercy and find grace to help us in our time of need"* (Hebrews 4:16).

God is not like the Wizard of Oz. When Dorothy, Toto, and her three friends arrived at the Emerald City and knocked on those big green doors, requesting an audience with the great and powerful Oz, they were rudely told by the doorkeeper, "The Wizard? But nobody can see the Great Oz. Nobody's ever seen the Great Oz."[68] Slam! By contrast, the New Covenant comes complete with an open-door policy. We are God's confidants. We are his friends.

No wonder we are *"very bold"* (2 Corinthians 3:12). It is not overstating it to say that as representatives of the New Covenant, our boldness with people finds its character and courage from our boldness with God. In short, we have a boldness for God that is from God. That kind of confidence is renewed by time spent alone with him.

Continuing to compare representatives of the New Covenant with Moses, the apostle points out that Moses, *"put a veil over his face to prevent the Israelites from seeing what was passing away"* (2 Corinthians 3:13). In that regard, Paul respectfully submits, *"We are*

---

[67] Greek: "parrēsia" (παρρησίᾳ). This term describes a person who is courageous, straightforward, and outspoken in the best sense of the term. The same word is translated *"courage"* in Acts 4:13 and *"boldly"* in Acts 4:31. In 1 John 2:28 it is rendered *"confident."* A bold person is someone who leaves nothing unsaid that needs to be said. Luke used this term to describe the demeanor of the apostles. He reports that the Sanhedrin *"Saw the courage of Peter and John"* (Acts 4:13). He uses it to describe the earliest Christians in general. *"And they were all filled with Holy Spirit and spoke the word of God boldly"* (Acts 4:31).

[68] *The Wizard of Oz*. Metro-Goldwyn-Mayer, 1939.

not like Moses" (2 Corinthians 3:13). This is not to say that we are personally superior to Moses. But, because of the Covenant we represent, we enjoy a superior status. Unlike Moses, the glow we get from being with God won't fade because the covenant we represent will never fade, much less disappear.

The veil imagery Paul has been using to contrast the Old and New Covenants nudges him to further apply the metaphor. Now, he transitions from references to the Israelites of the Exodus to the Jews of his own day. Characteristically, as a people they have been blind to the grace of God. It's as though there has always been an opaque membrane between them and the truth. Paul makes a sweeping assessment of their situation. *"But their minds were made dull"* (2 Corinthians 3:14).

Paul is not glib about such conclusions; he's heartbroken. *"My heart's desire and prayer to God for the Israelites is that they may be saved. For I can testify about them that they are zealous for God, but their zeal is not based on knowledge"* (Romans 10:1-2). It's an incessant sorrow. It is not careless hyperbole when he says,

> *I speak the truth in Christ — I am not lying, my conscience confirms it through the Holy Spirit — I have great sorrow and unceasing anguish in my heart. For I could wish that I myself were cursed and cut off from Christ for the sake of my people, those of my own race.* (Romans 9:1-3)

Paul viewed the dull hardness of the Jews toward the gospel as entrenched and perpetual. *"For to this day the same veil remains when the old covenant is read"* (2 Corinthians 3:14). For decades it had been the apostle's strategy to first visit the Jewish synagogue in every town on his evangelistic itineraries. He figured that there was no better place to get a hearing for the good news than a gathering of people longing for their Messiah. Sometimes it worked. In Antioch of Pisidia, Luke records, *"On the Sabbath they entered the synagogue and sat down. After the reading from the Law and the Prophets, the synagogue rulers sent word to them, saying, 'Brothers, if you have a message of encouragement for the people, please speak'"* (Acts 13:14-15).

Paul spoke and they were invited back. *"On the next Sabbath almost the whole city gathered to hear the word of the Lord"* (Acts 13:44). Luke sums it up. *"The word of the Lord spread through the whole region"* (Acts 13:49). But, the reception was not unanimously positive. *"When the Jews saw the crowds, they were filled with jealousy. They began to contradict what Paul was saying and heaped abuse on him"* (Acts 13:45).

These vivid memories forced the apostle to a regrettable conclusion about his own people. They had ears, but they didn't hear. The uniform witness of the Law and the Prophets was Christological, but they didn't see it. They couldn't hear it. They didn't get it. Jesus had the same experience. *"Though seeing, they do not see; though hearing, they do not hear or understand"* (Matthew 13:13). It had been that way for centuries. Jesus quotes Isaiah 69:9-10.

> *You will ever be hearing but never understanding; you will ever be seeing but never perceiving. For this people's heart has become calloused; they hardly hear with their ears, and they have closed their eyes. Otherwise they might see with their eyes, hear with their ears, understand with their hearts and turn, and I would heal them.* (Matthew 13:14-15)

What happened at Sinai keeps repeating itself. The words of Stephen continue to resonate. *"You stiff-necked people! Your hearts and ears are still uncircumcised. You are just like your ancestors: You always resist the Holy Spirit"* (Acts 7:51). The veil remains. *"It has not been removed...even to this day when Moses is read, a veil covers their hearts"* (2 Corinthians 3:14-15).

But, while stubborn resistance to the gospel is dispiriting, it's not hopeless. The veil blinding the unbeliever's eyes is real, but it is not inevitably permanent. Spiritual blindness can be healed. Paul knows that from personal experience. When he came to faith in

Christ, the scales fell from his eyes (Acts 9:18). For the first time in his life, he could see. He later testifies, *"Even though I was once a blasphemer and a persecutor and a violent man, I was shown mercy because I acted in ignorance and unbelief"* (1 Timothy 1:13). The truth of Christ dispels the darkness.

It's a paradox: faith alone can nullify unbelief. *"But whenever anyone turns to the Lord, the veil is taken away"* (2 Corinthians 3:16). Jews become Jews for Jesus. Those blinded by the devil, see God. There is but one all-determining stipulation: *"Only in Christ is it taken away"* (2 Corinthians 3:14). This is the gospel it is our sobering responsibility to preach. And, it's a joyful one. In this task, Paul rejoices for all of us. *"And we, who with unveiled faces all reflect the Lord's glory, are being transformed into his likeness with ever-increasing glory which comes from the Lord"* (2 Corinthians 3:18, NIV 1984).

When we take advantage of our privileged status and private access with God, the celestial glow from being in his presence continues to grow. We become living mirrors reflecting the Lord's glory. We are transformed—and transforming. It doesn't fade; it only gets brighter. It is an *"ever-increasing glory."* It is the *"glory of Christ who is the image of God"* (2 Corinthians 4:4).

We come now to a theological technicality that deserves our attention. Paul says, *"Now the Lord is the Spirit, and where the Spirit of the Lord is, there is freedom"* (2 Corinthians 3:17). What are we to think of the first phrase of this sentence? How are we to square such a statement with our orthodox convictions about the doctrine of the Trinity?

We know that Father, Son, and Holy Spirit, while inherently and essentially one, are at the same time distinct personages. Fret not, Paul is not fusing or confusing the persons of the Trinity. As awkward as the phrase seems, he is simply pointing out the quintessential unity of Jesus and the Holy Spirit. Christ transforms our lives so thoroughly through the activity of the Holy Spirit that they are virtually doing it together. There is no actual division of labor. We may speak of them as one, because they are one in purpose, though not in person. As Jesus said, *"I and the Father are one"* (John 10:30). He could have just as easily said, "I and the Spirit are one." Here, Paul says it for him. And he's comfortable with it. He repeats it. He describes the *"ever-increasing glory"* that characterizes our lives as that *"which comes from the Lord, who is the Spirit"* (2 Corinthians 3:18).

How cute the toddler who avoids eye contact with you by covering her face with her little hands. She figures that if she can't see you, you can't see her. Typically though, if you wait just a few seconds, she will open her fingers just enough to peek through to see if you are still there. And then, you can both have a good laugh. A small child knows intuitively that her face reveals herself.

Our faces tell people who we are. Laura Rosetree wrote a 300-page book called *I Can Read Your Face.*[69] She claims that every facial feature, from eyebrows to chin dimples, reveals who a person really is. If she's right, then people can tell what we are all about, just by looking at us. I want people to see God when they see my face. Don't you? And now, we know the secret to making sure they do—time spent alone with him.

THINK

1. What is a covenant?

2. How many covenants has God made with human beings? What are the two best known ones? What are their stipulations?

---

[69] Rosetree, Laura. *I Can Read Your Face.* New York: Dell Publishing, 1991.

3. In this section of Scripture Paul compares and contrasts the New Covenant with the Old Covenant. Is the Old Covenant still in place? Are there parts of it still in effect?

4. Paul describes the Old Covenant as being *"of the letter."* What does that mean?

5. What are the *"letters in stone"* that Paul refers to in 2 Corinthians 3:7? How did they bring *"death"* to the people under the stipulations of that covenant with God?

6. Read Exodus 33:12-23 and 34:29-38 and explain what Paul means in 2 Corinthians 3:7 by saying *"so the Israelites could not look steadily at the face of Moses."*

7. What has the fading glow of Moses' face got to do with the transitory nature of the Old Covenant?

8. As *"ministers of a new covenant"* Paul describes himself and the other apostles as being *"very bold."* Where does spiritual boldness come from? How do you get it?

9. Your face is reliable evidence that you have spent time alone with God. True or False?

10. Can everyone see the facial radiance of someone who knows God in a personally intimate way?

ACT

1. Spend sixty seconds looking at your face in the mirror. What do you see? Write it down.

2. Make a list of Christ followers you know whose faces reflect their experience of him.

3. Repeat to yourself a few times a week: "I am a representative of the New Covenant. In that sense, I have an even higher status than Moses himself."

4. When you pray today, picture yourself in God's presence. See yourself as his friend.

5. Ask someone if your relationship with God can be seen on your face.

Chapter 6

The Power of Perpetual Optimism

2 Corinthians 4:1-16

In the junior high school that I attended, Mr. Eugene Grogan was the football and basketball coach as well as the boys' P.E. teacher. The bunch of us guys who got acquainted with him in all three capacities were convinced that he had missed his calling in life. Coach Grogan should have been a Drill Instructor in the Marine Corps. Under his eagle-eyed surveillance, the gymnasium, track, and fields of our small campus were transformed into a military base. He was General Patton. We were the grunts.

Coach Grogan had a sixth sense for the slightest sign of insolence. This did not bode well for a fourteen year old boy with an above-average rebellious streak—like me. One morning we were lined up outside for P.E. Coach was pacing back and forth calling roll, when from out of nowhere, he barked, "Crain, I don't like your attitude. Run the track!" Blindsided and dumbfounded as to just what it was that I'd done wrong, I had no choice but to comply. While my classmates engaged in the sporting activities of the hour, I ran laps until the bell rang. I would never have admitted it then, but I learned a lesson that day—attitude matters. And, it's unlikely you'll be able to completely conceal a bad one.

As we come to the fourth chapter of Second Corinthians, once again the Apostle Paul has a lot to teach us. This time, the topic is positivity. When we are positive, with God's help, we take responsibility for keeping our lives going in a beneficial direction.

It all starts with the realization that there are two basic ways of looking at life and living it; we are either optimistic or pessimistic. The latter is not a personality trait that contributes to effective leadership. Pessimists inspire no one. They are negative about the present and nervous about the future. Optimists, by happy contrast, invigorate everyone. They are enthusiastic and confident. They are persistently convinced that there's every reason to be hopeful. For them, the glass isn't half empty.

It goes without saying, Christ followers are people of faith. That is reason enough for us to be optimistic. After all, faith is *"Confidence of what we hope for and assurance of what we do not see"* (Hebrews 11:1). We can do courageous and even heroic things because we're certain that God can do anything: the unexpected, the incredible, and the miraculous. We join Paul in saying with conviction, *"I can do all this through him who gives me strength"* (Philippians 4:13). That's optimism. Everything will work out because we believe that *"He who began a good work in you will carry it on to completion until the day of Christ Jesus"* (Philippians 1:6). Since God is at work in us, our dreams—or many of them anyway—will come true. Our hopes will be realized. Optimists are completely sure that *"In all things God works for the good of those who love him and are called according to his purpose"* (Romans 8:28). God is good, all the time. All the time, God is good.

In 1913 Eleanor Porter wrote the now classic children's novel about an indomitably optimistic young girl, *Pollyanna.*[70] Her persona has since become synonymous with a subconscious bias toward the positive; i.e., the "Pollyanna Principle." Some are inclined to view this default disposition as unrealistic; concluding that such people are not in touch with reality.

No one would argue that being in touch with reality is a good thing. But are we negative or positive about the reality we presume

---

[70] Porter, Eleanor. *Pollyanna.* Boston: L. C. Page & Company, 1913.

to be in touch with? Is it possible to be perpetually optimistic? Yes! It's possible. And important. Paul puts it this way, *"We do not lose heart"* (2 Corinthians 4:1). But, as with all statements of faith, there are obstacles that have to be overcome.

DESPITE CRITICISM

One of the most common hindrances to optimism every spiritual leader must learn to cope with is criticism. In the congregation at Corinth there was an obstinate vocal minority who didn't hesitate to let their disapproval of the Apostle Paul be known, loud and long.

Jesus pointed out once that some people have a plank in their own eye, while they make it their business to concern themselves with the splinter in ours.[71] They are quick to expose our faults. And, it can get vicious. The Corinthians were saying malicious things about their spiritual father and his co-workers. Paul protests, *"We have renounced[72] secret and shameful ways."* These are the sorts of

---

[71] *"Why do you look at the speck of sawdust in your brother's eye and pay no attention to the plank in your own eye? How can you say to your brother, 'Let me take the speck of dust out of your eye,' when all the time there is a plank in your own eye? You hypocrite, first take the plank out of your own eye, and then you will see clearly to remove the speck from your brother's eye."* (Matthew 7:3-5)

[72] Paul wants to make it clear that his renunciation of the behavior he's being accused of is absolute and final. When he says *"we have renounced,"* he uses the Aorist tense of the Greek verb which describes definite action, once and for all completed in the past. The verb is also in the Middle Voice, which indicates an action Paul and his companions have imposed upon themselves.

accusations he is disavowing. He insists, *"We do not use deception,*[73] *nor do we distort*[74] *the word of God"* (2 Corinthians 4:2).

Paul's recalcitrant critics characteristically challenged him with being sneaky, but he knows better.

> *Now this is our boast: our conscience testifies that we have conducted ourselves in the world, and especially in our relations with you, with integrity and godly sincerity. We have done so not relying on worldly wisdom but on God's grace.* (2 Corinthians 1:12)

Later, he will sarcastically toss their criticisms back in their faces. *"Yet, crafty fellow that I am, I caught you by trickery"* (2 Corinthians 12:16). In point of fact, it is his opponents who have been deceptive.

> *For such people are false apostles, deceitful workers, masquerading as apostles of Christ. And no wonder, for Satan himself masquerades as an angel of light. It is not surprising, then, if his servants also masquerade as servants of righteousness. Their end will be what their actions deserve.* (2 Corinthians 11:13-15)

I remember the time a young man in our church invited me out to lunch. After some initial pleasantries and small talk, the other shoe dropped. With an abrupt change of tone, he said, "My wife and I are leaving the church. Your preaching isn't biblical enough." That shoe landed on my foot! Stunned, I challenged his allegation. He remained adamant. They were leaving. It was my fault. On another occasion, there was no subtly to the disapproval when a church

---

[73] Greek: "mē peripateō" (μή περιπατέω). The Greek syntax of this declaration of innocence puts the *"not"* at the front of the phrase; it literally reads, "not deception we use." Even the way the apostle arranges his words is a strong rebuttal of the charges against him.

[74] Greek: "doloō" (δολόω). This word means to corrupt or ensnare. It is the cultist's stock in trade; to entrap potential converts by distorting Scripture.

member came right out and called me a "false prophet" because I didn't see things his way.

When Christians are careless and cruel in their criticisms of us, it is tough to stay optimistic. The reality is, we've been misjudged and condemned. These are people we've loved, served, and stood beside for years. Now, what do we do? Let's start with a long look in the mirror. Is there any basis for their criticism? If not, we shake it off. *"On the contrary, by setting forth the truth plainly we commend ourselves to every man's conscience in the sight of God"* (2 Corinthians 4:2).

Baseless disapproval stings. One source of consolation is hidden in Paul's prepositional phrase, *"in the sight of God."* God is watching the conflicts we find ourselves in. He knows everyone's hearts and motivations. As leaders, if our conscience does not condemn us, then neither does God.[75] Paul has already reminded the Corinthians, *"I care very little if I am judged by you or by any human court; indeed, I do not even judge myself"* (1 Corinthians 4:3). With our own conscience clear, we can confidently appeal to our critics to listen to theirs. *"We commend ourselves to everyone's conscience"* (2 Corinthians 4:2).

We can only pray that the cynics we have to contend with will apply to themselves the standards they apply to us. Sadly, this doesn't typically happen. In situations like these, our realism could easily turn pessimistic. Not Paul. Characteristically, he maintains a buoyant attitude about his ministry. As his successors, it is vital that we do the same.

DESPITE REJECTION

Part of perpetuating an optimistic attitude is to think clearly. Paul was good at that. He knew why people were rejecting him and his

---

[75] This is generally true; but not absolute. As Paul acknowledges in 1 Corinthians 4:4, *"My conscience is clear, but that does not make me innocent. It is the Lord who judges me."*

preaching. *"The god of this age*[76] *has blinded the minds of unbelievers, so they cannot see the light of the gospel that displays the glory of Christ who is the image of God"*[77] (2 Corinthians 4:4).

Paul was up against the devil, and he knew it. He has been clear about this cosmic conflict from the day he first came face to the face with the glory of Christ. How could he forget it?! Three times in Acts, Luke records that dramatic event. *"As he neared Damascus on his journey, suddenly a light from heaven flashed around him. He fell to the ground"* (Acts 9:3-4). Paul later testifies, *"About noon as I came near Damascus, suddenly a bright light from heaven flashed around me. I fell to the ground...My companions led me by the hand into Damascus, because the brilliance of the light had blinded me"* (Acts 22:6-7, 11). That blindness lasted for three days. So severe was the trauma of it all, he didn't eat or drink anything.

In retelling the story to King Agrippa, the apostle adds: *"As I was on the road, I saw a light from heaven, brighter than the sun, blazing*

---

[76] Only here in Scripture is Satan referred to as *"the god of this age."* Jesus described the devil in slightly different but equivalent terms, calling him *"the prince of this world"* (John 12:31; 14:30; 16:11). The world-system is where the devil reigns—for the time being. But, this age is coming to a precise and certain end. Jesus says, the prince of this world *"will be driven out"* (John 12:31). Already, he *"stands condemned"* (John 16:11). But for now, earth is his territory and he rules it ruthlessly. *"The great dragon was hurled down – that ancient serpent called the devil, or Satan, who leads the whole world astray. He was hurled to the earth, and his angels with him"* (Revelation 12:9). Still, he makes war on God's people and keeps the population of this planet under his thumb. He is *"the ruler of the kingdom of the air"* (Ephesians 2:2). Paul reminds us that *"this"* age is in clear contrast with the one to come. Within the confines of time, the devil reigns (with God's permission). In eternity, he burns. Hell is *"eternal fire prepared for the devil and his angels"* (Matthew 25:41). *"And the devil...was thrown into the lake of burning sulfur, where the beast and false prophet had been thrown. They will be tormented day and night forever and forever."* (Revelation 20:10)

[77] The Greek syntax of this verse is made up of an accumulation of genitives expressing origin and possession, each introduced with the preposition *"of"*: *"of this age...of unbelievers...of the gospel of the glory of Christ, who is the image of God."*

around me and my companions" (Acts 26:13). It was not only bright, it was hot. His eyelids were toasted. On the third day *"something like scales fell from Saul's eyes, and he could see again. He got up and was baptized, and after taking some food, he regained his strength"* (Acts 9:18-19).

Non-Christians are confused. It's not all the devil's fault; but, he doesn't hesitate to do his best to keep them in the dark. The assaults are relentless. Sinister spiritual forces are already defeated, but they don't act like it. To the contrary, most of the time they seem to be winning the invisible battle for human souls. We should not be surprised. The war is being fought in enemy territory. The devil remains *"the prince of this world"* but, ultimately, he *"will be driven out"* (John 12:31). For now, though, he is holding his ground. The battle rages on.

Paul faced the reality of spiritual warfare. *"And even if our gospel is veiled, it is veiled to those who are perishing"*[78] (2 Corinthians 4:3). Once again, he takes up the language of chapter 3 where he recounts the fact that Moses wore a veil to shield the people from the glory of God's radiance on his face; they were terrified of it. Then by way of analogy, the apostle applies the imagery to the Jews of his own time. *"Even to this day when Moses is read, a veil covers their hearts"* (2 Corinthians 3:15).

---

[78] Greek: "apollumi" (ἀπόλλυμι). This verb has military connotations. It can mean to demolish, to put out of the way entirely, to end, abolish, ruin, render useless, destroy, or kill. Here, it is in the present tense, describing an ongoing and desperate condition. Paul joins the rest of the apostles in making a clear distinction between Christ followers and non-Christians; the first are saved and the latter are lost. It all depends on their response to the gospel. Early on in the Corinthian correspondence, Paul said, *"The message of the cross is foolishness to those who are perishing, but to us who are being saved it is the power of God"* (1 Corinthians 1:18). Jesus underscored the same simple truth. *"For God so loved the world that he gave his one and only Son, that whoever believes in him shall not perish but have eternal life...Whoever believes in him is not condemned, but whoever does not believe stands condemned already because he has not believed in the name of God's one and only son"* (John 3:16,18).

This explains the persistent rejection Paul has faced from them since the start of his life's work for Christ. He knows the reason for their resistance. He knows too the miraculous remedy required. *"But whenever anyone turns to the Lord, the veil is taken away"* (2 Corinthians 3:16).

Rejection will not stop him. Optimists don't give up. Most hearers of the gospel may say no, but some will say yes. The devil has blinded the eyes of most. But, Jesus can make many see. We preach. He heals. Miracles happen. The veil is removed.

Paul summarizes this determination of his ministry: *"For what we preach is not ourselves, but Jesus Christ as Lord, and ourselves as your servants for Jesus' sake"* (2 Corinthians 4:5). The apostle preaches Christ-centered good news.

The preacher's business is to always draw attention to Christ. We preach Christ as Savior, and we preach Christ as Lord. The recent ascendency of the term "Christ-follower" to describe Christians, is a subtle but important reminder that not only are we to believe in Jesus, but to obey him too.

As Watchman Nee suggests in his powerful classic, *Spiritual Authority,* believers would best be called "obeyers."[79] Undoubtedly, Dietrich Bonhoeffer was right too when he said, "To obey is to believe. To believe is to obey."[80] We have a clear mandate: *"Go and make disciples of all nations, baptizing them…and teaching them to obey everything I have commanded you"* (Matthew 28: 18-20). With rightful indignation Jesus asks, *"Why do you call me 'Lord, Lord' and do not do what I say?"* (Luke 6:46)

Paul contrasts his preaching of the gospel with the carpet-bagging propaganda of his opponents in Corinth. *"Unlike so many, we*

---

[79] Nee, Watchman. *Spiritual Authority.* New York: Christian Fellowship Publishers, 1972.

[80] Bonhoeffer, Dietrich. *The Cost of Discipleship.* New York: Macmillan Publishers, 1963.

do not peddle the word of God for profit. On the contrary, in Christ we speak before God with sincerity, as those sent from God" (2 Corinthians 2:17).

Cults owe their origin to preachers peddling a fraudulent gospel for selfish gain. That's what happens when Jesus is not kept in his rightful place. Paul is stubborn about maintaining the Christ-centeredness of his preaching. *"And so it was with me, brothers and sisters. When I came to you, I did not come with eloquence or human wisdom as I proclaimed to you the testimony about God. For I resolved to know nothing while I was with you except Jesus Christ and him crucified"* (1 Corinthians 2:1-2). It is the crucified Savior and risen Lord that we too are obligated to proclaim.

Like Paul, we preach Christ as Lord and *"ourselves as your servants"*[81] (2 Corinthians 4:5). We are not just at Christ's beck and call; we are in the service of his people too. Paul speaks of himself, Timothy, Titus, Luke, and his other apostolic companions, as though their time was not their own. That's the tone the apostle set for his ministry — hardworking, uncomplaining, and consistently available. He does it all *"for Jesus' sake"* (2 Corinthians 4:5). Our service to others is obedience to Christ. And, we know what's really going on. *"I tell you the truth, whatever you did for the least of these brothers and sisters of mine, you did for me"* (Matthew 25:40).

There's a mysterious energy that stimulates a selfless life of service to others in the name of Jesus. Paul explains it. *"For God, who said, 'Let light shine out of darkness,' made his light shine in our hearts to give us the light of the knowledge God's glory displayed in the face of Christ"* (2 Corinthians 4:6).

It's been a long time since Paul had to ask, *"Who are you, Lord?"* (Acts 9:5) Ever since Damascus, he has known Jesus for who is. *"So from now on we regard no one from a worldly point of view. Though we*

---

[81] Greek: "doulos" (δοῦλος). The word describes a slave; someone who belongs to another and is at their disposal day and night.

once regarded Christ in this way, we do so no longer" (2 Corinthians 5:16). Paul speaks cognitively and emotively when he says,

> *I thank Christ Jesus our Lord, who has given me strength, that he considered me trustworthy, appointing me to his service. Even though I was once a blasphemer and a persecutor and a violent man, I was shown mercy because I acted in ignorance and unbelief. The grace of our Lord was poured out on me abundantly, along with the faith and love that are in Christ Jesus.* (1 Timothy 1:12-14)

Now that he sees things as they are; it is something that cannot be contained. It's the essential element of his commission. Jesus said,

> *Now get up and stand on your feet. I have appeared to you to appoint you as a servant and witness of what you have seen of me and what I will show you. I will rescue you from your own people and from the Gentiles. I am sending you to them to open their eyes and turn them from darkness to light.* (Acts 26:16-18)

Paul loves the analogy between initial Creation and his own personal re-creation. God said, *"Let there be light. And there was light"* (Genesis 1:3). The apostle sees his conversion as equally astounding. And, it's all of Christ. To see *"the face of Christ"* is to behold *"God's glory"* (2 Corinthians 4:6).

Each of us have had our own experience of that glory. God has *"made his light shine in our hearts"* (2 Corinthians 4:6). We have not met Christ on the road to Damascus, heard his voice, or spent time alone with him in the Arabian Desert,[82] but we too have been blinded by the light. And now, we see. This impels us to preach with

---

[82] *"But when God, who set me apart from my mother's womb and called me by his grace, was pleased to reveal his Son in me so that I might preach him among the Gentiles, my immediate response was not to go up to Jerusalem to see those who were apostles before I was, but I went into Arabia and later returned to Damascus"* (Galatians 1:15-17).

apostolic conviction. We have a priceless treasure to share with the world.

DESPITE WEAKNESS

In Bible times, most household pots, cups, and dishes were made of baked clay. Cheap and easy to come by. You used them as long as they were useful. They were temporary utensils. They were sturdy, but not indestructible. If you dropped one and broke it, you didn't try to repair it; you swept it up and replaced it. They were *"jars of clay"* (2 Corinthians 4:7). Expendable.

With this word picture Paul describes those who preach *"the gospel that displays the glory of Christ"* (2 Corinthians 4:4). He calls it a *"treasure in jars of clay"* (2 Corinthians 4:7). At first, the analogy strikes us as strange. We don't keep treasures in Styrofoam. The invaluable artifacts we've seen displayed in museums or art galleries are typically encased in bulletproof glass, roped off, with armed guards to watch every suspicious move, and security systems to make sure any malefactor is apprehended fast. That makes sense. Something of incalculable worth should be kept and protected with appropriate dignity and strength.

By contrast, the most costly treasure of all time is contained in people. Like Paul. Like you and me—human beings who are temporal, breakable, oftentimes frail, and ultimately disposable. As usual, God does the unexpected. As usual, he has his reasons for doing so. In this case, it's *"to show that this all-surpassing power is from God and not from us"* (2 Corinthians 4:7).

Paul had to learn this lesson the hard way. As a human vessel of the gospel, his body not only showed all the normal signs of wear and tear, but also clearly visible were the scars on his skin and bumps from broken bones that never healed quite right. Added to that, he had to endure an unrelenting physical malady that he called *"a thorn in my flesh"* (2 Corinthians 12:7).

111

We admit that this principle is counterintuitive. Does it make sense to put something priceless in a fragile receptacle? Evidently. We must never forget our expendability. We are useful until we finally break into pieces. Then we are swept up and replaced. To God be the glory!

DESPITE PERSECUTION

Optimism is sustained despite our individual human weaknesses. But, for some, the challenges are even greater. That was certainly the case with the Apostle Paul. He lists a series of situations he had to face; all of which would sorely test anyone's optimism.

He begins by saying, *"We are hard pressed on every side"* (2 Corinthians 4:8). My step-dad was from Kansas. He had a folksy saying to describe such situations. When he was in a tight spot, he called it being "between a rock and a hard place." Paul often found himself in such circumstances. When you are *"hard pressed,"* you have little room to maneuver. An enemy combatant has you cornered. Your very life is at risk. But how do you defend yourself when you can't move? Or there's no way to escape?

In the first *Star Wars* movie, Luke Skywalker, Han Solo, Chewbacca, and Princess Leia were trapped in a trash compacter on Death Star I. The automated walls were closing in, threatening to squish our heroes to a premature death. But, alas, they were squeezed, but not squashed. The same was true for Paul. *"We are hard pressed on every side, but not crushed"* (2 Corinthians 4:8).

Next, our apostle admits to being *"perplexed"* (2 Corinthians 4:8). The original word suggests another uncomfortable situation: facing a problem without enough resources to solve it. We can all recall circumstances in our own lives when this was the case for us too. How did we respond? Those who are perpetually optimistic stay positive. Paul says that he was *"perplexed, but not in despair"* (2

Corinthians 4:8). There's a play on words here that we don't see in our translations. Paul is saying, "We were at a loss, but not a loss."

The apostle continues by saying that sometimes he was *"persecuted"* (2 Corinthians 4:9). He recalls being hunted down. The picture is one of hostility and violence. A veteran missionary friend of mine has been threatened, run out of town, and shot at, simply for bringing the gospel to the mountain villages south of Mexico City. Despite multiple close calls, he shrugs it off. Like Paul, some Christ followers in some parts of the world still have to face perilous situations on a daily basis. But, they know that with God's ever-present protection they are *"not abandoned"* (2 Corinthians 4:9).

Think how hard it would be to stay positive if your life was on the line. Paul recalls being *"struck down"* (2 Corinthians 4:9). Lystra comes to mind. Early in his missionary work, Paul and Barnabas were preaching the gospel and performing miracles in Galatia. They made such an impression on the townsfolk that they started to worship them, shouting, *"The gods have come down to us in human form!"* (Acts 14:11).

While the evangelists tried to dissuade the mob from their misdirected adoration, some fractious Jews showed up and *"won the crowd over"* (Acts 14:19). Next thing you know, *"They stoned Paul and dragged him outside the city, thinking he was dead"* (Acts 14:9). He was *"struck down, but not destroyed."* That day he was as good as dead, or maybe, he really was dead. Temporarily. Luke reports, *"But after the disciples gathered around him, he got up and went back into the city"* (Acts 14:20). Paul picked up where he left off and kept preaching the good news. The apostle apparently got so used to violent opposition that he grew to expect it. He testifies, *"We always carry around in our body the death of Jesus"* (2 Corinthians 4:10). This is an enigmatic way of talking. What does he mean?

I'll never forget the day when I arrived to speak in chapel at a Christian college—a 25 year old novice of a Christian who knew nothing of suffering persecution. In a scheduling snafu, another man showed up to preach that day too. His name was Richard Wurmbrand. I was awestruck. My jaw must have dropped as we shook hands. I had read his book, *Tortured for Christ*, documenting the fourteen years he'd spent in a Romanian prison for the simple crime of being a pastor.[83] He literally bore on his back the scars of Christ. By contrast, I hadn't even been treated rudely for being a Christian. When I wonder about the meaning of what Paul is saying here, I think of Richard Wurmbrand.

Still, it is the willingness to risk our lives for Christ that matters. Some get the chance to actually do so. Paul could testify, *"I bear on my body the marks of Jesus"* (Galatians 6:17). Shortly, he will tell the Corinthians, *"Five times I received from the Jews the forty lashes minus one. Three times I was beaten with rods, once I was pelted with stones"* (2 Corinthians 11:24).

Paul tells us why we should be willing to be tortured for Christ. He says, *"So that the life of Jesus may also be revealed in our body"* (2 Corinthians 4:10). Grammarians draw our attention to what they call a "purpose clause" in this statement; i.e., *"so that."* This is the reason we would choose martyrdom, if it comes to it. It is the essence of what Jesus meant when he said, *"Very truly I tell you, unless a kernel of wheat falls to the ground and dies, it remains only a single seed. But, if it dies, it produces many seeds"* (John 12:24). In plainer terms, he added, *"Anyone who loves their life will lose it, while anyone who hates their life in this world will keep it for eternal life"* (John 12:25). I'll confess, I do not hate my life in this world. Not enough, anyway. Because of that lapse in commitment, my witness for Jesus is hampered.

I long to say with Paul, *"I have been crucified with Christ and I no longer live, but Christ lives in me"* (Galatians 2:20). There were no crucifixes in the first century, but I can picture Paul wearing one. If

---

[83] Wurmbrand, Richard. *Tortured for Christ.* Bartlesville, OK: Living Sacrifice Book Company, 1967.

not around his neck, surely in his heart. He repeats himself, *"For we who are alive are always being given over to death for Jesus' sake, so that his life may be revealed in our mortal body"* (2 Corinthians 4:11).

In Paul's case this aspiration would come true in just a few years. He tells Timothy, *"For I am already being poured out like a drink offering, and the time of my departure is near"* (2 Timothy 4:6). This was not merely some sort of premonition, but he has been forewarned. Jesus said on the day of his conversion, *"I will show him how much he must suffer for my name"* (Acts 9:16). As tradition has it, in AD 68 Nero ordered him beheaded.[84] In the end, every jar of clay that contains the treasure of the gospel will be shattered and swept away. Until then, may the life of Christ be revealed in our mortal bodies.

The readiness to die for Jesus transforms itself into spiritual vitality. Such joyful self-denial is fundamental to perpetual optimism. The conviction that everything is going to turn out just fine keeps us putting one light-hearted foot in front of another. We are not deterred by criticism, rejection, weakness, or even persecution. After all, everything we do is for Christ's sake. Far from dejected resignation, Paul triumphantly concludes, *"So then, death is at work in us, but life is at work in you"* (2 Corinthians 4:12). But what is it that fuels this persistent positivity? First off, it's faith.

MOTIVATED BY FAITH

Paul knows his Bible. *"It is written: 'I believe; therefore I have spoken'"* (2 Corinthians 4:13). He quotes David's statement of faith in Psalm 116:10. On the run for much of his life, from real not imagined danger, David bemoans, *"The cords of death entangled me, the anguish of the grave came over me"* (Psalm 116:3). But in his despair he reached out to God. He says, *"I trusted the LORD when I said, 'I am greatly afflicted'"* (Psalm 116:10). Paul could relate to David's testimony: *"For*

---

[84] Pollock, John. *The Apostle, A Life of Paul*. Garden City, NY: Doubleday, 1969.

you, LORD, have delivered me from death, my eyes from tears, my feet from stumbling, that I may walk before the LORD in the land of the living" (Psalm 116:8-9). He adds, *"Since we have that same spirit of faith we also believe and therefore speak"* (2 Corinthians 4:13). This is faith-driven, death-defying bravery. Only optimists have it.

The apostles shared remarkable courage when it came to life-threatening situations. Remember Peter and John? When browbeaten by Israel's highest court, the Sanhedrin, their comeback was civil but forceful. *"Which is right in God's eyes: to listen to you, or to him? You be the judges! As for us, we cannot help speaking about what we have seen and heard"* (Acts 4:19-20). A few days later, after being flogged by the same panel of inquisitors, and ordered not to speak in the name of Jesus ever again, Luke records, *"The apostles left the Sanhedrin, rejoicing because they had been counted worthy of suffering disgrace for the Name. Day after day, in the temple courts, and from house to house, they never stopped teaching and proclaiming the good news that Jesus is the Messiah"* (Acts 5:41-42).

These men were all marching to the beat of the same drum—proud, confident, and joyfully optimistic. The prospect of death did not dampen their determination to speak for God. Like Jeremiah, they couldn't keep the message to themselves. *"His word is in my heart like a fire, a fire shut up in my bones, I am weary of holding it in; indeed, I cannot"* (Jeremiah 20:9). Optimism is born of faith. Faith bursts into flames of zealous courage.

The linchpin of such fortitude is confidence in the power of God. *"Because we know that the one who raised the Lord Jesus from the dead will also raise us with Jesus and present us with you to himself"* (2 Corinthians 4:14). Like David, Paul is convinced of God's ability to deliver his people from danger and death.

The apostle's courage is not careless swagger. It's certitude. He's convinced that whether we die young or old, from accidental or natural causes, or an executioner's blade; one thing is for certain—

God will raise us up. Someday we will all be standing together in his presence.[85] Faith in this fact is our motivation. It is the basis of our optimism. With Paul we triumphantly say, *"The perishable must clothe itself with the imperishable, and the mortal with immortality"* (1 Corinthians 15:53). Death's stinger has been removed. *"Where, O death is your victory?"* (1 Corinthians 15:55).

Courageous optimism is contagious. *"All this is for your benefit, so that the grace that is reaching more and more people may cause thanksgiving*[86] *to overflow to the glory of God"* (2 Corinthians 4:15). Herein lies another secret to suffering — focusing on its benefit to others. This others-orientation keeps us from feeling sorry for ourselves and is fundamental to an optimistic outlook on life. As the happy recipients of God's unconditional love, we are filled with gratitude. The result is that in everything we say and do — God is praised. Hallelujah!

INSPIRED BY HOPE

Like a bow being tied around a gift, Paul now repeats what he said at the start: *"Therefore, we do not lose heart"* (2 Corinthians 4:16). Practically speaking, attitude is more important than reality. *Though outwardly we are wasting away, yet inwardly we are being renewed day by day"* (2 Corinthians 4:16).

The Apostle Paul is a realistic optimist. There's no question that his sufferings, while not yet fatal, were exacting a toll. And, he knew

---

[85] *"After this I looked and there before me was a great multitude that no one could count, from every nation, tribe, people and language, standing before the throne and before the Lamb. They were wearing white robes and were holding palm branches in their hands. And they cried out in a loud voice: 'Salvation belongs to our God, who sits on the throne, and to the Lamb'"* (Revelation 7:9-10).

[86] Greek: "eucharistia" (εὐχαριστία). This term means "good grace." It gets transliterated into English as "eucharist," which is what we celebrate every time we take the Lord's Supper. It is a giving of thanks for God's grace; repeated around the world millions of times every week.

it. This is jars of clay talk. We are all fragile, breakable, and ultimately expendable.

Paul contrasts the two elements of our humanity. Physically, we are deteriorating. We get daily reminders of it—aches and pains, sagging muscles, wrinkled skin, and graying hair. Spiritually though, *"we are being renewed day by day"* (2 Corinthians 4:16). Paul may not have heard of the second law of thermodynamics, but intuitively he understood the concept. Everything, including the universe itself, is slowing down. Everything—and everyone—is wearing out. Inevitably, it will all stop. But, God trumps entropy.

Ultimately, physical vitality is not renewable. But spiritual vitality is another story. The inner renewal optimistic Christ followers experience is the opposite of their physical atrophy. This is a miracle that happens every day. Paul sees the things that take their toll on us now as mysteriously contributing to the immortality awaiting us in the world to come. *"For our light and momentary troubles[87] are achieving for us an eternal glory that far outweighs them all"* (2 Corinthians 4:17). This is the perspective of perpetual optimism.

Tribulation in this world is inevitable. Sometimes we say to ourselves, "This is going to break me before it makes me." But the optimist knows better. Our trials and troubles won't break us. In fact, in a paradoxical way, our troubles contribute to our triumph.

Note the contrasts here: momentary versus eternal, light versus heavy, troubles versus glory. Hardships don't create glory, but they are the means used by God to accomplish his glorious purposes. Optimists realize this. All earthly troubles are *"light"* because they are *"momentary."* The glory of what lies ahead is *"eternal."* There is just no way to compare the two. The one *"far outweighs"* the other.

---

[87] Greek: "thlipsis" (θλῖψις). This word connotes a pressing together, resulting in pressure. Paul used it soon after he was left for dead in the Galatian city of Lystra. He said, *"We must go through many hardships to enter the kingdom of God"* (Acts 14:22). The term is variously translated as hardships, sufferings and troubles.

One day, what strikes us as so troublesome now, most likely, will not even come to mind.

Paul summarizes the optimist's mindset. *"So we fix our eyes not on what is seen, but on what is unseen. For what is seen is temporary, but what is unseen is eternal"* (2 Corinthians 4:18). It's an expansive perspective of things.

> *We know that the whole creation has been groaning as in the pains of childbirth right up to the present time. Not only so, but we ourselves, who have the first fruits of the Spirit, groan inwardly as we wait eagerly for our adoption to sonship, the redemption of our bodies. For in this hope we were saved. But hope that is seen is no hope at all. Who hopes for what they already have? But if we hope for what we do not yet have, we wait for it patiently.* (Romans 8: 22-25)

This kind of thinking requires concentration. We set our sights on what we can't see, recalling the words of Isaiah, *"No eye has seen, no ear has heard, no mind has conceived what God has prepared for those who love him"* (Isaiah 64:4; 1 Corinthians 2:9, NIV 1984). We can't see the other side, but we can sense it. Daily, we tell ourselves, "This too will pass. Heaven will last." The eternal triumphs over the temporary. That's what keeps us motivated. That's the optimist's incentive. And, it's powerful!

THINK

1. Attitude is more important than reality. True or false?

2. Are you basically an optimist or a pessimist? Is there another option?

3. Has a bad attitude on your part ever resulted in a negative experience of some kind?

4. What kind of circumstance is most likely to evoke a pessimistic attitude in you?

5. If you're a Christian, you should be perpetually optimistic. True or false?

6. Describe what happens to a person who loses heart.

7. How does disapproving criticism make staying optimistic a challenge?

8. What does it mean to describe ourselves as *"jars of clay"*?

9. What part does faith play in practicing perpetual optimism?

10. How does hope keep us optimistic?

ACT

1. Talk to yourself today about your general outlook on life. Challenge any negativity that crops up, repeating, "This situation is going to turn out okay. I will not lose heart."

2. Make a list of the names of your most persistent critics. Now, pray for them. Every day.

3. Pay attention to your conscience. If it is condemning you for anything, ask God's forgiveness. And, if you've offended someone, ask for their forgiveness too.

4. Ask yourself if you are deceiving anyone or practicing any *"secret and shameful ways."* Confess them to God and repent.

5. Discipline yourself to describe the difficult situations in your life right now as *"light and momentary troubles."* Repeat this shift in thinking until your attitude toward it changes.

Chapter 7

Energized by Hope

2 Corinthians 5:1-10

Lots of people love to go camping. Just mention the word and you can start them daydreaming about the great outdoors and getting back into it. The call of the wild. They smell bacon crackling on the cook stove. They hear birds chirping in the trees. They see the bass jumping in the lake and chipmunks scurrying from one big rock to the next. They envision themselves sitting by a late-night campfire, roasting marshmallows or toasting s'mores. They are enticed by the prospect of snuggling into a cozy sleeping bag, dropping off into a satisfying slumber to the mixed chorus of crickets and frogs, and waking up the next morning to sunshine peeking through the pine trees. A leisurely day beckons them to hike a mountain trail or dangle their feet in an icy creek. Oh, the joys of nature!

Backpackers usually sleep under the stars. But indispensable to a traditional camping trip is a tent; that tried and true synthetic-fabric home away from home. Tents serve an important purpose; they provide shelter—from wind, rain, mosquitos, snakes, scorpions, and pesky raccoons. They even give the illusion of making us safe from hungry bears and mountain lions.

In Old Testament times, it was common for people to live in tents. A tent wasn't a home away from home; it was home. But for us today, a tent is a temporary place. Even the most avid camper doesn't set one up in the backyard and live in it year-round. We presume a tent is a shelter with a time limit. It's where we stay when we are away.

The Apostle Paul, purportedly a tentmaker by trade, describes our entire human experience on this planet as living in a tent. He calls our body a tent. It's a temporary dwelling until we go home. To Heaven. All camping enthusiasts eventually look forward to going home.

Home is where we belong. A memorable song from the early years of Contemporary Christian Music was written by a young troubadour named Pat Terry. It was called *"Home Where I Belong."*[88] The lyrics went like this: "They say that Heaven's pretty. Living here is too. And, if they said that I would have to choose between the two, I'd go home. Yes, I'd go home, where I belong." Verse two added these sentiments: "Sometimes when I'm dreaming, it comes as no surprise that if you look you'll see the homesick feeling in my eyes. I'm heading home. Yes, I'm going home, where I belong."

Heaven is about hope. Hope inspires us to believe that what we long for now, one day we will have. Hopeless people, with little to look forward to, lack energy and enthusiasm. But, hopeful people are invigorated; they are full of purpose and optimism. Hope is a powerful motivator. For Christ followers, the hope of Heaven enables us to outlast the hardships of Earth. It transforms us into Energizer bunnies — "Still going!" But how to stay hopeful? In this section of Second Corinthians we find out.

CARELESSLY

The hope of Heaven enables us to live each day carelessly, in the most literal sense of the term. We know that just as surely as we will die physically, we will live spiritually. Just as certainly as we are alive in this world, we will be alive in the next. This empowers us to be careless.

---

[88] Terry, Pat. *Songs of the South.* Myrrh, 1976.

We've all heard the old adage: "Life is hard. Then you die." True enough. But the Christian version of that dictum is better. "Life is hard. Then you die—and go to Heaven!" Paul is triumphantly confident about that. He says, *"For[89] we know[90] that if[91] the earthly tent we live in is destroyed, we have a building from God, an eternal house in heaven, not built by human hands"* (2 Corinthians 5:1). If our earthly body is like a tent, our heavenly body will be like a house. I like the sound of that. Suburbanite that I am, I'm not much of a camper. I prefer four walls and a roof, lights you can turn on with a switch, a bathroom at the end of hall, a toilet you can flush, and a real bed.

In Heaven, we will have an eternal home. For now, though, we are in this world. And, in these bodies. The longer we stay on this camping trip, the more worn out and frayed our "tents" are going to get. It's as it should be; this *"earthly tent"* was not designed to last. It was Moses who said, *"Our days may come to seventy years, or eighty, if*

---

[89] This conjunction serves to connect what is being said here with something that's already been said. Looking at 4:16-18, we see the connection. *"Therefore we do not lose heart. Though outwardly we are wasting away, yet inwardly we are being renewed day by day. For our light and momentary troubles are achieving for us an eternal glory that far outweighs them all. So we fix our eyes not on what is seen, but on what is unseen. For what is seen is temporary, but what is unseen is eternal."* True to form, the entire New Testament is written with an eschatological point of view. The true New Age has already dawned, and did so with the coming of Christ. He proclaimed *"The Kingdom has come near"* (Mark 1:15). The full realization of God's sovereign reign is yet to come.

[90] Greek: "oidamen" (οἴδαμεν). Two Greek words are rendered *"know"* in our English translations of the New Testament. One, "ginōskō" (γινώσκω), speaks of experiential knowledge; to perceive and feel something. It describes personal intimacy. The complementary term is used here. It connotes a knowledge based on factual information and evidence. It is meant to emphasize the certainty of what is comprehended.

[91] Greek: "ean" (ἐάν). This term is often translated as *"if,"* which is a tentative way of saying "when." The word could also be rendered as "since." But, unless we are alive when the Day of Resurrection arrives, we will all die.

our strength endures; yet the best of them are but trouble and sorrow, for they quickly pass, and we fly away" (Psalm 90:10).

Moses had a long and vital life. *"Moses was one hundred and twenty years old when he died, yet his eyes were not weak, nor his strength gone"* (Deuteronomy 34:7). He died strong. But died he did. We will too. George Bernard Shaw was right about human mortality. "The statistics on death are impressive. One out of one dies."[92] Sooner or later, we will all be gone. But, so what! We're going to Heaven. That kind of hope keeps us kicking. Care is a troubled state of mind. We are carefree.

Paul describes the day we die as breaking camp. The NIV renders it *"destroyed"* (2 Corinthians 5:1). But literally, the word means "to pull up the tent pegs." Sooner or later, every camper does that. Sometimes reluctantly. Sometimes gladly. Either way, like all adventures, every camping trip comes to an end. That's why we say we are "going" camping. It's presumed we are coming back. Once we pull up the tent pegs—we are headed home.

Our bodies are *"earthly"* (2 Corinthians 5:1). They are physical. And, we know that *"Flesh and blood cannot inherit the Kingdom of God"* (1 Corinthians 15:50). Not to worry. We have *"an eternal house in heaven"* (2 Corinthians 5:1). It's not a temporary, fragile, and fraying dwelling. It's permanent. It's solid. It's imperishable. Jesus said, *"Do not let your hearts be troubled. You believe in God; believe also in me. My Father's house has many rooms; if that were not so, would I have told you that I'm going to prepare a place for you?"* (John 14:1-2)

The aging process itself is a reliable reminder that someday, we will indeed break camp and go home. The physical bodies we live in for seventy or eighty years were never meant to last. They are wearing out. Paul describes it as *"wasting away"* (2 Corinthians 4:16). Each passing day underscores the fact that we are just that much closer to our final destination.

---

[92] scriptureunion.org.uk. Accessed January 22, 2016.

The death of our earthly bodies then, is not the end of anything. It is the beginning of a new and everlasting life. This physical body will be replaced with a spiritual one. *"If there is a natural body, there is also a spiritual body"* (1 Corinthians 15:44). Our new bodies, like Christ's Resurrection body, will be as superior to this present one as a well-built house is to a tent. Contrary to ancient Greek thinking, we will not be disembodied spirits in the world to come. What kind of hope is that?! No, we will have new bodies that will never wear out, never be weak, never grow old, and never die.

God is the architect and builder of the *"eternal house"* that will be our resurrected spiritual body. It is *"not built by human hands"* (2 Corinthians 5:1). I have a powerful leaf-vacuum machine. It's one tough, reliable piece of equipment. It's Troy-Bilt. Someday, we will have a spiritual body to replace this physical one. It's a durable dwelling for our spirit and soul. It's God-Bilt.

By contrast, a tent is temporary. You put it up, you take it down. You pitch it, you un-pitch it. Our human bodies are like that. Even with the best of genes, a good diet, and heart-healthy exercise, few of us will last more than ninety years. People without biblical faith figure that's the best you can hope for. We know better.

REALISTICALLY

As Christ followers, we have a hope that inspires us to outlast the troubles of this life. But, *"meanwhile we groan"* (2 Corinthians 5:2). We may be carefree, but we are also realistic. From the start, Christians have understood that we live between the ages; i.e., betwixt the sin-cursed existence of this old world and the full deliverance of our redemption in the new heavens and the new earth. As Gordon Fee and Douglas Stuart describe it in, *Reading the Bible for All Its Worth*, we live in the interlude between the already and the not yet.[93]

---

[93] Fee, Gordon and Douglas Stuart. *How to Read the Bible for All Its Worth*. Grand Rapids, MI: Zondervan, 1982.

Already we know God's free and full forgiveness, but we are far from fully perfected (Philippians 3:10-14). Already we are assured of victory over death (1 Corinthians 3:22), but we will still die (Philippians 3:20-21). We remind ourselves of these paradoxical truths every time we participate in Communion, proclaiming *"the Lord's death until he comes"* (1 Corinthians 11:26). We are in the Kingdom and still pray *"your Kingdom come"* (Matthew 6:10). There's a tension to living in-between the beginning of the end and the consummation of the end. We are down to earth about it. We have a defined and proactive strategy; we *"fix our eyes not on what is seen, but on what is unseen"* (2 Corinthians 4:18).

As people of faith, we look forward to the unseen. But for the time being, we groan. Involuntarily, we make inarticulate sounds when we are weary, frustrated, in pain, or grief. And, it seems, the older we get the more we do it. Though we know that we are *"being renewed day by day"* (2 Corinthians 4:16), the sheer weight of living in this world gets heavier as time goes by. One of these days though, every bone-tired old soul will have a new, young, strong, stand-up-straight, wrinkle-free body. No reading glasses. No cane. No walker. No railings in the bathtub. No hearing aids. No Rogaine. No Oil of Olay.

Until then, we groan. But, we don't gripe. There's a difference. We are realistic, but not discontented. We are weary, but not peeved. We acknowledge that life is hard, but we don't complain. The apostle explains that what we are really doing is *"longing to be clothed with our heavenly dwelling"* (2 Corinthians 5:2).

Abruptly switching metaphors, Paul shifts from talking about the shelter of a tent to the protection and comfortability of clothing. It's another way to describe our longing for eternity.

Physically and psychologically, we feel safer with our clothes on. Less vulnerable. More secure. Paul says, *"When we are clothed, we will not be found naked"* (2 Corinthians 5:3). Being unclothed is a frightening prospect for the human psyche. We feel threatened by it. This dates back to Eden (Genesis 3:21). When Paradise is restored we will be clothed, not only with the righteousness of Christ, but with a body that has risen from the grave—just like his. Paul keeps talking about that hoped for transformation, as if the point needed to be emphasized. *"For while we are in this tent, we groan and are burdened, because we do not wish to be unclothed but to be clothed instead with our heavenly dwelling, so that what is mortal may be swallowed up by life"*[94] (2 Corinthians 5:4).

It's an expectation the apostle loves to contemplate. He spent an entire chapter talking about it in First Corinthians, saying things like: *"If the dead are not raised, 'Let us eat and drink, for tomorrow we die'"* (1 Corinthians 15:32). *"The body that is sown is perishable, is raised imperishable; it is sown in dishonor, it is raised in glory; it is sown in weakness, it is raised in power; it is sown a natural body, it is raised a spiritual body"* (1 Corinthians 15:42-44). *"The spiritual did not come first, but the natural, and after that the spiritual"* (1 Corinthians 15:46). *"And just as we have borne the image of the earthly man, so shall we bear the image of the man from heaven"* (1 Corinthians 15:49). The hope of Heaven invigorates us. We join Paul in the exhilarating expectation of the wonder of it all.

> *Listen, I tell you a mystery: We will not all sleep, but we will all be changed — in a flash, in the twinkling of an eye, at the last trumpet. For the trumpet will sound, the dead will be raised imperishable, and we will be changed. For the perishable must clothe itself with the imperishable, and the mortal with immortality. When the perishable has been clothed with the imperishable, and the mortal*

---

[94] Greek: "zōē" (ζωή). This term is used in contradistinction to mere biological life. Biological life is temporary. It is the *"natural body"* Paul talks about in his discussion of the Resurrection in 1 Corinthians 15. The natural body is Adam's legacy. It has its limits. Spiritual life is forever; it is derived from Jesus himself. *"If there is a natural body, there is also a spiritual body. So it is written, 'The first man Adam became a living being; the last Adam, a life giving spirit'"* (1 Corinthians 15:44-45).

with immortality, then the saying that is written will come true: "Death has been swallowed up in victory. 'Where, O death, is your victory? Where, O death is your sting?'" (1 Corinthians 15:51-55)

In his book, *The Jesus I Never Knew,* Philip Yancey spends a chapter trying to figure out the Beatitudes in The Sermon on the Mount.[95] He calls it "Lucky Are the Unlucky." He asks if Jesus was guilty of dangling pie-in-the-sky promises to his gullible listeners. Was he irresponsibly tossing pieces of bread to the desperate masses hanging on his every word? No, Yancey maintains. Christ's bold assurances were genuine promises central to his message. Jesus was not a politician making pledges just to get elected. To the contrary, he was genuinely offering his audience eternal rewards. Those who mourn *will* be comforted; the meek *will* inherit the earth; the hungry *will* be filled; the pure *will* see God. The prospect of such an assured inheritance stimulates hope.

Yancey concludes, "Like a bell tolling from another world, Jesus' promise of rewards proclaims that no matter how things appear, there is no future in evil, only in good." He caps this contention by telling the story of his wife, Janet, who was working near a Chicago housing project, judged by many to be the poorest community in the country. About half of her clients were white, half were black. In their lifetimes, all of them had survived plenty of hardships, including two world wars — with the Great Depression in between. They lived in daily awareness of death and dying. What was surprising was the way in which the whites and the blacks faced their deaths. Exceptions notwithstanding, a trend emerged. As the inevitability of it all closed in, many of the whites became increasingly fearful and anxious about dying. They complained a lot about their lives and their deteriorating health. The blacks, on the

---

[95] Yancey, Philip. *The Jesus I Never Knew.* Grand Rapids, MI: Zondervan, 1995.

other hand, maintained good humor and a triumphant spirit, even though they arguably had better reason for bitterness and despair. The difference between the two was hope. In the black community there was a bedrock belief in Heaven, summarized in slave era hymns like, "All God's children got shoes. When I get to Heaven, gonna put on my shoes, and walk all over God's Heaven." The unlucky are indeed lucky!

There is a realism to our hope of Heaven. When Paul talked of groaning, he wasn't theorizing. *"We are hard pressed on every side, but not crushed; perplexed, but not in despair; persecuted but not abandoned; struck down, but not destroyed"* (2 Corinthians 4:8-9). One day, though, all this mortality will be *"swallowed up by life"* (2 Corinthians 5:4). What has relentlessly burdened us down will be gulped up. *"For our light and momentary troubles are achieving for us an eternal glory that far outweighs them all"* (2 Corinthians 4:17).

CONFIDENTLY

As a rule, I do my best to avoid visiting convalescent hospitals. Not that I haven't made many a pastoral call on people confined to such places. And, I've joined carolers at Christmastime going from room to room, singing, and stopping to visit with the patients or just smile and hold their feeble hands. But, there's no getting around it; most of those folks are there—waiting to die. And, they know it.

When my own mother ended up in such a facility, despite the two-hundred mile round trip, I went to see her as often as I could. There she was, day in and day out, confined to her tiny room, bed-ridden. But, instead of being depressed, she was consistently cheerful and up-beat. She never complained and never pleaded with me to stay a little longer. Not once. It was her hope that enabled her to live. And to die. She never left that place—until she went Home. The hope of Heaven enables us to live carelessly and realistically. It also empowers us to live confidently.

So, where does all this confidence come from? In short, it finds its source in the eternal purposes of God. Paul proclaims *"Now the one who has fashioned us for this very purpose is God"* (2 Corinthians 5:5). This world is not our home; we're just passing through.

A while back my wife and I went to the memorial service for a twenty-seven year old young man, the only son of my wife's friend, killed in a car crash. He was too young to die. But, his funeral had the aura of a celebration. They called it a "homecoming." And when the organist, there at Shiloh Baptist Church, soulfully played and sang, "I'm going up yonder, I'm going up yonder, I'm going up yonder to be with my Lord," the tears streamed down everyone's cheeks. Tears welling up from hope.

Inventor and innovator, Ray Kurzweil, has recently teamed up with the "Do no evil" guys at Google. They are dead serious about ending human mortality. Call me skeptical, but they aren't going to pull that one off. Still, when he dies, Kurzweil is having his body cryogenically frozen, so that if they don't find the fountain of youth before he shuffles this mortal coil, he can be resuscitated when they do. Jesus said, *"The one who believes in me will live, even though they die"* (John 11:26). What Ray Kurzweil calls resuscitation, Christians call resurrection.

God's promises are based on his character. In this case, he backs up what he says with a reliable promise. He *"has given us the Spirit as a deposit,*[96] *guaranteeing what is to come"* (2 Corinthians 5:5). This is no limited warranty. It's an iron-clad guarantee. God is the guarantor. He has given us a deposit, which is nothing less than the indwelling presence of the Holy Spirit.

---

[96] Greek: "arrabōna" (ἀρραβῶνα). This word was used to describe earnest-money, forfeited if a purchase was not completed. It came to refer to a pledge or promise of any kind.

On the Day of Pentecost Peter preached the gospel for the first time. With stabbing guilt for crucifying their own Messiah, the crowd interrupted his sermon. *"Brothers, what shall we do?"* (Acts 2:37) Peter promptly answered their question. *"Repent and be baptized, everyone one of you, in the name of Jesus Christ for the forgiveness of your sins. And you will receive the gift of the Holy Spirit"* (Acts 2:38).

We call this promise the indwelling presence of the Holy Spirit. It is a pledge, not speaking of the gifts the Spirit gives, but the gift of the Spirit himself. It's the possession of this gift that guarantees our salvation. Paul promises,

> *And you also were included in Christ when you heard the word of truth, the gospel of your salvation. When you believed, you were marked in him with a seal, the promised Holy Spirit, who is a deposit guaranteeing our inheritance until the redemption of those who are God's possession – to the praise of his glory.* (Ephesians 1:13-14)

I worked my way through college as a stocker for a California chain of grocery stores. Every day we waited for "the load" to arrive in a semi-trailer from the warehouse. A thin aluminum ribbon attached to the lock on the rear doors of the truck verified that the contents had not been tampered with. It was evidence that they were in fact, intact. The Holy Spirit's presence does the same for us.

This kind of glad assurance creates some very pleasant results. *"Therefore we are always confident"* (2 Corinthians 5:6). The promises of God are backed up by our personal possession of the Holy Spirit himself. This is the source of our confidence. And, it becomes the reason for our sustained courage while *"we are away from the Lord"* (2 Corinthians 5:6).

FAITHFULLY
The hope of eternal life is a uniquely Christian way of thinking. Many today are hopeless. As bluesman B.B. King used to sing,

"When you're dead you're done; so let the good times roll." That is the life philosophy of millions of people. But in the end, the prospect doesn't make for a joyful funeral. I prefer the Christian conviction: death is the portal to an intensely relational union with God – and everyone else who has claimed Christ as Savior. No wonder Paul was eager to be *"away from the body"* (2 Corinthians 5:8). *"I desire to depart and be with Christ, which is better by far"* (Philippians 1:23). This is the biblical perspective of human existence.

Old Testament saints, like Job, wondered about the dynamic between this world and the next. Life here is hard. When all hell broke loose, he cried out, *"If someone dies will they live again?"* (Job 14:14) But, what Job vaguely hoped for, we anticipate with confidence.

Christian hope is fixed on unseen realities; realities for which we have to wait. But, realities nonetheless. Our departure from this life, means instantaneous arrival in the next. It is nothing less than being *"with the Lord"* (2 Corinthians 5:8).

Peter expressed the same confident expectation when he said that God *"has given us new birth into a living hope through the resurrection of Jesus Christ from the dead, and into an inheritance that can never perish, spoil or fade. This inheritance is kept in heaven for you"* (1 Peter 1:3-4).

Faith creates hope. We are certain of what we do not see (Hebrews 11:1). This is not faith in faith; it is faith in God. Paul says *"we are confident"* (2 Corinthians 5:8). We know what we believe in. We have a clear sense of this world, and the world to come. Each day, it gives us a steadily optimistic perspective.

In his commencement address at Stanford University in 2005, Steve Jobs told the graduates, "If you live each day as if it were your last, someday you'll most certainly be right."[97] Six years later, Jobs

---

[97]   news.stanford.edu/news/2005/june15/jobs-061505.html.   Accessed January 25, 2016.

himself was dead. He was 56. Most folks dread the date of their death. Christians don't. We anticipate it.

My wife has already picked one of the songs she wants everyone to sing at her memorial celebration. It's the southern gospel foot-stomper, *Goodbye, World, Goodbye,* by Mosie Lister. The lyrics go like this: "A day or two then goodbye, goodbye to each sorrow and each sigh. Heaven is near and I can't stay here. Goodbye, world, goodbye!" When that day comes, people will be crying their eyes out and stomping their feet at the same time.

According to James Sire in his book, *The Universe Next Door,* one of the bedrock philosophical questions that every thinking person must contemplate sooner or later is, "What happens when we die?"[98] It's a persistent mystery.

Death happens. To all of us. But, what happens next? There are three basic responses to that fundamental question, each representing a widely held worldview. The first answer is simple: when we die, we cease to exist. This is the naturalist's conclusion. This life is all there is. Our ultimate destiny is annihilation.

The second answer can be abridged by saying that after we die, we come back. And we keep coming back. Until we get it right. Right enough to be absorbed into cosmic nothingness. Nirvana. One billion Hindus consider this explanation sacred. So do 500 million Buddhists.

The third answer is the biblical one. Human beings have been fashioned by a relational Creator. And, wonder of wonders, we've been invited to join the fellowship shared by the Father, the Son, and the Holy Spirit. Forever! Such togetherness starts here and extends into eternity. It's this kind of hope that keeps us relaxed, realistic and confident—care-less and faith-full. *"We live by faith, not by sight"* (2 Corinthians 5:7).

---

[98] Sire, James. *The Universe Next Door.* Downers Grove, IL: InterVarsity Press, 1997.

Everyone builds their view of reality on what seems to be true. They make sense of life by what they choose to believe. If we choose to conclude that humans are all alone in the universe, we roll the dice and take our chances. The French mathematician and theologian, Blaise Pascal, argued that if Christians are wrong, we have lost nothing. On the other hand, if atheists are wrong, they have lost everything.[99] The assertion is called "Pascal's Wager." Granted, it's a gamble.

Jesus promised, though, that if we choose to put our trust in him we will be blessed for doing so. When Doubting Thomas saw Christ's wounds and touched them, he overcame his disbelief. *"Jesus told him, 'Because you have seen me, you have believed; blessed are those who have not seen and yet have believed'"* (John 20:29). Some may find such faith foolish. But, as Christ followers, we decide to *"fix our eyes not on what is seen, but on what is unseen"* (2 Corinthians 4:18).

Before moving to a new thought, Paul feels compelled to restate the confidence of his faith and the exuberant hope it creates. *"We are confident, I say, and would prefer*[100] *to be away from the body and at home with*[101] *the Lord"* (2 Corinthians 5:8). Amen! Given a choice, we'd just as soon pull up the tent pegs.

RESPONSIBLY

Our destiny is decided. The date of our death may be set,[102] but it remains known only to God. In the meantime, our responsibility is

---

[99] peterkreeft.com/topics/pascals-wager.htm. Accessed Jan. 28, 2016.

[100] Greek: "eudokeō" (εὐδοκέω). This verb literally means to "think good." It describes the preference of our thoughts; to determine what we think and to take pleasure in our conclusions.

[101] Greek: "pros" (πρός). This preposition is more "toward" than *"with."* In this case it connotes being toward the Lord; i.e., face to face. This is a repeat of 2 Corinthians 5:6, with the added emphasis on personal preference. See Philippians 1:21-23 for the same longing.

[102] Some infer this to be the meaning of passages like Psalm 139:16. *"All the days ordained for me were written in your book before one of them came to be."*

clear. We share the Apostle Paul's determination. *"So we make it our goal to please him, whether we are at home in the body or away from it"* (2 Corinthians 5:9).

Christians are goal-oriented people. We have an earnest desire for achievement and distinction. But not in the typical sense. We have a newfound and abiding ambition — to please God. For us, pleasing him is the one thing more important than anything. Lesser aspirations are paltry by comparison. There's an accountability to this purposefulness that keeps us responsible. Each of us will have to stand up to the scrutiny of divine judgment.

The Bible is clear. Everyone is *"destined to die once, and after that to face judgment"* (Hebrews 9:27). There are two court appearances each Christ-follower must make. Along with all of humanity, both living and dead, we will appear before God in what is called the Great White Throne Judgment, described in Revelation 20:11-15. One thing, and one thing only, matters then — that our name is in *"the book of life"* (Revelation 20:15). If our name is written in that registry, everything is settled. But, if our name is not found on that roster, the verdict is grim, indeed. *"Anyone whose name was not found written in the book of life was thrown into the lake of fire"* (Revelation 20:15). *"The lake of fire is the second death"* (Revelation 20:14). For those of us in Christ, it will be an awesome, but not fearsome, experience. Our salvation is not based on works, but on the grace of God and our faith in Jesus.

Yet, there is a second judgment each Christ-follower must face. Paul declares, *"For we must all appear[103] before the judgment seat,[104] of*

---

[103] Greek: "phaneroō" (φανερόω). This word means to make visible what has been hidden, the manifestation of which may be in words or actions. It also connotes being exposed to view so that something is plainly recognized or thoroughly understood. In this instance, the verb is in the passive voice which means that it is an event that will happen to us. And, it is an appearance we *"must"* make. It is consoling to know that our judge is, at the same time, our staunchest advocate.

Christ that each of us may receive what is due us for the things done while in the body, whether good or bad" (2 Corinthians 5:10). The Great White Throne Judgment is a salvation adjudication. The Judgment Seat of Christ is a stewardship hearing. It has to do with how well we spent the life we've lived as Christians. It could even include the things we've said. *"But I tell you that everyone will have to give account on the day of judgment for every empty word they have spoken"* (Matthew 12:36).

Jesus alluded to this event in his parable about the talents when he said, *"After a long time the master of those servants returned and settled accounts with them"* (Matthew 25:19). The issue at hand is what we've done with what we've been given. Time, talent, and opportunity. It's different for everyone. But, we are all answerable. That audit will be meticulous.

In his letters to the seven churches in Revelation, Jesus puts it more sternly. Speaking to the Christians in Thyatira, he says, *"I am he who searches hearts and minds, and I will repay each of you according to your deeds"* (Revelation 2:23). Elsewhere, in the red-letter sections of Revelation, we hear Jesus pressing his people about their *"deeds."* Repeatedly, he says to them, *"I know your deeds"* (Revelation 2:2; 2:19; 3:1; 3:8; 3:15). He warns the church in Sardis, *"Wake up! Strengthen what remains and is about to die, for I have found your deeds unfinished in the sight of my God"* (Revelation 3:2). In the very last chapter of Scripture, he makes a promise and extends a warning: *"Look, I am coming soon! My reward is with me, and I will give to each person according to what they have done"* (Revelation 22:12).

---

[104] Greek: "bēma" (βῆμα). This term translated as *"judgment seat"* literally describes the space a human foot covers in a single step. Secondarily, it was used to depict a raised platform mounted by steps. The bema was a section of pavement in first century Corinth where court was held and verdicts rendered. It was the platform on which the judge's chair was located. In Acts 18:12 it is translated "court." The prospect of this judgment is sometimes referred to as the "bema" seat of Christ.

Paul told the Christians in Rome, *"So then, each of us will give an account of himself to God"* (Romans 14:12). The writer of Hebrews reminds us that *"Nothing in all creation is hidden from God's sight. Everything is uncovered and laid bare before the eyes of him to whom we must give account"* (Hebrews 4:13). Ultimately then, we will *"receive what is due us"* (2 Corinthians 5:10), for what we've done.

Now is the time to ask ourselves about the quality of the work we are doing in the name of Christ. Paul admonished the Corinthians, *"Each one should build with care"* (1 Corinthians 3:10). He explains. *"If any one builds...using gold, silver, costly stones, wood, hay or straw, their work will be shone for what it is, because the Day will bring it to light. It will be revealed with fire, and the fire will test the quality of each person's work"* (1 Corinthians 3:12-13).

Clearly, high quality effort — gold, silver and costly stones — will survive. Shoddy work and cheap materials — wood, hay and straw — won't. Not that our salvation is at risk. *"For it is by grace you have been saved, through faith — and this is not from yourselves, it is the gift of God — not by works, so that no one can boast"* (Ephesians 2:8-9). Paul reassures us, *"If what has been built survives, the builder will receive a reward. If it is burned up, the builder will suffer loss but yet will be saved — even though only as one escaping through the flames"* (1 Corinthians 3:14-15). Still, the truth remains that we are *"God's handiwork, created in Christ Jesus to do good works, which God prepared in advance for us to do"* (Ephesians 2:10). It is this aspect of our hope that keeps us responsible.

Officiating at funeral services is part of the job description for individuals in professional ministry. Over a lifetime, every pastor will do dozens of them. On such occasions the task is simple; you comfort those mourning the loss of a loved one. You read the eulogy, preach a short message, and do your best to console people in their grief. Most pastors see the responsibility as sacred. They prepare head and heart to do it well. I know I did. Except once.

A relative of a church member had died. Suddenly. Hit by a car. The family decided that they wanted me to do the service. The only trouble was that there was a slip-up in their plans for the memorial. I was not notified of their wishes for me to officiate. When my wife and I arrived at the service, to join in paying our respects to the departed and his family, the funeral director approached me and said, "Everyone's here, pastor, are you ready to begin?" Dumbfounded, I responded, "Are you sure? I didn't know I was supposed to do the service." In response, he pointed to my name in the printed program.

I politely said, "Give me a minute." I rushed back to the car, retrieved my Bible, frantically thinking about just what I would say. The deceased young man was a dedicated Christian; there was no doubt about his eternal destiny. That simplified things. In a flash of last-minute inspiration, this passage came to mind as the text from which I would make my remarks. What you've been reading in this chapter is a refined version of what I decided to say that day. By the grace of God, the passage preached itself. It is the hope of Heaven that enables us to outlast the hardships of this life.

THINK

1. How often does the hope of Heaven enter your thoughts on a given day?

2. Why is a tent an apt analogy in describing the human body?

3. How does the hope of Heaven enable us to be care-less about the hardships of our lives here and now?

4. When will your *"earthly tent"* be *"destroyed"*? Is that destruction already happening?

5. Contrast our *"earthly tent"* with our *"eternal house in heaven."* (See 1 Corinthians 15.)

6. In 2 Corinthians 5:2, Paul admits that he *"groans."* Is it okay to groan?

7. Paul lives with an increasing *"longing."* What is he longing for? Have you ever felt it?

8. What does it mean to be described as *"mortal"*? Contrast that with what it means to be immortal.

9. Life is hard, and then you die. True or False?

10. The prospect of the Judgment Seat of Christ has motivational power. What is it?

ACT

1. Discipline yourself to think about Heaven a few times every day.

2. Take some time to plan your own funeral service. Pick the songs and the Bible verses you want to be used to celebrate your homecoming.

3. Thank the Holy Spirit that his indwelling presence is the guarantee of your salvation.

4. On a scale of 1 to 10, rate the certainty of your own sense of salvation. Now, write out a prayer to God in gratitude for his gift of grace.

5. If you are a spiritual leader, review the last several sermons you've preached, lessons you've taught, meetings you've conducted, conversations, and counseling sessions you've had. In each instance, was the quality of your work gold, silver, and precious stones; or wood, hay, and straw?

Chapter 8

Agents of Reconciliation

2 Corinthians 5:11-21

On January 1, 1970 the state of California enacted into law legislation that is now in effect in all fifty states—no fault divorce. Such statutes make the dissolution of a marriage possible without proving wrongdoing by either party. The petitioner need not produce evidence that the defendant has committed a breach of the marital contract. In most states, the only prerequisite is that the couple no longer gets along and wants to go their separate ways, stating their reason for doing so.

The most common cause cited for ending a marriage these days is "irreconcilable differences." Two words; that's all it takes. A man and a woman who promised to love, respect, and cherish each other "until death do you part" are parting. They just can't work it out. They have lost the will and energy to try. The impasse is so formidable that nothing can be done about it. Communication is broken. Trust is shattered. Hearts are cold. Hope is gone. The man and wife have become estranged. Two people who once loved each other enough to say, "I do" are now saying, "I don't."

Divorce rates are alarming—even among couples professing faith in Christ. It sounds simplistic, but there's some truth to it; a Christian marriage cannot end up in estrangement and divorce, unless one or both people in the union first become estranged from God. At the heart of the heartache is disaffection with him. And, in the end, that's the human condition, isn't it? People are alienated from each other because their sins have alienated them from God.

Loyalty and allegiance have been lost. But, there's hope; the differences aren't irreconcilable after all.

Spiritual leaders are agents of reconciliation. Paul reminds us that God has *"committed to us the message of reconciliation"* (2 Corinthians 5:19). In this role, we are *"Christ's ambassadors"*[105] (2 Corinthians 5:20). We have been commissioned to do whatever we can, whenever we can, to help people be reconciled to God. To reconcile is to settle a dispute, to bring into agreement and harmony, to cause to become friendly, or peaceable again. That's our responsibility and privilege — to mediate renewed harmony between God and individuals estranged from him by their sins. He dispatches us to approach them on his behalf in the hope that the discord can be resolved once and for all.

MOTIVATED BY THE FEAR OF GOD

What will move us to accept our responsibilities as ambassadors of Christ? Unexpectedly, Paul starts with fear as a proper motivation. He says, *"Since then, we know what it is to fear*[106] *the Lord"* (2

---

[105] Greek: "presbeuō" (πρεσβεύω). This word means to be older. It's the term from which we get our word "presbyter;" i.e., a church elder. It doesn't simply describe someone who is old, but rather a person who is experienced and, thereby, wise. Originally, in an extended sense, the term described someone who played the role of an ambassador. In the first century, political ambassadors were sent to Rome's provinces. There were two kinds of ambassadors; one was an emissary of the senate and the other an envoy of the emperor himself. Peaceful territories had senatorial delegates. Imperial ambassadors were dispatched to provinces occupied by Roman legions. Such ambassadors represented the authority of the Emperor himself. As ambassadors of Christ, we represent nothing less than the authority of the Kingdom of God.

[106] Greek: "phobos" (φόβος). This term describes fear, dread, or that which strikes terror. The word slips into English as "phobia," i.e., a persistent, irrational fear of a specific object, activity, or situation that leads to a compelling desire to avoid it. Of course, the fear of God is anything but irrational. It is the result of seeing God for who he is. His holiness demands a righteousness in us, which in turn presumes responsibility and obedience.

Corinthians 5:11). Connecting this statement with its immediate context, we again see the reason for this sobering incentive. *"For we must all appear before the judgment seat of Christ, that each of us may receive what is due us for the things done while in the body, whether good or bad"* (2 Corinthians 5:10).

A wholesome fear of accountability to Christ moves us to do and say things as his ambassadors. Consequently, *"We try to persuade others"* (2 Corinthians 5:11). This kind of conduct is not socially correct in contemporary culture. We live in times when everyone is supposed to be doing their best to mind their own business. They expect us to do the same. We are tempted to comply, even when the eternal destiny of people around us is in jeopardy. Too often, we've been intimidated. We are afraid to speak up. We don't want to be perceived as pushy. But perhaps we should be more afraid of God than public opinion.

Christians these days often fall short of a healthy fear of the Almighty. Jesus was forbidding about it.

> *I tell you, my friends, do not be afraid of those who kill the body and after that can do no more. But I will show you whom you should fear: Fear him who, after your body has been killed, has authority to throw you into hell. Yes, I tell you, fear him.* (Luke 12:4-5)

It has always been so. *"And now, Israel, what does the LORD your God ask of you, but to fear the LORD your God, to walk in obedience to him, to love him, to serve the LORD your God with all your heart and with all your soul, and to observe the LORD's commands and decrees that I am giving you today for your own good?"* (Deuteronomy 10:12-13). And, as with all God's expectations, there are always positive psychological and spiritual results. Job learned this lesson the hard way. He said, *"The fear of the Lord — that is wisdom"* (Job 28:28). We remember too, the perspective of Proverbs. *"The fear of the LORD is the beginning of knowledge"* (Proverbs 1:7). And, *"Through the fear of the LORD, evil is avoided"* (Proverbs 16:6). Paul maintains that he knows what it is to fear Christ. The verb form is an Ingressive Aorist, which points to an established fact that was formulated by a process; he had come to know the fear of Christ.

Being saved by grace is a glorious experience. But, may we never forget the disconcerting declaration that *"It is a dreadful thing to fall into the hands of the living God"* (Hebrews 10:31). We need a renewed awe of God; one that moves us to open our mouths to preach the gospel at every appropriate moment. Or, at times when we aren't so sure that it is appropriate. Paul exhorted Timothy, his timid protégé, to *"Preach the word; be prepared in season and out of season"* (2 Timothy 4:2). Peter echoes that admonition. *"Always be prepared to give an answer to everyone who asks you to give a reason for the hope that you have"* (1 Peter 3:15).

I teach homiletics. It's the art and science of preparing and preaching a sermon. I ask the students if they know the difference between preaching and teaching. Yes, there are lots of distinctions, but the main difference is that preaching is persuading. Effective teachers inform their listeners of God's Word. We teach. But, when we preach, it is our intention that they do something with the information they're hearing. There's an urgency to the exhortation.

As Fred Craddock says in his classic homiletics textbook, *Preaching*, we should never preach as if there was nothing at stake.[107] Everything is at stake! Failing to be urgent about it has serious consequences. We should be afraid not to do so. It is the prospect of divine judgment that produces in us a deep sense of godly dread. It provides the energizing incentive we need to take the Great Commission seriously and *"Go into all the world and preach the gospel to all creation"* (Mark 16:15). Paul lives and preaches with the judgment seat of Christ ever in mind. We would be wise to do the same.

Spiritual leaders with integrity are aware of their motivations. More importantly, we are aware that God is aware of our motivations. *"What we are is plain to God, and I hope it is also plain to your conscience"* (2 Corinthians 5:11). We know that the deepest

---

[107] Craddock, Fred. *Preaching*. Nashville, TN: Abingdon Press, 1985.

desires of our hearts are *"uncovered and laid bare before the eyes of him to whom we must give an account"* (Hebrews 4:13). We can only hope that others see our intentions as clearly as God does. The apostle longs for the Corinthians to give him a fair shake. It remains to be seen if they will. He pleads with them. *"We are not trying to commend ourselves to you again, but we are giving you an opportunity to take pride in us"* (2 Corinthians 5:12).

Paul's enemies in Corinth were insistently vocal in demanding that he meet their standards of authenticity. The apostle appeals to the rest of the congregation to reject such worldly expectations and to take his side in the distended argument about his integrity, *"so that you can answer those who take pride in what is seen rather than in what is in the heart"* (2 Corinthians 5:12). He has already expressed his bewilderment at the ambivalence of their love. *"Are we beginning to commend ourselves again? Or do we need, like some people, letters of recommendation to you or from you?"* (2 Corinthians 3:1)

Paul's adversaries in Corinth were unscrupulous in their slanderous rejection of his apostolic authority. They even accused him of being mentally unstable. He has heard the gossip they were spreading about him. He can quote what they've been saying. *"If we are 'out of our mind', as some say, it is for God"* (2 Corinthians 5:13). Paul refutes this charge by giving it supposed credibility. He's heard this kind of ridicule before.

One day, upon hearing the sensational testimony of his Damascus road conversion to Christ, the exasperated governor of Palestine, Porcius Festus, reacted to Paul in front of a roomful of people. *"You are out of your mind, Paul!"* (Acts 26:24) Now, you might expect that kind of consternation on the part of a pagan politician, but for the Corinthian Christians to countenance such an accusation was inexcusable.

In one sense though, the Apostle Paul probably prized the allegation of being out of his mind for God. Perhaps he recalled the account of the same thing happening to Jesus himself. Too busy helping and healing people to even stop to eat, Mark records: *"When his family heard about this, they went to take charge of him, for they said, 'He is out of his mind'"* (Mark 3:21). Paul is quick though to amend his brief concession to ostensible insanity. *"If we are in our right mind, it is for you"* (2 Corinthians 5:13). Ultimately, misunderstood zeal for God has an irresistibly positive effect on those within our sphere of influence.

A true Christian is often considered to be eccentric in the eyes of the world. How else to explain our apparent fanaticism? It's hard to beat Jim Elliot's pithy comeback to a critic who challenged his sanity one time. "I'm a fool for Christ," Elliot admitted. Then he asked the man, "Whose fool are you?!"[108]

COMPELLED BY THE LOVE OF CHRIST
Paul has conceded that the fear of Christ was his incentive for being a persuasive preacher and avid ambassador of the gospel. Now, he acknowledges an even stronger motivation. *"For Christ's love[109] compels[110] us"* (2 Corinthians 5:14).

Compulsion is not normally seen as a healthy incentive. The psychological definition of the word says that it is a strong, usually

---

[108] Elliot, Elisabeth. *The Journals of Jim Elliot.* Grand Rapids, MI: Fleming H. Revell, 1978.

[109] Greek: "agapē tou Christou" (ἀγάπη τοῦ Χριστοῦ). Literally translated, this phrase is "the love of Christ." It presents us with a grammatical challenge. Is it Christ's love for us, or our love for Christ, that compels us to be agents of reconciliation between God and humankind? Both are viable possibilities. The NIV opts for the first, translating the phrase as *"Christ's love;"* i.e., it is the love of Christ for us, rather than our love for him, that motivates us to be his ambassadors.

[110] Greek: "sunechō" (συνέχω). This verb means to hold something together, to keep it from falling into pieces. The word also creates a variety of vivid mental images. It was used to describe a strait which forces a ship into a narrow channel, a corralled cow, or a besieged city. In this case, it is a positive force controlling behavior in a prescribed direction.

irresistible, impulse to perform an act; especially one that is irrational or contrary to one's will. Admittedly, if we are compelled to do something destructive or dangerous, then let's get some counseling. But to believe the gospel so deeply that we can't do anything else but preach it—what's healthier than that?!

This is a Christ-like compulsion. Jesus made no apologies for his zeal. *"I have come to bring fire on the earth, and how I wish it were already kindled! But I have a baptism to undergo, and what constraint I am under until it is completed"* (Luke 12:49-50). When he talks about the cross as a baptism he must *"undergo,"* Luke puts the same verb in Jesus' mouth that Paul uses here. Christ was compelled to Calvary. He was inexorably driven to die for the sins of the world. And now, we share that compulsion. Being constrained to act as an agent of reconciliation to a lost and desperate humanity is a healthful mentality. Let's be obsessive about it.

CONVICTED BY THE TRUTH OF THE GOSPEL

Paul gives us a deeply theological reason for his preoccupation with preaching the gospel of reconciliation. *"Because we are convinced that one died for all, and therefore all died"* (2 Corinthians 5:14). Theologians call the doctrine embedded in this statement the "substitutionary atonement." We are all destined to die for our sins unless someone else takes our place. This is the essence of our message. Christ has become our substitute. *"For the wages of sin is death, but the gift of God is eternal life in Christ Jesus our Lord"* (Romans 6:23).

Philip Bliss's 1875 hymn "Hallelujah! What A Savior" is thrilling to sing—still.

> Man of Sorrows, what a name
> For the Son of God, who came
> Ruined sinners to reclaim.
> Hallelujah! What a Savior!

Bearing shame and scoffing rude
In my place condemned he stood
Sealed my pardon with his blood.
Hallelujah! What a Savior!

Guilty, vile, and helpless we
Spotless Lamb of God was he
Full atonement! Can it be?
Hallelujah! What a Savior!

When Christ died, we died with him. Spiritually speaking, we were with him on the cross. Christ died for all, *"therefore, all died"* (2 Corinthians 5:14). No wonder Paul says, *"I have been crucified with Christ and I no longer live, but Christ lives in me"* (Galatians 2:20).

The apostle underscores this reality more than once in his writings. *"Or don't you know that all of us who were baptized into Christ Jesus were baptized into his death?"* (Romans 6:3). *"If we have been united with him like this in his death, we will certainly also be united with him in his resurrection"* (Romans 6:5). *"For we know that our old self was crucified with him so that the body ruled by sin might be done away with…Now if we died with Christ, we believe that we will also live with him"* (Romans 6:6, 8). *"For you died, and your life is now hidden with Christ in God"* (Colossians 3:3). Somehow, his death is our death. And, the result of both is resurrection.

There are practical ramifications to our spiritual participation in the death and resurrection of Christ. *"He died for all, that those who live should no longer live for themselves, but for him who died for them and was raised again"* (2 Corinthians 5:15). The sacrificial love of Jesus inspires us to be his ambassadors of goodwill to the world. There has been a paradigm shift in our value system. We are not reservoirs, but conduits — channels through which the love of God can flow.

As the preachers from my childhood used to point out, the Sea of Galilee is alive and vibrant because of its headwaters in the north and the Jordan River in the south. The Dead Sea is dead because it has an inlet, but no outlet. Christians who live only for themselves are stagnant. Lifeless, even. The love of Christ does not compel them to give what they have to others. By contrast, we flow like a river. We are driven on a course that allows for no deviation. We are confined to a single purpose. We are in a narrow, walled-in passage going in one direction. We are single-mindedly living for him. What a magnificent obsession!

Constrained by the love of Christ, we see things differently now. We see people differently now. *"So from now on we regard no one from a worldly point of view"*[111] (2 Corinthians 5:16). Paul speaks from dramatic personal experience when he talks like this. Before that day on his way to Damascus, his concept of Christ was distorted. He was convinced that Jesus was an imposter and that the movement devoted to him was a threat to the identity and well-being of God's people. His perception of Jesus was without spiritual insight. It was worldly. Logic was mixed with prejudice.

Could an obscure, albeit miracle-working, Galilean who died a criminal's death, be the Messiah? Not on the face of it. But then, Paul got the blazing answer to his question: *"Who are you, Lord?"* (Acts 9:5) Everything changed. *"Though we once regarded Christ in this way, we do so no longer"* (2 Corinthians 5:16). His myopia had been healed. Once sightless, he now began to see clearly. For the first time.

When any estranged sinner sees Jesus as he really is and himself as he really is—new life can begin. Reconciliation can occur. *"Therefore, if anyone is in Christ, the new creation has come: the old is*

---

[111] Greek: "kata sarka" (κατά σάρκα). Literally this phrase is translated "according to the flesh." The NIV has chosen to interpret Paul's intent; "from a worldly point of view."

gone,[112] *the new is here!"* (2 Corinthians 5:17). It turns out that there are no irreconcilable differences between God and human beings, after all.

When an individual is *"in Christ"* all is changed. This two-word prepositional phrase is a favorite with the Apostle Paul. One of my academic colleagues wrote his doctoral dissertation on these two words. Four hundred pages worth! Let me summarize his research. There are 163 references to *"in Christ"* in Paul's epistles. It was a dominant thread in the fabric his Christology. Paul often substitutes *"in the Lord"* and *"in him"* for the more specific *"in Christ."* There is no formula here, but there is surely a common kernel of meaning. The nuances of each phrase are dependent on their individual contexts. That being said, there is clearly a mystical/spiritual dimension being described in saying that Christians are *"in Christ."* The phrase also implies an instrumental element, looking at the fact of our being *"in Christ"* as being done *"through Christ."* In short, we are *"in"* Christ by being placed *"into"* Christ, *"through"* Christ. He is the agent and the object of this permanent re-creation. In every sense of the term, a new relationship has been established between us and Christ. It's wondrously true — we are in Christ and Christ is in us!

This was the Apostle John's assertion when he said, *"We know that we live in him and he in us"* (1 John 4:13). And, it is the fulfillment of Christ's prayer when he said, *"Father, just as you are in me and I am in you, may they also be in us"* (John 17:21). This is the basis and reality of our Christian identity.

The question is often raised regarding the part we play in the initiation of our new status with God. St. Augustine (354-430 AD) contended that we have no part in it. We can do nothing. We did

---

112 Greek: "parerchomai" (παρέρχομαι). This word means to pass by, or to pass away, as in the permanent loss of a loved one who has died. Hence James' use of it when describing the rich as those who will *"pass away like a wild flower"* (James 1:10). The Aorist tense of the verb here denotes a specific action in the past, definitely completed.

nothing. It's called Monergism. Those disagreeing would argue for Synergism. God offers the gift, independently and presciently. What he offers; we actively receive. But, whatever our leanings are on this controversy, we can surely all concur that, in the end, *"All this is from God, who reconciled us to himself through Christ"* (2 Corinthians 5:18). It's a done deal. Notice the past tense of the verbs. The old *"has"* gone; the new *"has"* come. Surprisingly, in translating 2 Corinthians 5:17, the NIV doesn't include the original Greek exclamation "Behold!" —but, it truly is something to see. Look at what God has done!

Once reconciled to God, we become reconcilers for God. What we've received, we offer to others. We've been commissioned to do so. God *"gave us the ministry[113] of reconciliation"* (2 Corinthians 5:18). On behalf of Christ and in his place, we are now in the service of others. In such an ambassadorship, there is no more fundamental duty than to extend the offer of reconciliation to everyone who recognizes their estrangement from God. We are ambassadors— agents of reconciliation.

Paul reminds us that the reconciliation process is initiated by God. He is *"reconciling the world to himself in Christ, not counting men's sins against them"* (2 Corinthians 5:19). Here is the essential feature of relationship restoration; God does not hold our sins against us.

Careful interpreters of Scripture are quick to point out that it is not God who is reconciled to us; but us who are reconciled to him. We are the ones who ruined the relationship. We created the estrangement between ourselves and our Creator. But, because of his grace, all that can be reversed. We can rejoice with King David. *"Blessed is the one whose transgressions are forgiven, who sins are covered.*

---

[113] Greek: "diakonia" (διακονία). This word describes service to others. It is the source of our word "deacon;" i.e., those who serve the needs of people in the local church, under the leadership and supervision of the elders. In a wider sense, we are all deacons of the Great Commission.

Blessed is the one whose sin the Lord does not count against them" (Psalm 32:1-2).

The United States has diplomatic relationships with 180 countries in the world. An ambassador is a high ranking official. He or she not only represents the president, but our entire nation. Ambassadors live in the country in which they serve. The analogy is a strong one for those of us who represent Christ in the countries where we live. As Paul reminds us here *"We are therefore Christ's ambassadors, as though God were making his appeal through us"* (2 Corinthians 5:20). God is speaking through us. Amazing!

Ambassadors are professional diplomats. They are tactful and skillful—especially in delicate and serious situations. Calm and deliberate, courteous, and patient, they are determined to find a solution to conflict. When necessary, they urge, beseech, and plead. We do too. *"We implore you on Christ's behalf: Be reconciled to God"* (5:20). It's not just our appeal; it's God's. There's a begging quality to the original word, which is not an idea easily applied to God. But, the spirit of urgency in his efforts to re-establish harmonious relationships with alienated human beings should not be dismissed as below his dignity. Quite to the contrary. We serve a humble God, who is Love itself.

We are ambassadors of the one, *"who being in very nature God, did not consider equality with God something to be used to his own advantage, but rather he made himself nothing by taking the very nature of a servant, being made in human likeness. And being found in appearance as a man, he humbled himself"* (Philippians 2:6-8).

Contrary to the common tenets of religion, reconciliation with God is not a matter of placating an easily irritated deity. Instead, a loving Creator graciously initiates the restoration of broken relationships with sinners. The question is whether or not people will respond. That's where we come in.

Paul summarizes the theological basis for the conciliatory plea of every Christian evangelist. *"God made him who had no sin to be sin for us, so that in him we might become the righteousness of God"* (2 Corinthians 5:21).

Reconciliation with God is possible because the sinless was sacrificed for the sinful. The innocent takes the place of the guilty. Sin is paid for. Relationship is restored. The Apostle Peter confirms this principle. *"He himself bore our sins in his body on the cross"* (1 Peter 2:24). Six hundred years earlier, Isaiah made a prediction so certain it was stated in the past tense. *"Surely he took up our pain and bore our suffering...he was pierced for our transgressions, he was crushed for our iniquities, the punishment that brought us peace was on him, and by his wounds we are healed"* (Isaiah 53:4-5). Paul concurs. *"Christ redeemed us from the curse of the law by becoming a curse for us, for it is written, 'Cursed is everyone who is hung on a pole'"* (Galatians 3:13). It was Christ's voluntary act that enabled God to make him our atoning sacrifice. *"I lay down my own life – only to take it up again. No one takes it from me, but I lay it down of my own accord"* (John 10:17-18). Hallelujah! What a Savior!

In First Corinthians Paul declares that Christ is *"our righteousness, holiness and redemption"* (1 Corinthians 1:30). Now, he takes it a step further. Not only is Christ our righteousness, we have the potential to *"become the righteousness of God"* (2 Corinthians 5:21). As we have received the righteousness of God through faith in Christ, we now have the opportunity to become the embodiment of it. Because of Jesus, we are right with God. We experience it. We live it. We personify it. We proclaim it. We are agents of reconciliation. Our mission is to bring that message of hope and peace to a world of heartbroken and desperate people.

THINK

1. What does it mean to say a relationship between two people is over because of "irreconcilable differences"? What word is used to describe a husband and wife in such a condition?

2. Are most people today estranged from God? Are they aware of it?

3. In your own words, what is reconciliation?

4. What role does a third party play in reconciliation between estranged individuals? Have you ever played such a role?

5. Is fear a proper motive to serve God?

6. How effective are you at persuading people to be reconciled to God? When was the last time you did it? Or, tried to?

7. How is *the love of Christ* compulsive?

8. Have you experienced the truth of 2 Corinthians 5:17? What is the evidence of the newness of your life?

9. Does God need to be reconciled to us, or do we need to be reconciled to him?

10. Do you have compassion for people who need to be reconciled to God?

ACT

1. Make a list of individuals within your sphere of influence (family, friends, co-workers, neighbors) who need to be reconciled to God. Commit yourself to consistent prayer on their behalf. Look for ways to minister to them.

2. Every morning tell God that you are ready and willing to act as an ambassador of Christ to those you meet who are estranged from him. Give him enthusiastic permission to use you as an agent of reconciliation.

3. Identify and address the reasons why you are not an effective agent of reconciliation; i.e., fear of rejection, inadequate knowledge of Scripture, time constraints, indifference, etc. Repent and commit yourself to positive change.

4. Enlist three to five friends that will agree to join you in holding each other accountable as agents of reconciliation.

5. Photocopy this section of 2 Corinthians. Paste it on a 3x5 card and carry it with you daily; internalizing it by reading it every chance you get.

Chapter 9

Being Emotionally Consistent

2 Corinthians 6:1-13

Once I was thumbing through one of those mail-order catalogues full of inexpensive novelty items you can't find in most stores. Page after page featured things like ear-muffs for your dog, monogrammed golf balls, Chia Pets, Billy Bass mounted fish, and t-shirts with sayings like "World's Greatest Lover." You get the idea.

One product caught my eye. It was called the "Mood-O-Meter." It was kind of a PG-13 item designed for married couples. Those of us who are married, even happily, sometimes aren't exactly sure if our spouse is in the mood for romance, come the end of the day. That's where the Mood-O-Meter comes in. You mount it on the bedroom wall. It has a little dial and an arrow that you can move with your hand. The dial-face has options to choose from, like: "Tonight's the night!" or "I have a headache." Or "Don't even think about it." When you come in the room to go to bed, you know what to look forward to. Or, not. All you have to do is check the Mood-O-Meter.

I've known some people who could have done a service for all their family members, friends, and co-workers if they had a mood-meter on their foreheads. Then, at least we'd know what dimension of their mercurial personality we were going to be dealing with that day.

What we're talking about here is moodiness. We laugh it off with products like the Mood-O-Meter, but moodiness can be a serious personality disorder. And, it has all kinds of adverse effects on interpersonal relationships. Spiritual leaders with integrity work hard to have an even temperament. They do their best to be consistently predictable and pleasant to everyone.

Being even-tempered is a challenge. More so for some than others. Our youngest daughter is married to a guy who is ridiculously the same in every situation. In all the years they've been together, she's seldom seen him be anything but patient, polite, and pleasant—with her, and everyone else. How can someone be blessed with that kind of composure? But, what comes naturally to my son-in-law has to be worked at by the rest of us.

Mood swings can be a stubborn psychological problem and spiritual disability. It's little comfort to hear that Martin Luther was irritable and Charles Spurgeon was despondent. Or, that some of God's greatest representatives were melancholy much of the time. It's hard work managing our moods, but oh, so important to enhancing our influence with others.

By the very nature of things, emotions are inevitably subject to change. If you're alive, you know that. You're going along fine and then out of the blue, sometimes without notice and always without permission, your mood shifts. For some people it's genetic. Or they suffer from a serious chemical imbalance of some kind. They need medication. Most of us can manage our temperaments without pharmaceuticals, but we do need to attend to our ups and downs.

Sometimes that means talking to ourselves. Like King David did. *"Why, my soul, are you downcast?"* (Psalm 42:5) As Martin Lloyd-Jones counsels in his book, *Spiritual Depression*, if we don't talk to ourselves, our selves will talk to us.[114] And we won't like what our worst self has to say.

Moods, it seems, are affected by at least three things—circumstances, relationships, and our own disposition. To manage the turbulence that each of these can bring, we are going to need lots

---

[114] Lloyd-Jones, Martin. *Spiritual Depression*. Grand Rapids, MI: Wm. B. Eerdmans Publishing, 1965.

of God's grace. Thankfully too, we can learn from the example of others. Once again, the Apostle Paul is a first-rate role model for us to imitate.

Paul knew about God's grace. He'd been transformed by it. In his first letter to Timothy he testifies,

> *I thank Christ Jesus our Lord, who has given me strength, that he considered me trustworthy, appointing me to his service. Even though I was once a blasphemer and a persecutor and a violent man, I was shown mercy because I acted in ignorance and unbelief. The grace of our Lord was poured out on me abundantly, along with the faith and love that are in Christ Jesus.* (1 Timothy 1:12-14)

The apostle advises us to do the same—to let God's unconditional loving kindness work its wonders in our personalities. *"As God's co-workers*[115] *we urge you not to receive God's grace in vain"* (2 Corinthians 6:1).

Everything I do as a spiritual leader, including the management of my moods, is going to be in partnership with God. That privileged opportunity comes from the cornucopia of God's grace that has been lavishly offered to us all. In short, God is nicer to us than any of us deserves. He's eager to help and bless. That's what makes grace so amazing. But to have it, experience it, to be blessed and enabled by it, we have to *"receive"* it. Like ourselves sometimes, the Corinthians were not letting God's grace have its full effect in their lives. The grammar of the original Greek construction of this sentence implies that they should stop doing what they've been doing and do something else. In this case, to let God fully bless them.

---

[115] Greek: "sunergeō" (συνεργέω). This verb is the origin of our word "synergy." Synergy happens when two things work together, the result of which is greater than what could have been accomplished by themselves. The sum is greater than the parts. This single word is rendered in the NIV by a phrase, "God's co- workers."

Paul underscores this admonition with a reference to Isaiah. The mighty prophet had faithfully quoted Yahweh as saying, *"In the time of my favor I heard you, and in the day of salvation I helped you"* (2 Corinthians 6:2). *"Favor"* is another word for grace.

Have you ever been invited to a party at someone's house and when you arrived the host or hostess gave you a gift? They're called party "favors." The feeling engendered in us by such a gesture is one of surprised gratitude. Our friends have invited us to enjoy their home, a delicious meal, and engaging conversation. To complete such warm hospitality, they've given us a gift for coming. God's grace is like that; it's a favor. It makes us feel special. Paul exults, *"I tell you, now is the time of God's favor, now is the day of salvation"* (2 Corinthians 6:2).

Salvation literally means to be made healthy or whole. It is God's grace that makes today, and every day, an opportunity for spiritual healing and renewed vigor, even when we're up against things that all too often rob us of our vitality.

CIRCUMSTANCES

Circumstances are the situations we find ourselves in. The Latin word *circumstantia* means to stand in what's around us. Circumstances have the power to influence us because of the emotions they can generate. Our challenge is to stand up to the situation we are standing in. As Viktor Frankl reminded us in his memoirs of Auschwitz, *Man's Search for Meaning,* "the last of human freedoms is the ability to choose one's attitude in a given set of circumstances."[116] God's saving grace enables us to maintain our psychological equilibrium in whatever our current environment might be.

Some poor souls are uncontrollably S.A.D. They suffer from Seasonal Affected Disorder. An overcast day makes them feel gloomy. Many of us are plagued with some sort of mood malady.

---

[116] Frankl, Viktor. *Man's Search for Meaning.* Boston: Beacon Press, 1959.

We worry that someone will see through our pretense of stability and artificial composure. The Apostle Paul's vulnerable candor is liberating for those of us hiding behind a facade of equanimity. He describes a litany of his own potentially mood-altering circumstances. *"Troubles, hardships[117] and distresses...beatings, imprisonments and riots...hard work, sleepless nights and hunger"* (2 Corinthians 6:4-5).

Let's be honest; if these kinds of situations don't affect our mental outlook, we aren't authentically human. Paul's life was awash with circumstantial turbulence, but he characteristically triumphed over it.

I think of the time that he and his friend Silas were jailed on false charges in Philippi. There they were; stuck in stocks, still bleeding and bruised from a severe flogging, sleepless and hungry in the middle of the night—but, what were they doing? Singing![118] God's grace created composure and joy, in spite of their circumstances.

Paul's emotional consistency added to the credibility of his character. He could say of himself and his apostolic coworkers, *"As servants of God we commend ourselves in every way"* (2 Corinthians 6:4). Despite adverse, and often, injurious circumstances, these men commended themselves by displaying *"great endurance"*[119] (2 Corinthians 6:4). There was a steadiness to Paul's temperament that even *"beatings, imprisonments and riots"* (2 Corinthians 6:5) couldn't displace. Daily hardships and even life-threatening events converged to create what he describes as *"troubles, hardships and distresses"* (2 Corinthian 6:4). That last term is a word that means to be caught and

---

[117] Greek: "anagkē" (ἀνάγκη). This term depicts forced necessity; imposed by circumstances or duty. It implies calamity and distress.

[118] *"About midnight Paul and Silas were praying and singing hymns to God, and other prisoners were listening to them"* (Acts 16:25).

[119] Greek: "hupomonē" (ὑπομονή). Literally, this term means to "stand up under." It suggests steadfastness, constancy, and perseverance.

cramped in a narrow place, with no room to move and no way to get out.

It brings to mind the 2010 movie, *127 Hours*, about the life-threatening ordeal of Aron Ralston, who cut off his right arm with a dull knife blade after it was pinned between two boulders for several days in a remote canyon near Moab, Utah. The film was based on a book by Ralston called *Between a Rock and a Hard Place*.[120]

It seems Paul's whole life was between a rock and a hard place. But, in every desperate situation he received a fresh supply of God's grace. Such merciful compassion empowers us to get the better of situations that could easily get the better of us. Paul continues to describe the circumstances that can be endured by such enabling grace.

RELATIONSHIPS

At times, the challenges to our emotional stability get personal. In fact, there aren't many difficulties in life that are not directly or indirectly related to people. Not that others create our problems; although they can and often do. But inevitably, they play a part in the volatility of our emotional state. Then, what do we do?

Nowadays, we hear a lot about "toxic" people. I have a book in my library called, *Toxic Parents: Overcoming Their Hurtful Legacy and Reclaiming Your Life,* by Susan Forward.[121] Believe me, I have known plenty of students who are trying to do just that. We can't control other people, but we can seek a quality of character that will help us to cope with them when they are at their worst. The apostle itemizes his successes at such character-development: *"In purity, under-standing, patience and kindness"* (2 Corinthians 6:6).

---

[120] Ralston, Aron. *Between a Rock and a Hard Place.* New York: Simon & Schuster, 2004.

[121] Forward, Susan. *Toxic Parents: Overcoming Their Hurtful Legacy & Reclaiming Your Life.* New York: Random House, 2002.

Paul starts with purity. If something's pure it is unmixed; free of contaminants. Pure people have moral integrity. Roman Catholicism finds itself reeling from the sex-abuse scandals seemingly rampant with priests around the world. Protestant pastors are not exempt. It's called C.S.A. Clergy Sexual Abuse. The label describes spiritual leaders who take advantage of individuals who trust them. Impurity is poisonous. How wide the damage caused by such needy, emotionally unstable individuals. Personal purity is our responsibility. Paul made it a priority.

The apostle's persona was also characterized by *"understanding"* (2 Corinthians 6:6). Moody people are typically preoccupied with how they are feeling. They lack the capacity to walk a while in someone else's shoes. Their primary concern is being understood by others. They don't typically have the energy or the inclination to understand someone else.

People almost always test our *"patience"*[122] (2 Corinthians 6:6). Paul knew this from firsthand experience, especially with the Corinthians. Still, his mindset and manner of ministry was to be patient. A moody person, by contrast, is easily irked and agitated. Quick to explode; their moodiness creates their impatience. Let's not let that happen to us.

As patience cultivates a positive response to exasperating people, *"kindness"* (2 Corinthians 6:6) is the good-natured initiative we take toward them. Hard to define, kindness is something we all intuitively recognize when we see it. And especially so, when we are the recipients of it. Kind people are polite, attentive, generous, and gracious. Kindness is active goodness. It is love in action. It is loving kindness.

---

[122] Greek: "makrothumia" (μακροθυμία). This term was commonly applied to one's capacity to not be annoyed by people. Longsuffering is an old word to describe this discipline to not react or seek revenge. Such a person can endure injury, trouble, or provocation patiently.

Moodiness is mitigated by Christ-likeness. But, where are we going to get all these Christ-like qualities Paul has been enumerating? The answer comes in the form of a prepositional phrase. We are not going to get purity, patience, understanding, and kindness *from* something, but rather, *in* something—to be specific, *"In the Holy Spirit"* (2 Corinthians 6:6). When the Holy Spirit is the atmosphere in which we live, then we become like Christ. It's that simple.

Paul continues to delineate the emotional consistency characteristic of our relationships with others. Fundamental, is *"sincere love"* (2 Corinthians 6:6). Genuine love is essentially *"sincere"*[123] (2 Corinthians 6:6). It was a term the ancient Greeks used to describe a piece of pottery without any cracks.

Back in those days, crooked merchants often sold pots and vases with cracks by sealing up the fissures with wax and glazing it over. The unsuspecting buyer was easily fooled. But the savvy shopper would run a flame of some sort over the surface of the clay. As the wax melted out of the cracks, the "hypocrites" would soon be revealed for the phonies they were. Truly loving people don't fake it. No wax in the cracks. Their love is sincere.

Leaders with integrity embody authentic love. One way they consistently do that is in *"truthful speech"* (2 Corinthians 6:7). As Paul put it in another place, *"Speaking the truth in love"* (Ephesians 4:15).

We realize too, that getting mastery over moodiness is part of a much larger spiritual battle. Oftentimes it's akin to hand to hand combat. *"In the power of God with weapons of righteousness in the right hand and in the left"* (2 Corinthians 6:7). We need to be armed if we are going to win the fight.

---

[123] Greek: "anupokritos" (ἀνυπόκριτος). This term described things that were unfeigned or undisguised. It is transliterated into English as "un-hypocritical."

It's a good bet that Paul had been to more than one sports arena where men, brandishing knives, swords, spears, and spiked clubs, fought to the finish. "Those who are about to die, salute you," the gladiators shouted to the crowds. Without a weapon of some kind, the combatants would be defenseless. And dead. When it comes to emotional consistency, the battle is oftentimes internal; the opponent is us. We are up against the stubborn manifestations of our own depravity.

DISPOSITION

Paul next outlines nine sets of extremes that commonly bring out the worst in even the best of us. The details emerge from his personal experiences in each category; we can easily imagine our own variations of them.

> *Through glory and dishonor, bad report and good report; genuine, yet regarded as imposters; known, yet regarded as unknown; dying, and yet we live on; beaten and yet not killed; sorrowful, yet always rejoicing; poor, yet making many rich; having nothing, and yet possessing everything.* (2 Corinthians 6:8-10)

As all experienced college professors can testify, every semester students manifest a distinct mood shift right after midterms. The day before the test everything is hunky-dory, despite their nervousness about the imminent exam. For many of them, though, the day after the test is a different story. "Down in the dumps" my mom would call it. They didn't do as well as they'd expected. They are depressed over points lost. It takes a week or more for amiable rapport to return between the test-giver and the test-takers. It's an academic example of *"bad report, good report"* (2 Corinthians 6:8). Of course, there are always those whose grades matched or exceeded their expectations; no mood swings there. What we're talking about is the intersection of circumstance and disposition. They impact each other.

167

It's the human condition. For some of us it is a bigger challenge than for others. But, it's nonetheless real for everyone.

Another aspect of academia that illustrates what Paul alludes to here pertains to *"glory and dishonor"* (2 Corinthians 6:8). At the end of every school year, our university has an awards assembly. We call it "Celebration Chapel." It's an event where scholarships, grants, certificates, and plaques are handed out. Sometimes the amounts of money that go with the awards are sizable. Everyone hopes to get something. But, not everyone does. For those who walk to the front to the applause of their classmates, it's nothing short of *"glory."* They've been recognized. They've been honored. But, for those who don't get public appreciation, or scholarship money, the result is often resentment and bitterness at being overlooked and left out.

In the overall scheme of things, GPAs and scholarships are not serious concerns. Now that we are out of school, we don't think in those terms much anymore. There are greater challenges to face. For example, trying to keep our emotional equilibrium when we see ourselves as *"genuine, yet regarded as imposters"* (2 Corinthians 6:8). Even if the opinion of such people doesn't really count, it still hurts.

I remember a painful experience like that. In the small church I was pastoring, one of the families had been going through a tidal wave of trouble. One evening, one of the elders and I paid a visit to their home. The dad was still at work; the wife was alone, and at wit's end. We listened sympathetically to her woes. You can imagine our shock though when, in exasperation, she turned her frustrations on the church and the two of us. She blurted it out, "You don't care!" It was like a sharp blade to the heart. We were genuine; but she was convinced we weren't. And said so. I left there that night, depressed. To be regarded as phony, when I knew I wasn't—that was hard to handle.

Paul would have done better, I think. His priorities supplied the motivation for rising above predictable and understandable mood swings. *"As servants of God we commend ourselves in every way"* (2 Corinthians 6:4). Even more explicitly, he says, *"We put no stumbling block in anyone's path, so that our ministry will not be discredited"* (2 Corinthians 6:3).

I was colleagues once with a professor who sometimes left students in tears. Revered for his expertise, he was equally disregarded for his capricious personality. Some days he was jovial and outgoing, laughing, joking, and glad to see you. On other days, he was distant, cranky, and occasionally downright cruel. The students didn't know just which teacher they were going to get. His depth of learning, incisive wit, command of ideas and language couldn't compensate for his unpredictability. Sadly, he did not *"commend"* himself to those of us who were witnesses of his moodiness. His personality was a stumbling block.

We are who we are. Still, the old dictum that people change—but not much—need not be inevitable. We owe it to God, ourselves, and those we lead to make the changes necessary to represent him rightly and serve them well. We must resolutely commit ourselves to never let our emotional inconsistency trip people up.

Paul continues his enumeration of mood-altering contrasts. *"[We are] known, yet regarded as unknown"* (2 Corinthians 6:9). Who doesn't want to be significant? Who doesn't want to be somebody to someone? Or better yet, to everyone.

Francis Schaeffer wrote a short little book entitled, *No Little People, No Little Places.*[124] It's an encouraging reminder to those of us laboring away in anonymity, that everyone is significant in God's estimation. Even if we feel like a lonely farmer working forty acres of hardpan out in the middle of nowhere, we are not small and what

---

[124] Schaeffer, Francis. *No Little People, No Little Places.* Wheaton, IL: Crossway Books, 2003.

we do is not unimportant. Still, to not have our worthiness acknowledged can be a downer — but, it shouldn't be.

Getting older also presents some unique, and sometimes unexpected, mood-swings. Aging can be depressing. Paul maintains a triumphant tone in facing such realities. He's determined to not let its challenges discredit his witness. *"[We are] dying, yet we live on"* (2 Corinthians 6:9). He has already described himself as *"wasting away"* (2 Corinthians 4:16). Now, he owns up to the subtle reality that his work on earth was almost done. But, in the meantime he lives each day he has left to the fullest.

And then, there's money. Each of us has a knee-jerk response to money — or the lack of it. What power those greenbacks have to lift our spirits when we have some extra cash, or deflate us when we don't. Yet, dare we let money matters sway us so much?

By the world's standards, Paul was a pauper. But, did he feel sorry for himself? I don't think so. He sees himself as being *"Poor, yet making many rich"* (2 Corinthians 6:10). The lack of capital did not affect his outlook on life. *"I know what it means to be in need and I know what it is to have plenty. I have learned the secret of being content in any and every situation, whether well fed or hungry; whether living in plenty or in want"* (Philippians 4:12).

Not all moods are unfounded mental states. Sometimes we are down because we have good reason to be. In this world, there is a lot to be sad about. The Apostle Paul was in touch with reality. He admits that at times, he was *"sorrowful"* (2 Corinthians 6:10). Jesus himself was sorrowful too — often enough to be called a *"man of sorrows and acquainted with grief"* (Isaiah 53:3, NIV 1984). Being sorrowful is not being moody. But, how we handle our legitimate sadness is crucial. Paul testifies that he was *"sorrowful, yet always rejoicing"* (2 Corinthians 6:10). Again, our Savior sets the example. *"For the joy set before him endured the cross"* (Hebrews 12:2).

Paul closes out his treatment of the topic of moodiness by acknowledging one of the fiercest enemies of emotional equilibrium — unrequited love. What will we do if the people we love don't reciprocate? What did Paul do? Never one to deny or mask his true feelings, he pleads with the Corinthians, *"We have spoken freely to you, Corinthians and opened wide our hearts to you. We are not withholding our affection from you, but you are withholding yours from us. As a fair exchange — I speak to you as to my children — open wide your hearts also"* (2 Corinthians 6:12-13). When someone we love, won't or can't love us in return; that hurts. But, we keep loving them anyway.

Unmanaged moodiness is a sin. It is especially so for spiritual leaders, because it trips up the people we lead and love. It confuses them. They wonder where they stand with us. Arguably, it would be better to always be difficult than to be unpredictable.

Let me end this chapter with a true confession. I've been rightly criticized in the past for being one thing when I'm up in front of a group of people — energetic, funny, friendly, and affable. And then, being something quite different once I'm "off stage" — quiet, withdrawn, lost in my own thoughts. I don't intend to baffle people; but sometimes I do. Still, there's no excuse for that kind of inconsistency. Leaders have a public persona and a private one. But the difference between the two should be minimal. Those who look to us for leadership need us to be the same person. All the time.

THINK

1. Would your family and friends consider you a moody person?

2. Isn't it natural to experience a wide spectrum of emotions as a human being? Shouldn't we expect and accept a certain degree of moodiness?

3. Why is a moody disposition a *"stumbling block"* to those we live with and love?

4. Why does Paul introduce this passage about emotional consistency with two verses about God's grace?

5. What is the broader sense of the term *"salvation"*?

6. How do we *"commend"* ourselves to others?

7. In 2 Corinthians 6:4-5 Paul lists a set of circumstances that tend to have a negative effect on our moods. What comes to mind when you think of each of these nine trying situations?

8. Is your mood affected negatively by fatigue or the lack of sleep or food?

9. In 2 Corinthians 6:6-7, Paul enumerates several positive qualities that demonstrate emotional consistency. Which ones are your strong points? Your weakest?

10. Do you love people who don't or won't return your affection? How does that affect your mood?

ACT

1. Ask some people who know you well if they think you are a moody person.

2. Make a list of individuals you may have hurt by being in a bad mood lately. Ask their forgiveness at the first opportunity you get.

3.   Make up your mind to not be bothered by being over-looked or under-appreciated.

4.   Practice preventative measures to keep you from unmanageable mood swings. Get enough sleep, eat better, and exercise regularly.

5.   Make a list of the Christ-like characteristics that you consistently demonstrate to others. Pat yourself on the back for your success.

Chapter 10

Resisting Compromise

2 Corinthians 6:14-7:1

On the theory that visual aids improve the effectiveness of oral communication, one Sunday I introduced the sermon for the morning holding a big green ceramic frog. With everyone paying rapt attention, I explained to the audience that if my stoneware frog was a real frog and you put it into a pan of water and slowly increased the temperature of the water, the frog, being a cold-blooded creature, would not realize that it was gradually boiling to death — until it was too late.

I went on to say that though human beings aren't reptiles, the principle still applies. Few of us intentionally get ourselves involved in behaviors that we know are going to hurt us. We certainly wouldn't say, "Today, I'm going to purposefully put myself in harm's way." To the contrary, we typically get entangled in spiritually perilous situations without realizing it. Little by little, imperceptibly, it happens. It's called compromise.

Compromise occurs when we make seemingly negligible adjustments to our moral values for some perceived immediate benefit. Like the proverbial frog in boiling water, we are oblivious to what we are doing to ourselves. The incremental modification of our ethical standards is slight, slow, and subtle — but deadly. We are in extended jeopardy, but we aren't aware of it.

Before William Jessup University had its new state-of-the-art dining commons, we all ate in a simple no-frills cafeteria. At morning snack time, you made your selections, tabulated the cost and then dropped your nickels, dimes, and quarters into a muffin tin the cooks left on the countertop. Or, you slipped a dollar or two under the corner of the pan. It was the honor system.

One day I watched a hungry student work the system. He made his choices of what to eat and drink. And then I watched him make another choice—not to pay. Instead of dropping the correct change into the tin, he flicked it with his finger, giving the cooks, working a few feet away, the impression he had paid for his snacks. But, he didn't. No one knew that but him. And me. Some might say "Big deal! It was less than a couple of bucks." True. And, maybe he intended to come back and pay later in the day. Maybe he did. But, that morning he took some food and didn't pay for it. He compromised. He made a slight adjustment to his moral values for the immediate benefit of getting something to eat. He wasn't a thief. Or, was he? That's the trouble with compromise; it doesn't seem so serious. At least, not at the moment. But in time, it will. The temperature's rising.

One thing you learn in the study of biblical interpretation is that stories in Scripture are typically told without comment as to the behavior of the participants in the drama. The writers don't pause to say, "Now don't miss the moral of this story." They just tell it.

For example, take the episode in Genesis starting in chapter 13. Lot and his uncle Abraham have been blessed by God with overwhelming prosperity. Their wealth was so extensive that their combined flocks and herds were running out of grazing room. Conflicts kept erupting between the herdsmen of each man. Ever gracious, Abraham suggested that they go their separate ways, offering his nephew first choice of the prospects for their continued mutual success.

Lot could have the rocky hill country where they were currently located, or the lush flatlands below. It was an easy decision to make—if you were thinking only of immediate gain. Looking out for himself, Lot chose the fertile plain. The only catch was that the two main cities in that expansive greenbelt were Sodom and Gomorrah, known by all to be owned and operated by practicing homosexuals. But Lot decided to chance it. He chose the valley below. Scripture says he *"pitched his tents near Sodom"* (Genesis 13:12). The only comment Moses makes in telling the story was to say, *"Now the men of Sodom were wicked and were sinning greatly against the LORD"* (Genesis 13:13, NIV 1984).

In the next chapter of Genesis, we find Lot, his wife, and daughters, living in Sodom (Genesis 14:12). Before long, Lot had become so integrated into the daily life of the town, that he was a member of what amounted to the city council (Genesis 19:1).

In the meantime, Yahweh told Abraham of his plans to incinerate both Sodom and Gomorrah because of their sexual depravity. Concerned for Lot and his family, Abraham pleads with God. *"What if there are fifty righteous people in the city? Will you really sweep it away and not spare the place for the sake of the fifty righteous people in it?"*(Genesis 18:23). He courageously negotiates with God, eventually persuading him to not obliterate the place, if at least ten righteous persons could be found there. Yahweh momentarily capitulates, telling Abraham, *"The outcry against Sodom and Gomorrah is so great and their sin so grievous, that I will go down and see if what they have done is as bad as the outcry that has reached me. If not, I will know"* (Genesis 18:20-21).

In Genesis 19, God carries through with his plan in the person of two angels. But the angels were undercover; they looked like young men. No wings. No glow. They meet Lot, who promptly insists that they accept his hospitality and lodge in his home for the night, rather than spreading out their bedrolls in the city square as they'd planned.

Word soon spread that two young strangers were in town. The Bible is explicit about what happened next. *"Before they had gone to bed, all the men from every part of the city of Sodom — both young and old — surrounded the house. They called to Lot, 'Where are the men who came to you tonight? Bring them out to us so that we can have sex with them'"* (Genesis 19:4-5). That prospect so mortified Lot that in inexplicable desperation, he offers his two daughters to the mob instead, saying, *"Do what you like with them"* (Genesis 19:8).

Long story short, the angels had to forcibly escort the reluctant family from the city. Lot's daughters' intended husbands were incredulous when the angel said, *"Hurry and get out of this place, because the LORD is about to destroy this city."* Moses adds, *"But his sons-in-law thought he was joking"* (Genesis 19:14). With the clock ticking, the angels grabbed the foursome and dragged them out of town. *"As soon as they had brought them out, one of them said, 'Flee for your lives! Don't look back[125], and don't stop anywhere on the plain! Flee to the mountains or you will be swept away!'"* (Genesis 19:17)

Once safely holed up in a cave in the hills miles away, Lot's compromised character continued to have a ruinous effect. With Sodom and Gomorrah reduced to ashes, his daughters conspire to commit incest with their father, for the stated purpose of perpetuating the family line. They got their dad drunk and then took turns having sex with him. Both girls got pregnant. Nine months later, two sons were born (Genesis 19:36-38). They preserved the family line alright, but the descendants of those boys became the Moabites and the Ammonites, a couple of clans that gave the ancient Israelites nothing but trouble for generations.

The sordid saga of Lot and his family can be traced to compromise. One small modification of moral standards on Lot's part led to another. And another. And another. The Apostle Peter's reference to this story underscores Lot's conflicted state of mind, speaking of him as *"a righteous man, who was distressed by the depraved*

---

[125] Lot's wife is infamous for ignoring the angel's warning. She was instantaneously calcified into a pillar of salt (Genesis 19:26).

conduct of the lawless (for that righteous man, living among them day after day, was tormented in his righteous soul by the lawless deeds he saw and heard)" (2 Peter 2:7-8). Tragically though, compromise had paralyzed him. Lot could no longer do what was right.

Compromise is typically imperceptible and often contagious. Lot's wife couldn't resist just one more glance at the city she'd grown to love. And she paid the price for it. Lot's daughters rationalized incest for the sake of preserving their father's legacy. But generations of hostility followed. Incremental, seemingly incidental, violations of conscience almost always result in catastrophic consequences.

Compromise is the theme that Paul develops here with the Corinthians.[126] He does so with a series of pointed questions.

> *What do righteousness and wickedness have in common? Or what fellowship can light have with darkness? What harmony is there between Christ and Belial? What does a believer have in common with an unbeliever? What agreement is there between the temple of God and idols?* (2 Corinthians 6:14-16)

These questions are preceded by the principle they are intended to support: *"Do not be yoked[127] together with unbelievers"* (2 Corinthians 6:14).

In the Old Testament God separated animals, birds, fish, and even insects, into two categories—the "clean" and the "unclean." This precept applied to foods that his people were allowed to eat in order to protect their health, and to set them apart from their pagan

---

[126] The apostle interrupts his appeal for mutual affection with the Corinthian congregation, just stated in 6:12. He will return to it in 7:2.

[127] Greek: "mē heterozugeō" (μή ἑτεροζυγέω). Grammatically, the verb here is a present imperative, preceded by a negative prohibition. Paul is not suggesting a preventative measure. Rather, he was telling the Corinthians to stop an activity they were currently engaged in; i.e., compromising. The original agricultural injunction is found in Deuteronomy 22:10.

neighbors. On a broader scale, the segregation of what was approved and disapproved was extended to fabrics woven together, seeds sown together, and to domesticated animals working together. Ones with cloven hoofs were prohibited from teamwork with those with un-cloven hoofs. The ox and donkey, for example, could not plow a field in tandem.

The same mandate applied to human beings in covenant relationship with Yahweh. He forbade his people from being teamed up with people who weren't his people. The Israelites were "clean;" the Egyptians, Assyrians, Philistines, Hittites, Amorites and Jebusites, etcetera, were "unclean." The two were incompatible. No intermingling allowed.

APPRECIATING OUR IDENTITY

Compromise is a fundamental threat to integrity. At any given moment, we either have integrity or we don't. We are living out what we claim to believe in, or we aren't. The Corinthians, despite their feeble rationalizations, were integrity-deficient. It was a double standard that had to be abandoned.

Paul begins where all repentant change must start—the recognition of who we are. He reminds the Corinthians that *"we are the temple of the living God"* (2 Corinthians 6:16). We live in God, and he lives in us. We are in covenantal relationship with each other. This sacred union must be marked by observable holiness. There is an exclusivity to the relationship that must be maintained.

There is a fundamental distinction between people in covenant relationship with God and those who aren't. That distinction is not always apparent or appreciated. But it needs to be. Paul insists that the Corinthians get unyoked from the unbelievers in Corinth. Time hasn't changed that mandate. We must stay out and get out of long-term or binding relationships that are spiritually incompatible.

These days this obligation has typically been applied to marriage and dating.[128] In pastoral ministry, when it came to wedding ceremonies in which I was asked to officiate, my policy was politely rigid. I would, and occasionally did, marry two non-Christians to each other, as well as two Christians to each other. But, I would never marry a Christian to a non-Christian. The reason is simple: the two are not equally matched. No matter what else they may have in common or how well they apparently get along, a Christian and a non-Christian do not have enough in common to ensure them of a lasting and harmonious relationship. To join them together would be an act of serious compromise.

While I've concluded that the principles and prohibitions Paul details here apply to marriage, it is not what he was thinking about when he made this strict prohibition. Romantic compromise wasn't his concern. It had to do, instead, with trade guilds.

In the first century it was common for trade guilds to be semi-religious organizations. The labor unions in those days—tentmakers, silversmiths, butchers, candle makers, and the like, were almost always associated with a pagan deity. The god was their patron. Union meetings were often held in the idol's temple. Typically, after the business of the day was conducted, there was food and drink. And, debauchery.

As a rule, Paul was open-minded regarding matters of conscience; like eating meat sacrificed to idols.[129] But, he was quite unyielding when it came to Christians actually being inside idols' temples, whether it was for a meal or a union meeting. He argues, *"What agreement is there between the temple of God and idols? For we are*

---

[128] Technically, this is called the "extended application" of Scripture. For a helpful discussion of the concept, see *How To Read the Bible for All Its Worth*, 3rd edition by Gordon D. Fee and Douglas Stuart, pp. 76-77. The challenge to make a text apply to a social-historical context foreign to the original one is real. Proceed with caution.

[129] See 1 Corinthians 10:25-30.

the temple of the living God" (2 Corinthians 6:16). He has already made this conclusion clear to the Corinthians.

> *The sacrifices of pagans are offered to demons, not to God, and I do not want you to be participants with demons. You cannot drink the cup of the Lord and the cup of demons too; you cannot have a part in both the Lord's table and the table of demons.* (1 Corinthians 10:20-21)

Paul is of one mind with James, who reminds us that *"Friendship with the world means enmity against God"* (James 4:4). That understood, staying clear of compromise is often tricky territory to navigate. In Corinth, to get or keep a job typically required trade guild membership that was more often than not affiliated with idols, idol worship, and all the promiscuity that went with it. What's a Christ-follower to do when it comes to association with such people and their practices? Paul, takes a hard line on this one.

That same high standard still applies today. It is a violation of God's will for a Christian to establish or remain in a long-term, binding, or intimate relationship with a non-Christian.

Notice please that Paul does not prohibit associating with non-Christians. He doesn't say we can't socialize with friends, classmates, coworkers, or next door neighbors who don't share our commitment to Christ. As he's already explained to the Corinthians, to avoid that we would *"have to leave this world"* (1 Corinthians 5:10). But, the apostle does outlaw irrevocable relationships with them. It comes back to being *"yoked together"* (2 Corinthians 6:14).

Most of us have a mental image of a yoke. A yoke is a substantial, unyielding length of timber. Usually, it consists of a crosspiece with a pair of bow-shaped loops, each placed on the neck of two animals, binding them together. Under the control of the plowman, both animals go in the same direction, at the same speed. But, without someone at the reins, the animals take the path determined by the strongest and most stubborn of the two. They can't go their separate ways.

I had a Christian friend once who was business partners with a non-Christian. They'd been working together for years. Tens of thousands of dollars and endless hours had been invested in their venture. In discussing this text with him one day, he admitted to me that incompatibility between the two of them was a common occurrence, as they clashed over how to manage their company. His conscience was not clear about many of the decisions he was forced to make. He found himself having to go in the direction his partner thought was best. What else could he do? They were bound together, financially and contractually. Most of the time, where his partner went, he went. The two of them were in a binding, yet incongruous relationship. It's those kinds of affiliations we are being warned of here. Christians and non-Christians simply don't have enough in common to make a go of it. Such partnerships invite repeated compromise. So, we are to stay out of an alliance like that. Or, to get out of it.[130]

Paul continues his prohibition of compromise with the first of five pointed questions. *"What do righteousness*[131] *and wickedness*[132]

---

[130] There is one biblical exception to the termination of such an incompatible relationship: a marriage between a Christian and a non-Christian. This course of action does not apply in such cases. Paul advised the Corinthians, *"If any brother has a wife who is not a believer and she is willing to live with him he must not divorce her. And if a woman has a husband who is not a believer and he is willing to live with her, she must not divorce him"* (1 Corinthians 7:12-13).

[131] To be righteous is to be right with God. Jesus Christ is the means and focus of our righteousness with God (1 Corinthians 1:30). Not being united with him by faith, makes a person un-righteous by definition. In short, a Christian is right with God; a non-Christian isn't. There is an absence of spiritual compatibility between the two of them.

[132] Greek: "anomia" (ἀνομία). This word means to be without law or lawless. It connotes status as well as behavior.

have in common[133]*?"* (2 Corinthians 6:14) The implied answer is as simple as it is unyielding: not enough! What essential commonality can there be between someone who is right with God and someone who is wrong with God? To be sure, a Christian and a non-Christian are alike sinners; but one is a sinner saved by grace (Ephesians 2:8). The other is not. Regardless of whatever affinity may exist between them, Christians and non-Christians are fundamentally and inalterably incompatible. Their essential identities make partnership impossible.

Paul now asks his second rhetorical question. *"What fellowship can light have with darkness?"*[134] (2 Corinthians 6:14) This is an appeal to common sense. It's basic physics. There are shades of gray, but light and darkness can't be experienced at the same time. Darkness is the absence of light. Light dispels darkness. As Martin Luther King, Jr. reminded us, "Darkness cannot drive out darkness; only light can do that."[135]

Christians are *"children of the light"* (1 Thessalonians 5:5). We live in the light. We are light. Non-Christians live in spiritual darkness.

---

[133] Greek: "metochē" (μετοχή). This term connotes partnership. It means "to have together." It is the same word used in Luke 5:7 of the fishing partnerships shared by the first four disciples, Peter and Andrew, James and John.

[134] Light's incompatibility with darkness is one of Scripture's most persistent analogies. This is especially true under the New Covenant. Christ is the light of the world (John 8:12; 9:5). His coming was like light shining in darkness (Matthew 4:16; Luke 1:79; John 1:4). The reason people reject him is because they love darkness rather than light (John 3:19). As believers, we have been called out of darkness into spiritual and moral light (Colossians 1:13; 1 Peter 2:9). Hell itself is *"outer darkness"* (Matthew 8:12, 22:13, 25:30). Satan rules spiritual darkness (Ephesians 6:12). And, ultimately, he will be confined to it (2 Peter 2:17). God, by contrast, is personified as light. *"God is light; in him there is not darkness at all"* (1 John 1:5). The rudimentary purpose of Christian ministry is to persuade people to turn from darkness to light (Acts 26:16). Paul describes conversion itself in such terms (2 Corinthians 4:6).

[135] Nobel Peace Prize acceptance speech, Stockholm, Sweden, December 11, 1964.

They are darkness. Compatibility is impossible. Partnership is prohibited. All else is compromise.

Paul next makes reference to the spiritual entities at war in the invisible conflict all human beings are caught up in, whether they know it or not. In this war, there is no chance of détente. He asks, *"What harmony[136] is there between Christ and Belial[137]?"* (2 Corinthians 6:15) Belial is a rude nickname for the devil, meaning "worthless one." What does the most worth-full person in the universe have in common with the most worth-less one? Nothing! Paul picks a musical term to describe the contrast. A Christian and a non-Christian cannot make beautiful music together. There can be no *"harmony"* between the two. The score of such a collaboration would be gratingly dissonant. We should stay out of such relationships. We must get out of such relationships. That's the message Paul is driving home with these repeated questions.

Leaving figures of speech and analogies behind, the apostle wraps up his argument with a plain, straightforward question: *"What does a believer have in common with an unbeliever?"* (2 Corinthians 6:15). There is no basis for community.

---

[136] Greek: "sumphōnia" (συμφωνία). This is the origin of our word "symphony." The Greek term is a hybrid of "together" and "voice." In Matthew 18:19 Jesus used it to depict an agreement between two individuals. *"If two of you on earth agree about anything you ask for, it will be done for them by my Father in heaven."*

[137] This term describes someone who is without restraint. It is only found here in the New Testament as an alias for Satan. In the Septuagint, the Greek translation of the Hebrew Old Testament, it was used as a proper name. Why Paul made the decision to describe Satan this way is uncertain. Perhaps it was in an effort to belittle the devil or to draw a starker contrast between him and Christ. It underscores the essential adversarial relationship between the two. Christ's mission is to destroy the devil's power (Hebrews 2:14). And, vice-versa. The contrast is absolute. There is no agreement between them in character or purpose.

Paul applies his argument to the specifics of the situation in Corinth. *"What agreement*[138] *is there between the temple*[139] *of God and idols?"* (2 Corinthians 6:16) There couldn't be a greater contrast between the people of God, among whom and in whom he takes up residence, and worshipers of artistically crafted substitutes for his existence, power, and presence. The Corinthian Christians needed to keep their distance from the idolatrous practices of their non-believing friends, neighbors, and coworkers. God is stubbornly strict in forbidding idolatry. He wants, expects, and demands spiritual monogamy. He won't share our devotion with any other supposed deity. His people can't leave the world, but they can stay out of idols' temples.

The school where I teach sponsors international education and service trips around the world. Recently a group of our students went to Thailand. One day, a visit to a Buddhist temple was on the itinerary. Most of the students went. After all, it was a unique exposure to Far East culture and religion. None of them thought for a moment that the golden Buddha inside stood for any kind of

---

[138] Greek: "sungkatathesis" (συγκατάθεσις), meaning "to put alongside another." This word is kindred to a verb that means "to consent." Luke used it to describe Joseph of Arimathea, as a member of the Jewish Sanhedrin, who had not "consented" to the decision to crucify Christ (Luke 23:51).

[139] Greek: "naos" (ναός). In contrast to the entire temple compound in Jerusalem, this term specifies the inner sanctuary itself, the Holy Place and the Holy of Holies, representing the very presence of God. The Tabernacle and the Temple of the Old Testament were impressive visual reminders that Yahweh himself was in the midst of his people and they were not to transfer their affections or allegiance to any of the heathen deities all around them in Canaan. To bring an idol into God's holy presence would be the ultimate in blasphemy (2 Kings 21:1-9; 23:3; Ezekiel 8:3-18). There is an absolute distinction between Creator and Creation. Paul has clearly instructed the Corinthians on this issue (1 Corinthians 10:7, 14). Idolatry is on his sin-lists (1 Corinthians 5:10; 6:9). It is consistently prohibited. The church has become the new temple of God (1 Corinthians 3:19; Ephesians 2:20; 1 Peter 2:5). Individually, our bodies are his temple too (1 Corinthians 6:19). There is no compatibility between the temple of God and the temple of idols.

spiritual reality. Other students, conscience-stricken, opted to do something else with the afternoon. Cultural exposure notwithstanding, they couldn't bring themselves to get that close to idolatry. It was a judgment call on everyone's part. I think Paul, a self-described "strong" brother,[140] would have sided with those who skipped the tour of the Buddhist temple that day. Better safe than sorry.

Idols' temples in first century Corinth weren't tourist attractions. They were part and parcel of the pagan way of life. Paul had no inclination toward compromise on this. For him, it was an identity issue. The church is the dwelling place of the Holy Spirit. We are God's temple; collectively and individually. *"For we are the temple of the living God"* (2 Corinthians 6:16). Paul has already made this explicitly clear to the Corinthians. *"Don't you know that you yourselves are God's temple and that God's Spirit dwells in your midst?"* (1 Corinthians 3:16) *"Do you not know that your bodies are temples of the Holy Spirit, who is in you, whom you have received from God?"* (1 Corinthians 6:19).

On two counts then, the Corinthians were to steer clear of idols' temples. Granted, we know that there is no spiritual reality to handcrafted chunks of stone or metal. *"We know that 'an idol is nothing at all in the world' and that 'there is no God but one'"* (1 Corinthians 8:4). Still, the evil spirits who traffic in such religious superstition are frighteningly real. *"Do I mean then that food sacrificed to an idol is anything, or that an idol is anything? No, but the sacrifices of pagans are offered to demons, not to God, and I do not want you to be participants with demons"* (1 Corinthians 10:19-20). This was enough reason for the Corinthians to stay out of such places. And, of any relationships that might have obligated them to be there. *"Are you trying to arouse the Lord's jealousy?"* (1 Corinthians 10:22)

---

[140] See Romans 14:1-23.

It is not the sexual shenanigans that often accompany idol worship that arouses God's jealousy and judgment. It's the idolatry that goes with the self-indulgence that is his primary concern. But, in Bible times, the two typically went together.

The Old Testament's Golden Calf episode is the prototype of such behavior. When the ancient Israelites had bowed the knee to Aaron's handiwork, he inexplicably declared, *"These are your gods, Israel, who brought you up out of Egypt"* (Exodus 32:4). The record then states: *"Afterward they sat down to eat and drink and got up to indulge in revelry"* (Exodus 32:6). The idolatry was augmented with an orgy.

Jesus himself connects sexual immorality and pagan idolatry in warnings to two of the seven churches in the Book of Revelation. He says to the congregation in Pergamum, *"I have a few things against you: You have people there who hold to the teaching of Balaam, who taught Balak to entice the Israelites to sin so that they ate food sacrificed to idols and committed sexual immorality"* (Revelation 2:14). To the church in Thyatira, he writes, *"I have this against you: You tolerate that woman Jezebel, who calls herself a prophet. By her teaching she misleads my servants into sexual immorality and the eating of food sacrificed to idols"* (Revelation 2:20). Paul echoes these admonitions to the church in Corinth.

When we lose sight of our identity as the covenant people of God, then we put our intimacy with him at risk—even if it's only in seemingly minor ways. Why would we take that chance when there are so many wonderful reasons not to? Paul quotes Leviticus 26:12 as applicable to Christians as well as our old covenant predecessors. *"As God has said, 'I will live among them and walk among them, and I will be their God and they will be my people"*[141] (2 Corinthians 6:16).

---

[141] The same words were part of Ezekiel's prophecy when he predicted Yahweh's presence with Israel upon their return from exile in Babylon. *"My dwelling place will be with them; I will be their God, and they will be my people"* (Ezekiel 37:27).

When the things that subtly call us to compromise steadily accumulate, the momentum becomes unstoppable. If the siren call was anything but faint, we would react in revulsion. Like Joseph's response to the shameless allurement from Potiphar's wife, *"Come to bed with me"* (Genesis 39:7). It was such an abrupt temptation, it shocked Joseph into immediate resistance. *"But, he refused"* (Genesis 39:8). He stated his reason for abstinence. *"How could I do such a wicked thing and sin against God?* (Genesis 39:9) To comply with her provocative come-on was incompatible with who he knew he was. His response was thus spontaneous and adamant. But more often than not, the most powerful temptations in our lives are not blatant, but understated. We are surreptitiously deceived. Frogs, in everhotter water.

We have acknowledged that these warnings and prohibitions to the Corinthians were not specifically about dating, marriage, and sexual temptation. But biblically, there is a connection between the disloyalty of idolatry and human hormones. That's the reason Yahweh strictly prohibited interracial marriage in the Old Testament. There was nothing inherently wrong in being an Egyptian, Philistine, Moabite, or Assyrian. It wasn't the ethnicity of the foreigner that was the problem. It was the foreignness of their religious commitments that made compatibility impossible.

Typically, when an Israelite did marry a foreign woman, she brought her gods along with her to her new home. Multiply that scenario a few thousand times, and there goes the covenant. Even Solomon, famous for his wisdom, disregarded this precept. The indictment against him was stinging.

> *King Solomon, however, loved many foreign women...Moabites, Ammonites, Edomites, Sidonians and Hittites. They were from nations about which the LORD had told the Israelites, 'You must not intermarry with them, because they will surely turn your hearts after their gods.' Nevertheless, Solomon, held fast to them in*

love... As Solomon grew old, his wives turned his heart after other gods and his heart was not fully devoted to the LORD his God, as the heart of David his father had been. He followed Ashtoreth the goddess of the Sidonians and Molech the detestable god of the Ammonites. So Solomon did evil in the eyes of the LORD; he did not follow the LORD completely, as David his father had done. (1 Kings 11:1-6)

Solomon remains a tragic example of the subtle dangers of compromise. Even smart frogs can boil to death.

Before we console ourselves by saying that we could never do such a thing, we should pause to recall the pastors, youth workers, and worship leaders we are personally aware of, who have. The temptation to compromise is subtle. And lethal. Sexual immorality is not incidental sin. But it's the disloyalty to God that is especially deplorable. It's not an oversimplification to say that anything or anyone who becomes more important to us than God is an idol. Idolatry is a possibility — for all of us. For any of us. *"Dear children, keep yourselves from idols"* (1 John 5:21).

ACCEPTING OUR RESPONSIBILITY

When it comes to compromising relationships, I have been repeating the same simple and strict advice: Stay out. Get out. You might be thinking that sounds a bit drastic. But I'm not sure there's any other way to interpret what Paul says next. *"Therefore come out from them and be separate, says the Lord. Touch no unclean thing, and I will receive you"*[142] (2 Corinthians 6:17). Not all the promises God makes are conditional, but intimacy with him is one of them.

---

[142] This is essentially a quote of Isaiah 52:11. Paul adds his own *"therefore"* to complete the application. Scripture reinforces Scripture. Christians, of necessity, are in the world, but we are, in fact, aliens here — at least from the values and practices of much of the world-system in which we must function. Originally, Isaiah's words called the Jews out of Babylon. They were to return to Israel, bringing the sacred vessels of the temple, leaving behind all that was defiled by the pagan culture in which they'd lived for

When Potiphar's wife repeatedly pressed Joseph to have sex with her, he was resolute in his resistance. *"And though she spoke to Joseph day after day, he refused to go to bed with her or even be with her"* (Genesis 39:10). Not one to take no for an answer, the promiscuous cougar persisted. One day when the house was empty, *"She caught him by his cloak and said, 'Come to bed with me!' But he left his cloak in her hand and ran out of the house"* (Genesis 39:12). Joseph understood Isaiah 52:11 long before it was written.

Standing up to compromise isn't a cake walk, but it can be done—or God wouldn't expect us to do it. An old hymn advises such a strategy. "Yield not to temptation, for yielding is sin. Each victory will help you some other to win. Fight manfully onward, dark passions subdue. Look ever to Jesus, he will carry you through."[143]

Paul advised the Thessalonians to *"Reject every kind of evil"* (1 Thessalonians 5:22). To our discredit, we sometimes try to see how close we can get to a compromising situation before we get caught up in it. That's risky. And irresponsible. Compromise is a drone-type assault weapon. Therein lies its power. Take cover!

When the ancient Israelites entered the Promised Land it wasn't empty. After 400 years in Egypt, that country's social mores, pagan religion, and depraved morality had worn off on them. But, they had been delivered. Egypt was behind them now. Yet, still ahead, was the even more nefarious culture of Canaan. Boundaries had to be drawn. And maintained. As Yahweh's spokesman, Moses was unambiguous about it.

When the LORD your God brings you into the land you are entering to possess and drives out before you many nations – the

---

seventy years. Fellowship with God, not rigid asceticism, was the purpose for the clean break. As we've already seen, Lot was a dramatic example of what happens when this kind of exhortation is ignored (Genesis 19:12-14).

143 Palmer, Horatio. *Yield Not To Temptation*, 1868. Public Domain.

Hittites, Girgashites, Amorites, Canaanites, Perizites, Hivites and Jebusites, seven nations larger and stronger than you – and when the LORD your God has delivered them over to you and you have defeated them, then you must destroy them totally. Make no treaty with them, and show them no mercy. Do not intermarry with them. Do not give your daughters to their sons or take their daughters for your sons, for they will turn your children away from following me to serve other gods, and the LORD's anger will burn against you and will quickly destroy you. (Deuteronomy 7: 1-4)

Despite their good intentions at the time, and their pledge to comply, God's people did not follow God's orders. Most of the Old Testament is the dismal record of their multiplied compromises. The oft-repeated refrain in the book of Judges summarizes the situation, *"Once again the Israelites did evil in the eyes of the LORD."*[144] The result? They didn't conquer the land. The land conquered them.

This stringent segregation policy was nothing new with Moses. Way back in Abraham's day the obligation of separation was clearly understood. When he commissioned his trusted attendant to get a wife for Isaac, he said,

Put your hand under my thigh. I want you to swear by the LORD, the God of heaven and the God of earth, that you will not get a wife for my son from among the daughters of the Canaanites, among whom I am living, but will go to my country and my own relatives and get a wife for my son Isaac. (Genesis 24:2-4)

A generation later, when it was time for Isaac and his wife Rebekah to guide their sons Jacob and Esau in finding wives, the Bible confirms their steadfast convictions. *"Then Rebekah said to Isaac, 'I'm disgusted with these Hittite women. If Jacob takes a wife from among the women of this land, from Hittite women like these, my life will not be worth living'"* (Genesis 27:46).

---

[144] See Judges 2:11-12; 3:12; 4:1; 6:1; 10:6; 13:1.

As we know, Jacob's headstrong and rebellious older brother had done just that. *"When Esau was forty years old, he married Judith daughter of Beeri the Hittite, and also Basemath daughter of Elon the Hittite. They were a source of grief to Isaac and Rebekah"* (Genesis 26:34-35). A person never known for being compliant, the Bible records, *"Esau then realized how displeasing the Canaanite women were to his father Isaac; so he went to Ishmael and married Mahalath, the sister of Nebaioth and daughter of Ishmael son of Abraham, in addition to the wives he already had"* (Genesis 28:8-9).

Esau set the pattern that many of the Israelites would imitate — to their own spiritual destruction. *"The Israelites lived among the Canannites, Hittites, Amorites, Perizites, Hivites and Jebusites. They took their daughters in marriage and gave their own daughters to their sons, and served their gods"* (Judges 3:5-6).

Shockingly, Moses himself didn't even practice what he preached. He married a foreign woman, violating the very law he reiterated to the people. He was subsequently censured for it by his older brother and sister. *"Miriam and Aaron began to talk against Moses because of his Cushite wife"* (Numbers 12:1). The woman in question was the infamous Zipporah, who treated the sign of the covenant with contempt. She called circumcision a bloody practice (Exodus 4:25). It wasn't the color of her skin, her nationality, or prickly personality that made Zipporah unacceptable. She was a pagan. She was outside the covenant. That was the source of the enmity between them. They were unequally yoked.

The intermarriage compromises in the Old Testament became a pattern — the rule rather than the exception. In a section that the 1984 edition of the NIV entitles, "Ezra's Prayer About Intermarriage," we find this summary:

> *The leaders came to me and said, "The people of Israel, including the priests and the Levites, have not kept themselves separate from the neighboring peoples with their detestable practices, like those of*

the Canaanites, Hittites, Perizzites, Jebusites, Ammonites, Moabites, Egyptians and Amorites. They have taken some of their daughters as wives for themselves and their sons, and have mingled the holy race with the peoples around them. And the leaders and officials have led the way in this unfaithfulness." (Ezra 9:1-2)

The Old Testament closes with the situation still out of control. *"Judah has been unfaithful. A detestable thing has been committed in Israel and in Jerusalem: Judah has desecrated the sanctuary the LORD loves, by marrying women who worship a foreign god"* (Malachi 2:11).

It is this history of compromise that Paul applies to the Corinthians. And to us. Do we long for intimacy with God? Then we must adopt a no-compromise mentality to make that affinity possible. *"Therefore come out from them and be separate, says the Lord. Touch no unclean thing, and I will receive you. I will be a father to you, and you will be my sons and daughters, says the Lord Almighty"* (2 Corinthians 6:17-18).[145]

When it comes to compromise, Paul is opposed to anything that even hints of legalism. As an ex-Pharisee,[146] he knew well the mentality of being a "separated one." Legalists characteristically make personal holiness a condition not just of fellowship with God, but of relationship with him too. But, salvation is not a carrot on a stick. At the same time, for Christians of every age, while our

---

[145] Now Paul adds the sentiments of 2 Samuel 7:8, 14 and Isaiah 43:6 to what he has to say. He spells out what it means to be *"received"* by God. The church is not only the temple of God, made of living stones, but his family as well. For centuries, *"the Lord Almighty"* was also a *"Father"* to his people, as in the passages here cited. The concept is intensified in the New Testament (Romans 5:6, 8, 10). This was especially meaningful to those who had lost their biological families or were experiencing strained relationships with them because of their commitment to Christ (Mark 10:29). It would be preposterous to put that new status at risk.

[146] See Philippians 3:5.

relationship with God does not depend on holiness, our intimacy with him does.

The pressures the Corinthians faced were economic as well as spiritual. Membership in idolatrous trade guilds was crucial to much of the employment in town. Without such unionized alliances, work could be hard to come by. What should they do? I like the attitude attributed to Tertullian (160-220 AD) when he was approached by a man in ancient Carthage, caught between listening to his conscience and losing his job. Rationalizing his frustration, he complained, "After all I must live!" To which Tertullian purportedly replied, "Must you live?!"[147]

Ever the pastor, Paul closes his urgent admonitions with a gentle, yet firm, exhortation. *"Since we have these promises, dear friends,*[148] *let us purify*[149] *ourselves from everything that contaminates body and spirit, perfecting holiness*[150] *out of reverence for God"*[151] (2

---

[147] knightforhire.com/sermons/no_compromise.htm. Accessed December 23, 2015.

[148] Greek: "agapētoi" (ἀγαπητοί). Literally translated, this term is "beloved." Paul is emotionally attached to the Corinthians as his spiritual children. He does not hesitate to tell them so. Aside from the Romans (Romans 12:19) and the Philippians (2:12; 4:1), he does not use this word to address other Christians.

[149] Greek: "katharidzō" (καθαρίζω). This is the source of our word "catharsis;" i.e., the purging of the emotions and relieving of psychological tension. Originally, it simply meant "to make clean." It was used to describe the removal of stains and dirt, as in the cleansing of utensils. And, of lepers being healed. In a moral sense, it meant to be purified from wickedness and freed from guilt; consecrated for service by cleansing. The verb here is in the Aorist tense, which indicates a definitive action in the past.

[150] The self-administered cleansing Paul calls for here accomplishes a higher goal: *"perfecting holiness."* Again, grammar plays a part in our correct understanding of what is expected of us. *"Perfecting"* is a Present Participle; the implication is that we must do this continually. And consistently. It literally means to "bring to a goal." The result is *"holiness."* The root of this term is translated elsewhere as being sanctified; i.e., separated from sin and sinful things. Such individuals are "holy ones" or saints.

[151] Greek: "en phobō theou" (ἐν φόβῳ θεοῦ). The healthiest of phobias is the fear of God. It is the most basic of motives for *"perfecting holiness."*

Corinthians 7:1). All sources of contamination must be expunged. It is crucial that we stay clean outside and in; body and spirit.

Compromise contaminates. It's a protracted and subtle process, unsuspected and undetected – until it's too late. Compromise pollutes the soul. More than that, it corrupts body and spirit. Realizing this, Paul exhorts us to get out and stay out of all compromising situations and relationships. It is our responsibility to purify ourselves. The middle voice of the Greek verb used here suggests that the action isn't done for us, but by us. This is our necessary part in the process of sanctification. Paul doesn't hesitate to put this obligation squarely in our laps. *"Everything that contaminates"* must be repudiated and done with (2 Corinthians 7:1).

Notice, Paul doesn't give us a list of specific polluting practices to eliminate from our lives. We are to eradicate everything that could corrupt us. These are activities and behaviors that are universally and timelessly wrong. They are not culturally relative. In the past, the Corinthians were well-practiced in such violations of God's will.

> *Or do you not know that wrongdoers will not inherit the kingdom of God? Do not be deceived: Neither the sexually immoral nor idolaters nor adulterers nor men who have sex with men nor thieves nor the greedy nor drunkards nor slanderers nor swindlers will inherit the kingdom of God. And that is what some of you were. But you were washed, you were sanctified, you were justified in the name of the Lord Jesus Christ and by the Spirit of our God.* (1 Corinthians 6:9-11)

Holiness is a state of separation from sin. Paul sets the standard high in encouraging us to maintain it. He talks about *"perfecting*[152] *holiness"* (2 Corinthians 7:1). This is a perpetual responsibility. The

---

[152] Greek: "epiteleō" (ἐπιτελέω). This verb means to bring something to an end; to accomplish, execute, or complete it. In this instance, it is a present tense participle, implying persistent and consistent effort.

apostle identifies our highest motivation for doing so—God deserves it.

I was in a pastoral counseling situation once with a young wife who was struggling to stay faithful to her still-new husband. She felt unloved. Bitterly so. She was frustrated, sad, and lonely. One day she called me from work. It turns out that a suave and handsome Don Juan at her office was giving her the attention she wasn't getting at home. He was attractive, attentive, sensitive, and gentle. And, a predator. She was falling in love with him.

One day, after finding herself flirting with him at the water cooler, she called me again, desperate to know what to do. My response was abrupt: "Stop talking to him. Stop smiling at him. Stop being around him. Be rude, if you have to. But, get away from him. Now!"

I'm sad to report that she didn't heed my advice. A month later, she left her young husband and ran off to South America with her new Latin lover. Of course, that little fling didn't last. She found herself unloved by yet another man—and doubtful if even God loved her anymore. She modified her moral values for the false promise of love and romance. She paid the price of compromise.

THINK

1. Which is more dangerous—a sudden, impulsive lapse into serious sin, or slow, subtle backsliding?

2. Define compromise.

3. Usually when we compromise we are not aware of it. True or false?

4. Why are wrong relationships an especially dangerous type of compromise?

5. What does it mean to be *"unequally yoked"*?

6. What is the best course of action regarding a spiritually compromising relationship?

7. If a Christian is married to a non-Christian, they should divorce their spouse and marry a true believer. True or false?

8. What big risks are we taking by entering spiritually compromising relationships?

9. What should you do if you are already entangled in a spiritually compromising relationship?

10. What is your heart-condition if you won't sever a spiritually compromising relationship?

ACT

1. Identify the areas of compromise you are engaged in right now. Repent and resolve to distance yourself from even the slightest modification of your moral standards.

2. If you are a pastor, commit yourself to never officiate at a wedding between a Christian and a non-Christian. Or, any couple that is not spiritually compatible.

3. If you work with young adults, go on record as being opposed to dating between believers and unbelievers. And, from this text, teach them why.

4. As a spiritual leader, commit yourself to teach your people about holiness, being unequivocal about it.

5. In counseling young men with porn-addictions, insist that they establish an accountability relationship with a mature Christian man.

Chapter 11

Risking Transparency

2 Corinthians 7:2-16

One of my good friends is a psychologist. Every now and then we get together for lunch, and along with the meal I get some free therapy. I've noticed that psychologists have their own way of talking. It's a professional kind of lingo that some outsiders refer to as "psycho-babble."

For example, people don't have problems; they have "issues." They aren't messed up; they are "dysfunctional." They aren't overpowered by others with serious short-comings; they are "co-dependent." You've heard the jargon yourself. What may surprise you is that "psycho-babble" isn't just pop culture slang. It's in the dictionary, where it is defined as "language that is used by people who talk about mental and emotional problems and that is seen as silly or meaningless." [153] Clearly, it's not always a complimentary term, and is often belittled as semantic mumbo-jumbo. But, let's not be too hasty. Our therapist friends may be on to something.

One psycho-babble phrase my psychologist chum introduced me to has proved to be quite useful. He talks about being "Big Circle" or "Little Circle," as a way to help people visualize their mental and emotional state at any given moment.

Here's how it works: If you are Big Circle that means that you are outgoing, enthusiastic, energetic, and optimistic. You are relaxed, contented, and grateful. You are smiling, talkative, friendly, open,

---

[153] merriam-webster.com/dictionary/psychobabble. Accessed March 1, 2016.

and others-oriented. You are approachable and receptive. Picture a Labrador Retriever. By contrast, if you are Little Circle, you are uptight, nervous, negative, and pessimistic. You are irritable, defensive, withdrawn, and aloof. You are snippy and yippy. Picture a Mexican Chihuahua.

As you can imagine, there aren't just two attitude circles. Between Big Circle and Little Circle are any number of in-between circles that reflect our current mental or emotional state. It goes without saying, you don't have to be a therapist to realize that the bigger Circle you are, the better.

Who would dispute it? Outgoing, enthusiastic, energetic, optimistic, relaxed, contented, grateful, smiling, congenial, open, others-oriented, and approach-able people are more pleasant to be around than uptight, nervous, negative, gloomy, irritable, defensive, and withdrawn ones. Spiritual leaders who are Big Circle most of the time, not only minimize their own dejection; they maximize their influence with everyone around them. The pastor who inspired me to commit myself to a lifetime of ministry was Big Circle to a fault. He was consistently pleasant and amiable. I wanted to be just like him. Still do.

The best thing about being Big Circle is that we are an open book to those around us. No one has to guess about what kind of mood we are in. They can see it. And what they see makes them feel good—about you, about themselves, and about God.

This is what happens when we take the chance to be transparent. Transparency is the condition of being "free from pretense or deceit, easily detected or seen through, readily understood."[154] Big Circle! Not everyone is. Regrettably, neither are some spiritual leaders. It's not their natural temperament. Or, because they've been hurt by being open with people in the past, they don't want to expose

---

[154] merriam-webster.com/dictionary/transparent. Accessed March 1, 2016.

themselves to the possibility of repeated pain. But they should. They must. Transparency in leadership, rightly practiced, is crucial.

OPEN AFFECTION

Big Circle people are blurters. In a good sense. Unwittingly, they divulge how they feel about you. They are innocently impulsive when they do it. For example, sometimes when I'm wrapping up a phone call with a friend, I find myself spontaneously saying, "Love you!" Or, to a whole roomful of students at the end of a class session—"Love you guys! See you next time."

Being openly affectionate sometimes takes people by surprise. They don't know what to do. Should they say, "Love you too!" Or just say, "See ya"? Well, it's the chance Big Circle people take. Occasional awkwardness won't kill you. Or the people you are awkward with. And, who knows, maybe you'll inspire some of them to be more demonstrative themselves.

I think of my son's dog, Chester. He's a golden Lab. Come into the room and he's moving toward you, tail wagging and eyes dazzling. He's looking for affection. He's expecting it. And, he's giving it. You could be the Wicked Witch of the West herself, it wouldn't faze Chester. The tail is still wagging. Eyes still sparkling.

The Apostle Paul is not coy with the Corinthians. He doesn't leave them wondering how he feels about them. He loves them and says so. He asks them to love him back. *"Make room[155] for us in your hearts"* (2 Corinthians 7:2).[156] In making emotional connection with

---

[155] Greek: "chōreō" (χωρέω). This verb connotes leaving space, which may be filled or occupied by another person. It can also imply moving forward, advancing, proceeding, or succeeding. Here, it is an imperative, doubly forceful by the inclusion of the pronoun "you" (not translated in the NIV). In other words, decisive action is being called for.

[156] Despite the inexplicable chapter division, 7:1 clearly belongs with the closing topic of chapter six. Paul now picks up where he left off in 2 Corinthians 6:13 when he said, *"As a fair exchange—I speak as to my children— open wide your hearts also."* If there is a connection between what he says here

others, Big Circle people try, and try again. They don't let the absence of a positive response stop them. They are irrepressible.

HONEST DISCLOSURE

Big Circle leaders are not just affectionate; they're honest. In love, we speak the truth. Paul is pleading with the Corinthians to open up their hearts to him. In doing so, he reminds them that they have no reason not to. *"We have wronged no one,*[157] *we have corrupted no one, we have exploited no one"* (2 Corinthians 7:2).

It's hard to be transparent when you have something to hide. Some Little Circle people are withdrawn for a reason. They've got skeletons in the closet. They are afraid to open the door. Paul was not plagued by such reticence.

In his appeal for reconciliation with the Corinthians, the apostle was honest, but not condemning. *"I do not say this to condemn you"* (2 Corinthians 7:3). Then he immediately lays his heart on the line— again. *"I have said before that you have such a place in our hearts that we would live or die with you"* (2 Corinthians 7:3). There seems to be no limit to how transparent Paul was willing to be with people who weren't willing, or able, to do the same.

When you are Big Circle you make commitments to people who won't or can't reciprocate. In his LP, *Big Horizon,* songwriter-singer,

---

with the parenthesis of 6:14-7:1, it's simply that the Corinthians should separate themselves from incompatible relationships with pagans and participating in their ungodly practices, but instead, pursue healthy rapport within the Christian community, including their spiritual leaders.

[157] With a technique not apparent in the English translation, Paul starts his rebuttal to the accusations against him with the same disclaimer: *"no one."* The Aorist tense of the verb in each denial indicates that he, and his coworkers, are not guilty of a single violation of integrity. He begins with *"no one wronged you."* The word indicates unfair treatment. Nor was their teaching or conduct *"corrupted"* in the slightest degree. Nor has anyone been *"exploited."* If the Corinthians can bring themselves to repudiate these charges, then a relaxed affinity will once again characterize their relationship with the man who led them to Christ in the first place.

David Wilcox, has a sorrowful song entitled *Break in the Cup*.[158] It's about a husband who continually pours love into his wife's life, like she was a cup. Trouble is, her cup has cracks in it from previous unhealed heartaches. No matter how much he fills it up, the love leaks out. She can't respond in kind.

Big Circle love is not "I'll love you, if you love me." It's not "I love you because you love me." Nor, "I'll love you, if you promise not to hurt me." No. It's "I love you, even if do you won't love me." It's "I love you — no matter what!"

POSITIVE CONFIDENCE

It's fun being around Big Circle people. You never have to wonder where you stand with them. Typically, what you get from them is affirmation. If there's anything positive about you to say, they say it.

I watched that kind of thing in action one summer at a Christian camp near Bass Lake, California. The entire staff was made up of youth pastors and other adults who thought teenagers were just the best people around. You could tell by the way they interacted with the students. Virtually everything they said and did was an exercise in self-esteem building. Even when they were correcting them, they expressed confidence in them.

One day at lunch, a table of boisterous boys was being especially loud and rowdy. The youth leader in charge was trying to get everyone's attention, and they weren't cooperating. But instead of becoming irritated or reacting in frustration, he looked at them and said for the whole room to hear, "That's what I like about you guys — enthusiasm!" Immediately, they settled down; corrected, but not belittled. Affirmation in every situation is smart leadership.

The Apostle Paul tries to find the best in even the worst of people. And then he verbalizes it. *"I have spoken to you with great*

---

158 Wilcox, David. *Big Horizon*. American Audio, 1994.

frankness;[159] *I take great pride*[160] *in you. I am greatly encouraged; in all our troubles*[161] *my joy knows no bounds"* (2 Corinthians 7:4).

Apart from Laodicea,[162] there were few first-century churches more cluelessly immature than the congregation in Corinth. They were not especially lovable, yet Paul loved them anyway. He looked for ways to affirm them. Despite their disturbing childishness, they did have some positive qualities that he could honestly commend. He expressed that confidence as often as he could. *"I am glad I can have complete confidence in you"* (2 Corinthians 7:16).

It's a demonstrable example of the power of suggestion — people tend to live up to our expressed opinions of them. Did you ever have a teacher or coach like that? Or, a parent? They watched for positive traits in you. When they saw something praiseworthy, they pointed it out. Their confidence inspired your own.

Spiritual leaders with integrity express their approval. And, they mean it. They empower those they influence. They infuse their followers with a belief in themselves. They create a psychological climate that inspires people to rise to their highest potential. The

---

[159] Greek: "parrēsia" (παρρησία). Typically translated as "boldness," this word usually refers to speech and the quality of holding nothing back. In this instance, Paul specifically responds to Titus' report of the Corinthians' repentant attitude (2 Corinthians 7:13-14). He doesn't hesitate to express his joy. For his other uses of the word see Ephesians 3:12 and 1 Timothy 3:13. The writer of Hebrews repeats it a lot too. (Hebrews 3:6; 4:16; 10:19, 35). As does John. (1 John 2:28; 3:21; 4:17; 5:14). The term is broader than just speech.

[160] Greek: "kauchēsis" (καύχησις). This is the noun form of the verb that figures so prominently in the last four chapters of Second Corinthians as Paul defends his apostleship, where it is rendered *"boast."*

[161] Greek: "thlipsis" (θλῖψις). Paul used the very same term the day after he was left for dead in Lystra from rocks thrown by an implacable mob that pummeled him to the ground in a pool of his own blood. *"We must go through many hardships to enter the kingdom of God"* (Acts 14:22). He uses it again when he says, *"We share in his sufferings in order that we may also share in his glory"* (Romans 8:17). It is variously translated in 2 Corinthians as hardships, sufferings, and troubles.

[162] See Revelation 3:14-22.

atmosphere around them is contagious with positivity. Everyone is encouraged.

It should be noted that churches have circle-sizes too. Generally, parishioners replicate the disposition of their up-front leaders. If the leaders are cordial and gregarious, the people will be too. If the leaders are self-occupied and distant—the whole congregation tends to be standoffish.

Many local churches these days have serious Big Circle deficiencies. The employees at my bank are friendlier than the members of lots of congregations I've visited in recent years. The folks at Wells Fargo say "Hi!" when you walk in the door. They smile. They ask how your day is going. They act like they are glad to see you. By contrast, church folk often treat you like you are invisible. No "Hello!" No "Hi!" No "How are ya?" No, "What's your name?" Sure, bank employees get paid to be friendly. Maybe we should do the same with Little Circle church members—give them a dollar for every guest they greet. (Just kidding! I think.)

Seriously though, let's reach out to people who take the chance to come to our churches. On the sprawling university campus where I teach, that's my MO. If I see someone I don't know, I say hello. I tell students and colleagues alike, "If you notice someone new, greet them! And smile too!" You can't overdo friendliness. Big Circle leaders are friendly; it's evidence of their integrity.

TRUE CONFESSION

Truth be known, the Apostle Paul hasn't been in a good place psychologically since he left Corinth. It's been a dismal several months—daily frustration and discouragement. One heartache after another. Most of it, the Corinthians' fault.

So, what do Big Circle people do when they get the blues? They say so. They risk transparency about their emotions, both good and not so good. *"For when we came into Macedonia, we had no rest, but we were harassed at every turn — conflicts on the outside, fears within"*[163] (2 Corinthians 7:5). Paul discloses his all too human vulnerabilities.

I have a pastor friend who took a big chance at being candid with his small congregation one Sunday morning. He'd been struggling with discouragement and depression for several weeks over the apparent lack of success in his ministry. That day, he told them so. To his joyful surprise, one by one, the people spontaneously came up to the platform and began to put their arms around him, adding their tears to his, reassuring him of their love and respect. It was a positive turning point in the dynamic between followers and their leader.

Paul takes his honesty a step further by describing himself as *"downcast"* (2 Corinthians 7:6). Downcast is an agricultural term. It describes what happens to sheep when they end up on their backs. They can't get up, no matter how hard they try. Without the assistance of a shepherd, they're stuck. The image of a downcast shepherd is startling.

I saw a billboard on the road recently. It showed the smiling face of a middle-aged man. The by-line read, "Church pastor living with depression." It was an advertisement for the psychiatric services of a local hospital. These things happen. Some of our greatest spiritual heroes have battled depression. Evidently, Saint Paul did too. He acknowledges it. But, to his credit, he quickly points to God as the source of his joyful relief.

---

[163] Paul is candid about his restless anxiety. In 2 Corinthians 2:4 he talks about having *"great distress and anguish of heart, and with many tears."* For the moment, there was no escaping it. He reports his dejection, but he doesn't belabor it. The conflicts he speaks of here, refer to interpersonal clashes with the Corinthians. His angst was psychological and physical; there were *"conflicts on the outside, fears within."* Earlier he admitted that he had *"no peace of mind"* (2 Corinthians 2:13). This kind of candor catches us by surprise. In a stronger frame of mind, his well-being doesn't seem to concern him (Acts 20:24). Not so, in this case.

Depression is circumstantial. God's deliverance from it is typically circumstantial too; he uses people and events to lift us up. *"But God, who comforts the downcast, comforted us by the coming of Titus, and not only by his coming but also by the comfort you had given him"* (2 Corinthians 7:6-7). Paul and Titus were proactive in encouraging the Corinthians. The Corinthians reciprocated — they encouraged Titus, who in turn, encouraged Paul. The apostle exults, *"He told us about your longing for me, your deep sorrow, your ardent concern for me, so that my joy was greater than ever"* (2 Corinthians 7:7). This is Big Circle talk.

The majority of the Corinthians have repented. They have decidedly renounced their worldly attitudes and childish conduct. They have reaffirmed their love for Paul and recommitted themselves to renewed submission to his spiritual authority. Like David, his mourning had been turned into dancing.[164]

Clinical depression is long-standing and persistent. Such a disorder may require medication, extended therapy, or both. Ordinary depression is common to human experience; we all have to deal with it. Eventually though, circumstances change, prayers are answered, others cheer us up. God is at work. We outlast being downcast.

In reviewing the recent turmoil between himself and the Corinthians, Paul takes a moment to reflect on the events which led up to his relief.

> *Even if I caused you sorrow by my letter I do not regret it. Though I did regret it — I see my letter hurt you, but only for a little while — yet now I am happy, not because you were made sorry, but because your sorrow led you to repentance. For you became*

---

[164] *"You turned my wailing into dancing; you removed my sackcloth and clothed me with joy, that my heart may sing to you and not be silent. LORD my God, I will give you thanks forever"* (Psalm 30:11-12).

sorrowful as God intended and so were not harmed in any way by us. [165] (2 Corinthians 7:8-9)

Paul had doubts about his stern letter to the Corinthian church. He knew it would hurt them *"for a little while"* (2 Corinthians 7:8). He wrote it anyway. It was a chance he had to take.

There's a beauty to transparency; it begets transparency. How did Paul know that the Corinthians had changed? How did he know that they were *"longing"* for him? That their concern for him was *"ardent"*? How did he know that their sorrow was *"deep"*? (2 Corinthians 7:7) They said so. They risked transparency because Paul risked transparency. That's how it works.

What if Paul had not taken the chance of hurting their feelings by telling them the truth about their conduct? If he hadn't opened up with them, most likely, they would never have opened up with him. Transparent communication results in repentance. *"Godly sorrow brings repentance that leads to salvation*[166] *and leaves no regret, but worldly sorrow brings death"*[167] (2 Corinthians 7:10).

---

[165] Scholars are divided as to which particular letter Paul is referring to; First Corinthians, or the now lost "stern letter." Both qualify as painful pastoral discipline. His regretful ambivalence stated here, may less apply to First Corinthians than to the stern letter; the tone of which was more like we find in Second Corinthians 10-13.

[166] Greek: "sōtēria" (σωτηρία). This noun is the source of our word "soteriology," the doctrine of salvation. It entails justification, sanctification, and glorification; the full and complete redemption of the whole person, body, soul, and spirit, from the consequences of sin. The original use of the word primarily means to be made healthy or whole. Secondarily, it speaks of deliverance, safety, and preservation.

[167] There's a difference between being sorry for what we've done and the resentment that we got caught doing it. *"Godly"* sorrow is oriented toward God. By contrast, *"worldly"* sorrow is self-centered regret for something lost or for the punishment that must be faced. The present tense verbs Paul uses here indicate on-going experiences. Worldly sorrow is a state of despair, clearly evidenced in the lives of biblical characters like Cain, Esau, Saul, and Judas. There's a stubbornness to it. The Book of Revelation predicts that in the End Times people will mourn over their loss of income (Revelation

Spiritual leaders with integrity take the chance of hurting people — for their own good. It's what love does. You tell people you love them before, during, and after the discipline. Compelling people to repent is painful. But, it is important. Without it, sinners will never get well. Repentance results in spiritual healing and wholeness.

> *See what this godly sorrow has produced in you: what earnestness,*[168] *what eagerness to clear yourselves, what indignation, what alarm, what longing, what concern, what readiness to see justice done. At every point you have proved yourselves to be innocent in this matter.*[169] (2 Corinthians 7:11)

Paul's prognosis for the Corinthian church is one of full recovery. There is no reason not to be optimistic.

> *So even though I wrote to you, it was neither on account of the one who did the wrong nor on account of the injured party, but rather that before God you could see for yourselves how devoted to us you are. By all this we are encouraged. In addition to our own encouragement, we were especially delighted to see how happy Titus was, because his spirit has been refreshed by all of you. I had*

18:11). But, they will refuse to grieve or repent for their sins (Revelation 9:20-21). Sorrow that doesn't lead us to God engenders on-going depression and despair. By contrast, godly sorrow results in spiritual wellness.

[168] Greek: "spoudē" (σπουδή). This term was used to describe diligence in pursuing or accomplishing something, or striving after it. It signifies total effort. If the problem of the incestuous man of 1 Corinthians 5 is the situation Paul had in mind here, they have expelled him from the congregation as they were told to do (1 Corinthians 5:13; 2 Corinthians 2:6). Truly repentant people are determined to wipe clean the record of their misdeeds. The Corinthians were earnest about scrubbing themselves clean of their sins.

[169] This is what John the Baptist meant when he insisted, *"Produce fruit in keeping with repentance"* (Luke 3:8). The consequences of remaining unrepentant are severe. *"The ax is already at the root of the trees, and every tree that does not produce good fruit will be cut down and thrown in the fire"* (Luke 3:9).

boasted to him about you, and you have not embarrassed me. But just as everything we said to you was true, so our boasting about you to Titus has proved to be true as well. And his affection for you is all the greater when he remembers that you were all obedient, receiving him with fear and trembling. (2 Corinthians 7:12-15)

HEARTFELT APPRECIATION

It is all too common among colleagues in ministry to commiserate with each other about the negative characteristics of their parishioners. Certainly Paul could have stooped to that kind of behavior regarding the Corinthians. There were plenty of things to grumble about. But, instead of bellyaching, he was boasting.

What's wonderful is that the Corinthian Christians lived up to Paul's affirmation of them. He proudly says it. *"Everything we said about you was true"* (2 Corinthians 6:14). The apostle is not faking it when he finishes this section of the letter with a statement melding positive confidence and sincere appreciation. *"I am glad I can have complete confidence in you"* (2 Corinthians 7:16). Paul is exuberant about the fact that rapport has been re-established with the congregation, and that most of them are once again fervent in their allegiance to him. Big Circle that he is, he tells them so.

Sow bugs are quizzical little creatures. They are harmless and cute in their own way. But friendly, they aren't. If you get down on your hands and knees to get better acquainted, they'll just keep moving. These diminutive arthropods prefer to stay out of sight, under rocks and logs. So, if you try to touch them, they will roll themselves up into a BB-sized ball until you lose interest and go away. They don't want to get to know you. Leave them alone. Some people are like that—they play Roly-Poly when you show them any kind of personal attention. Big Circle leaders aren't put off by that kind of behavior. They just keep loving people, until they get them to open up. Even if, it's only a little bit. Such leaders demonstrate the positive effect of risking transparency.

THINK

1. Why is it generally a good idea to be transparent in our relationships with other people? What does it mean to be transparent?

2. Are there any relationships in which it would not be a good idea to be transparent?

3. Explain the psychological concept of Big Circle and Little Circle.

4. On a scale of 1 to 10, rate your own level of transparency.

5. Why do we have to dare to be transparent?

6. Can you be transparent without being honest?

7. Paul admitted he was depressed. Should we do that very often?

8. What was it that caused Paul to feel *"downcast"*?

9. When we are transparent with people, they'll be transparent with us. True or false?

10. List the dramatic changes in the Corinthians' attitude that resulted from Paul's courage to be transparent with them.

ACT

1. Find five people who are willing to rate your level of transparency. Define Big Circle and Little Circle, then ask them to tell you which you are.

2. This week, tell three people that you love them. Say hello to five strangers.

3. At your first opportunity, give yourself permission to admit to a trusted friend that you have a less than positive attitude.

4. If you've been depressed lately, identify the reasons why. Then, reaffirm your faith. Tell yourself, "I refuse to be unhappy."

5. Resolve to never speak disparagingly about the members of your church to your partners in ministry, or anyone else. Instead, find something good to say about everyone.

Chapter 12

Getting Good at Giving

2 Corinthians 8:1-9:18

One summer on a road trip vacation, my wife and I were driving through southern Idaho. It was a Friday evening and we stopped at the KFC for some dinner in a town called Burley. As we placed our order, we chatted with the high school girl who was waiting on us. I joked with her a little and said, "What are you doing here on a Friday night when you could be out having fun with your friends?" She smiled and said, "Oh, I graduate this month and I'm going to Boise State in the fall. I need the money."

Once back in California I said to my wife, "Let's send some money to that girl." "What girl?" she asked. "The one at KFC. She's trying to put herself through college and it sounded like she could use some help." My wife said, "We don't even know her name." That was easy. I looked up the phone number of the KFC in Burley, Idaho and dialed it. The manager, Susan, answered the phone. I said, "I know this may sound a little strange, but Friday night we were in your restaurant and talked to one of your workers who is going to Boise State this fall. It sounded like she could use some extra money. My wife and I would like to send her some." She responded, "Oh, I was on duty that night. I remember you guys. Aren't you sweet! Her name is Lindsay Smith." I got the address of the restaurant and asked Susan not to say anything about what we were going to do. I hung up the phone and talked to my wife about how much money we should send. I said, "I was thinking about $100." She responded, "That won't help much, send her $300." We settled for $250 and put the check in the mail, with a short note wishing Lindsay Smith our best in her freshman year at college.

Chapters eight and nine of Second Corinthians are unique.[170] It is the largest block of Scripture devoted exclusively to the topic of financial stewardship. The principle is simple and fundamental: giving is loving. When we give, we extend ourselves for the well-being of others — whether it's time, attention, energy, or money. And it's always true, we can't love others without loving ourselves at the same time. That's just the way it works. When it comes to loving by giving, few things are as immediately rewarding as sharing the money we've got with someone who needs it. It's fun to be a philanthropist.

As Christ followers who understand God's grace, giving is second nature to us now. We've been the recipients of God's unmerited goodness. *"For you know the grace of our Lord Jesus Christ, that though he was rich,*[171] *yet for your sakes he became poor,*[172] *so that you through his poverty might become rich"* (2 Corinthians 8:9).

Authentic love consistently entails self-sacrifice. If what we are doing in the name of love doesn't have an element of giving up something for someone else, it may be a lot of things, but it isn't love.

---

[170] Second Corinthians is comprised of three distinct sections. Chapters 1-7 summarize the Apostle Paul's response to news from his assistant Titus that the majority of the members of the church had repented of their sinful immaturities and renewed their allegiance to him as their spiritual authority. In chapters 10-13, Paul vigorously defends his apostleship, threatening the defiant minority of church members in Corinth with severe consequences for their divisive rebellion. Sandwiched in between, Chapters 8 and 9 are devoted to instruction about financial stewardship.

[171] Greek: "plousios" (πλούσιος). This term connotes a condition in which there is an abundance of material resources. There is no limit to divine wealth. *"Every animal of the forest is mine, and the cattle on a thousand hills"* (Psalm 50:10).

[172] Greek: "ptōcheia" (πτωχεία). This word describes a destitute condition that has transformed its victim into a beggar.

Jesus is the personification of sacrificial love. He set the example and standard for us to follow.

Eventually, when we love people we are going to be parting with our money, to some extent or another. It's a shocking statistic that in the world, the people with the most money are the most miserly.[173] But, in the church it's the opposite. Or should be. True Christians, whether we have a lot or a little, are eager to share what we have with others. The Bible calls it stewardship. What we have isn't ours. It's God's. He has loaned it to us to invest and manage for him. He is trusting us to make decisions about his money and property that will benefit others.

Unlike many people who are driven to get, keep, and spend as much money as they can — on themselves — we operate on a different paradigm. We know "The one who dies with the most toys, wins." is nonsense. We are not here to accumulate. Instead, we keep what we need, and give the rest away. Like John Wesley used to say, "Earn all you can. Save all you can. Give all you can."[174] It was part of his larger philosophy of life as a steward of God's resources. "Do all the good you can. By all the means you can. In all the ways you can. In all the places you can. At all the times you can. To all the people you can. As long as ever you can."[175]

Contrary to the cynical conclusions of lots of folks, God isn't after our money. Why would he be? He doesn't need it. He owns everything. God is motivated to give, not to get. It's his nature to give. He wants us to experience his grace. And so, he lavishes it on us. What he gives, we joyfully receive. Then, over time, we become like him. We are eager to give away what we have, just as he is eager to give away what he has. As Jesus reminded his original disciples,

---

[173] patheos.com/.../shock-rich-tend-to-be-stingy-poor-tend-to-be-generous. Accessed April 8, 2016.

[174] goodreads.com/.../quotes/151350.John_Wesley. Accessed April 8, 2016.

[175] Ibid.

"Freely you have received; freely give" (Matthew 10:8). He also said, *"It is more blessed to give than to receive"* (Acts 20:35). Here Paul delineates the motivation, goal, secret, and purpose of our stewardship of the material resources God has entrusted to us. In doing so we receive Christ's promised blessing.

THE MOTIVATION FOR GIVING

When it comes to fiscal stewardship, it all starts with grace. *"And now, brothers and sisters,* [176] *we want you to know about the grace that God has given"* (2 Corinthians 8:1). Later Paul will simply call it, *"the grace of giving"* (2 Corinthians 8:7).

What motivated my wife and me to give a significant amount of money to a fast food worker whose name we didn't even know? We could have spent that money in many other ways. We could have treated ourselves to dinner at a fancy restaurant, or gone to a concert. We could have squirreled it away for a rainy day. Or, given it to one of our own kids, off to college themselves. Instead, we decided to bless a total stranger. We did it because we know what it's like to be on the receiving end of something freely given. God blesses people who don't deserve to be blessed; rain falls on the just and the unjust (Matthew 5:45). He blesses people who don't even know they are being blessed. That's what loves does. It gives.

The Apostle Paul is talking about the grace of God that moves us to pass that grace on to others in the form of goods, services, and cash. He's reminding us of the biblical principles on which financial stewardship properly stands. Sooner or later, the opportunity to practice those principles presents itself.

Paul was giving the Corinthians the chance to do just that. Christians to the east, in Palestine, were facing a serious famine. It

---

[176] Paul is a skilled communicator and he understands human nature. In broaching the typically touchy subject of financial stewardship, he addresses the Corinthians with affection.

was taking its toll on them. The crisis had wiped out their financial resources. They were destitute. The Corinthians and the rest of the Christians in Greece didn't have much, but they had more than their Judean sisters and brothers. It was time for them to share. Paul was raising an offering.[177]

In encouraging the Corinthians to be generous stewards, the apostle makes reference to *"the Macedonian churches"* (2 Corinthians 8:1). We are familiar with the congregations in this area of northern Greece—Philippi, Thessalonica, and Berea in particular. These local fellowships were small, but impressive. They embraced the premise that once we have freely received from God, we freely pass it on to others. Even if it's not much. If someone else needs what we've got, we give it.

When it comes to philanthropy,[178] people with the most money often give the least and those with the least typically give the most. It's impressive when modern-day billionaires give away millions of dollars; some even pledging to donate most of their fortunes to charity. But, they can afford it. The Macedonian Christians couldn't afford it. They were living at a subsistence level themselves. Paul compliments them. *"In the midst of a very severe trial,[179] their overflowing joy and their extreme poverty welled up in rich generosity"* (2 Corinthians 8:2). What a juxtaposition of circumstances! Severe trial and extreme poverty, overflowing joy and rich generosity. They

---

[177] Let's be clear about it; fundraising is not wrong, no matter what outside cynics may say, or how some television evangelists have used it for self-aggrandizement. Fundraising is, in fact, a responsibility spiritual leaders with integrity take seriously. But, when we raise money for the cause of Christ, it's vital that we do it his way.

[178] This term means the "love of people"; in particular, affectionate love for others.

[179] Greek: "thlipsis" (θλῖψις). Paul uses this term often in Second Corinthians. It is variously translated as hardship, tribulation, trial or pressure.

don't fit. It's illogical. Poverty results in generosity. Trouble results in joy. This is the paradox of God-like giving.

It's common for some Christians nowadays to postpone being faithful givers until they get their finances in order. One time, the elders of our church committed themselves to assist a single mom in the congregation with the monetary troubles she kept finding herself in. In addition to paying some of her pressing bills, they sat down with her to try to figure out a lasting solution to her fiscal problems. They helped her create a realistic budget. And, right at the top of the list of her weekly obligations, they included a financial commitment to the church. It was a big step of faith for her, but she dedicated herself to it. Before long, she found herself with a modest surplus in cash flow.

Even when we are poor, we give. How much we have, or don't have, doesn't change the equation. The Macedonian Christians didn't have any extra money. But, God's grace generates the desire to give, even when we don't have much. I remember a pastor in rural Nicaragua. He, his wife and eight kids lived in a one room, dirt floor house. When half a dozen of us Norte Americanos arrived for a visit one muggy afternoon, his face beaming with joy, he said, "Mi casa, es su casa!" God's grace motivates us to be generous with what we have, whether it's a lot or a little.

Another unexpected thing happens when the grace-driven desire to give wells up in our hearts. Somehow or another we are able to give, even beyond our means. When it came to the Macedonians, Paul was a proud witness to such financial serendipity. *"For I testify that they gave as much as they were able, and even beyond their ability"* (2 Corinthians 8:3). But, how can anyone give more than they have?

In the mid-1970s, there was a unique technique some pastors and parachurch leaders used to raise funds. It was called "Faith Promise." They challenged people to make a deal with God; not to give money they had, but money they didn't have — yet. When unexpected cash came along, they promised to give some of it away.

I remember the enthusiasm of a brand new Christian who had made such a faith-promise. In church one Sunday, he stood up to naively testify to the congregation that he'd won some lottery money that week. The way he looked at it, God provided the winning ticket. And now, it was his turn to pay it forward. Pass the offering plate!

Giving beyond our ability is the God-factor in Christian financial management. You won't read any articles about it in Money Magazine. It can't be explained or converted into a spread sheet. God does it. Paul will point out in a few paragraphs, *"Now he who supplies seed to the sower and bread for food will also supply and increase your store of seed and will enlarge the harvest of your righteousness"* (2 Corinthians 9:10).

God's grace motivates us to want to give. Paul pats the Macedonians on the back. *"Entirely on their own, they urgently pleaded with us for the privilege of sharing in this service to the Lord's people"* (2 Corinthians 8:3-4). What pastor wouldn't pinch himself to see if he was dreaming at the prospect of God's people being eager to part with their money? It happened then, it can happen again. Contemporary congregations might be relieved if we stopped passing the offering baskets, bags, or buckets every weekend, but not the Macedonians. They were eager to give; don't rob them of the opportunity. Paul was raising money for Christians in Judea. The Christians in northern Greece *"pleaded[180] with us for the privilege of sharing in this service[181] to the Lord's people"* (2 Corinthians 8:4).

Like Paul, I used to brag about the generosity of the congregation I pastored for several years. They had an easy

---

[180] Greek: "deomai" (δέομαι). This word connotes a strong desire, impelling someone to long for, ask, beg, or pray.

[181] Greek: "diakonia" (διακονία). This term is the origin of our word "deacon;" i.e., one who serves or ministers to meet the practical needs of others. Giving is a ministry.

willingness to give. And that, despite the absence of many among us with deep pockets. They were almost Macedonian. When a certain need arose, they would generously respond — with spontaneity and enthusiasm.

We saw a lot of Mormon churches on our summer vacation travels through Utah and Idaho. There's a uniformity to the way they look — rambling brown brick buildings, steeples and expansive lawns, immaculately maintained. All underwritten by Salt Lake City. But, it's the people's money that pays for those facilities. Every practicing Mormon is expected to tithe. A pledge card is signed each year indicating just how much money that will be. Many evangelical denominations do the same.

The Macedonian Christians didn't need an annual visit from the stewardship committee; they gave *"Entirely on their own"* (2 Corinthians 8:3). When God's grace motivates our giving, some guidance might be helpful, but we don't need any pressure to contribute. We want to give. Paul will comment on it again when he says, *"Each of you should give what you have decided in his heart to give, not reluctantly or under compulsion"* (2 Corinthians 9:7).

In the New Covenant giving is properly viewed as a privilege, not a duty. As much as contemporary pastors and Christian fundraisers are loathe to say so, there are no tithes in Christianity. Under the Old Covenant, the people of God were compelled to give ten percent of their income. The tithe was a tax. Additional revenues were also levied, bumping the yearly obligation to upwards of thirty percent. On top of that, there were freewill offerings. Preachers these days talk about "tithes and offerings;" but there are only offerings for those of us living in the era of God's grace. Tithing is as obsolete as the Old Covenant itself.[182]

---

[182] See Hebrews 8:13.

I know the reality church leaders face. With the average church-goer giving around three percent of their annual income[183], they are reluctant to turn loose of the ten percent minimum. But to continue to teach the obligation of a tithe is disingenuous. People should be told to give whatever they want to give. Once grace takes hold of our hearts, the dollar amount of our donations will most likely be way more than ten percent. Freely we've received; freely we give.

New Covenant giving is also people-focused. In the earliest years of church history, there were no facilities to maintain or staff salaries to pay. There was a simplicity to financial stewardship. It was all about someone, not something. Paul was raising funds for people, not capital improvements. Not that fundraising for places and projects is wrong—just because the first century church had no reason to do so, doesn't mean we can't. But, let's make sure that people in need don't take second place to building programs, parking lots, cameras, stage lighting, sound systems, and websites. Giving is primarily a ministry to people.

THE GOAL OF GIVING

When God's grace motivates us to give, it goes deep. Again, the Macedonians shine. Even Paul was taken by surprise. He says, *"And they exceeded our expectations: They gave themselves first to the Lord and then by the will of God also to us"* (2 Corinthians 8:5).

Stewardship is a matter of the heart. Jesus was the first to connect the two. *"Where your treasure is, there will your heart be also"* (Matthew 6:21). They are intertwined and reciprocal. He could have said, "Where your heart is, there will be your treasure also." We invest our money in what we value. Likewise, we value what we spend our money on. If our heart is not in our giving, something's missing. The Macedonian Christians gave themselves to Christ and

---

[183] huffingtonpost.com/.../the-flesh-is-weak-churchgoers-give. Accessed April 10, 2016.

then entrusted their money to their spiritual leaders to determine how it would be distributed.

I was a member of a church once where one of the staff members decided he wanted to be a missionary in South America. He presented the prospect of this change of ministry to the elders of the congregation, asking for their approval and financial support. After careful deliberation, they gently advised him that he needed more spiritual maturity before he pursued his aspirations. He didn't like the counsel. Or accept it. Without their approval or endorsement, he proceeded with his plans and started to raise the money he needed on his own. Some of the church members took his side and gave their money to him directly, ignoring the determination of the church leadership. The Macedonians wouldn't have done that. They entrusted themselves and their money to their duly appointed spiritual leaders.

Nowadays, many Christians give to whatever causes they deem worthy of their support. Not necessarily a bad idea. But a reasonable argument could be made for giving all our contributions through the local church of which we are a part. After all, if our spiritual leaders are men and women of integrity, we should have no cause to doubt their counsel or the wise management of the money we entrust to them.

The Macedonians were trusting Paul to carefully distribute the funds he was collecting. And, with integrity. The apostle was determined that he and the others who handled their contributions would be above reproach. *"We want to avoid any criticism of the way we administer this liberal gift. For we are taking pains to do what is right, not only in the eyes of the Lord, but also in the eyes of man"* (2 Corinthians 8:20-21).

From the start of his evangelistic ministry, Billy Graham was committed to being beyond suspicion in financial matters. He made himself accountable to a board of trustees, who set his salary and managed the millions of dollars that would eventually flow into and through that organization. Billy Graham was following the principle the Apostle Paul lays out here—going the extra mile to do what's right.

If the people who control the expenditures of any Christian enterprise aren't impeccably honest, then they deserve the disapproval they get. When it comes to money management, spiritual leaders have to pass muster with both God and human auditors. People expect that. They should.

Paul and his partners in ministry sought to minimize criticism when it came to the sizable amounts of money being raised in Greece for the drought-beset Christians in Palestine. The apostle was smart enough to not collect the cash himself. He had a team whose positive reputations preceded them. Topping the list was Titus, well-known, highly respected, and loved by the Corinthians. Paul says, *"Thanks be to God, who put into the heart of Titus the same concern I have for you. For Titus not only welcomed our appeal, but he is coming to you with much enthusiasm and on his own initiative"* (2 Corinthians 8:16-17).

Paul next mentions another man, without including his name. But he was clearly someone the Corinthians also knew and revered. *"And we are sending along with him the brother*[184] *who is praised by all the churches for his service to the gospel"* (2 Corinthians 8:18). Note too, that this person was not unilaterally selected by Paul for this ministry. He was approved by a consortium of local churches. *"What is more, he was chosen by the churches to accompany us as we carry the offering, which we administer in order to honor the Lord himself and to show our eagerness to help"* (2 Corinthians 8:19).

The reputation of Christ himself is hanging in the balance when comes to how spiritual leaders manage the money and material

---

[184] Traditionally, Luke has been seen as this unidentified man of God. Or perhaps, he is the other unnamed individual in 2 Corinthians 8:22. Of the three men mentioned, only Titus is named.

goods entrusted to them. Paul mentions yet another highly respected individual, who was also renowned enough to remain unnamed. *"In addition, we are sending with them our brother who has often proved to us in many ways that he is zealous, and now even more so because of his great confidence in you"* (2 Corinthians 8:22). Paul comes back to Titus, perhaps his most trusted envoy to Corinth. *"As for Titus, he is my partner and co-worker among you."* He then closes with one last tribute to the trio. *"As for our brothers, they are representatives of the churches and an honor to Christ"* (2 Corinthians 8:23).

When it came to money, Paul surrounded himself with people who shared his integrity. Finally, he tells the Corinthians how they should respond to such leadership. *"Therefore, show these men the proof of your love and the reason for our pride in you, so that the churches can see it"* (2 Corinthians 8:24).

Giving is *"an act of grace"* (2 Corinthians 8:6). Once we discover and experience God's unconditional love, we are motivated to duplicate it. We give things away—time, energy, possessions, and money. And, with each passing year, we get more enthused and skilled at doing so. The goal of giving is to excel at it. Paul encourages the Corinthians to do just that. *"But since you excel in everything—in faith, in speech, in knowledge, in complete earnestness and in the love we have kindled in you—see that you also excel in the grace of giving"* (2 Corinthians 8:7).

The Corinthian congregation was a charismatic[185] church in the truest sense of the term. Their childish immaturity notwithstanding, they were the recipients of God's grace and channels of it too. They had the full gamut of spiritual gifts and they were exercising them.

---

[185] Greek: "charis" (χάρις). This word describes that which affords joy, pleasure, delight, sweetness, charm, and loveliness. It is kindness, freely bestowed on those who might deserve it and those who definitely don't. It is grace extended to those who need it. It is the origin of our word "charismatic."

Now, Paul encourages them to add another element to their life of ministry. He challenges them to *"excel"* at giving.

When we excel, we do better at something than we've done before. We surpass ourselves. In doing so, we become excellent. The Corinthians were willing to give, but they needed to follow the example of their comrades in northern Greece and carry through with what they said they'd do. Paul exhorts them. *"Bring also to completion this act of grace on your part"* (2 Corinthians 8:6). It's not enough to resolve to give. We excel at it when we follow through with our intentions. Characteristically, Paul connects grace with giving. Giving must be grace-driven.

The Corinthians had pledged themselves to pitch in to help the hungry Christians in Palestine. Now it was time to put their money where their mouth was. Paul knows there's no tax in the New Covenant. Nor, is it his style to tell people what to do. But it's clear, he also knows how to tactfully apply pressure when it's needed. He leans on them a little. *"I am not commanding you, but I want to test the sincerity of your love by comparing it to the earnestness of others"* (2 Corinthians 8:8). In a paragraph or two, he will tighten the screws a bit more.

> *There is no need for me to write to you about this service to the Lord's people. For I know your eagerness to help, and I have been boasting about it to the Macedonians, telling them that since last year you in Achaia were ready to give; and your enthusiasm has stirred most of them to action. But I am sending the brothers in order that our boasting about you in this matter should not prove hollow, but that you may be ready, as I said you would be. For if any Macedonians come with me and find you unprepared, we — not to say anything about you — would be ashamed of having been so confident.* (2 Corinthians 9:1-4)

How's that for positive peer pressure? Paul doesn't make demands, but he forcefully recommends.

And here is my advice about what is best for you in this matter: Last year you were the first not only to give but also to have the desire to do so. Now finish the work, so that your eager willingness to do it may be matched by your completion of it, according to your means.[186] (2 Corinthians 8:10-11)

One of the ways we excel at giving is to do what we intend to do. God wants us to finish what we start. Plus, to do it better than we have in the past. I don't hesitate to tell people, that all things being equal, they should be giving more money this year than they did last year. If their income goes up, their giving should go up.

It's a common practice—and a mistaken one—to stick with a fixed amount of giving, year in and year out. In fact, that's the practical problem with the tithe; people give ten percent and never increase it. They've paid their tax. But, staying in the same place isn't moving ahead. It's not excelling. Excelling is making progress. It's going forward. In this case, giving more. More, than we ever have before.

THE SECRET OF GIVING

A secret is information that not everybody knows. It's hidden from sight. It's concealed. There is a stewardship secret in Scripture that now needs to be shouted from the housetops. It's right here. *"For if the willingness is there the gift is acceptable according to what one has, not according to what one does not have"* (2 Corinthians 8:12). There's nothing mysterious or complicated about it. How much we give is secondary to the desire to do so. The question is, are we willing?

When the poor widow put her two cents into the collection box at the Temple in Jerusalem, Jesus was watching. Luke reports, *"Jesus*

---

[186] While there is no fixed percentage of money we are prescribed to give under the terms of the New Covenant, we are to give a percentage, directly related to our income. Paul has already taught this principle to the Corinthians. *"On the first day of every week, each one of you should set aside a sum of money in keeping with your income"* (1 Corinthians 16:2).

saw the rich putting their gifts into the temple treasury. He also saw a poor widow put in two very small coins" (Luke 21:1-2). As you may have heard, the *"temple treasury"* was a big wooden box with a trumpet-shaped opening. Anyone nearby could hear the clanging of the coins people were putting in it.

From the context of this story, we learn that Jesus had already censured the teachers of the law for making a show of their righteousness in public. You can be sure, people like that made as big a racket as they could when they rolled their coins into the chute. By contrast, the widow's two pennies tinkled down the funnel. Jesus noticed the disparity. He commented, with an attention-getting alert. *"Truly I tell you, this poor widow has put in more than all the others"* (Luke 21:3). As far as Jesus is concerned, it's not how much we give, but how willing we are to give. That's what counts. That day at the Temple he pronounced, *"All these people gave their gifts out of their wealth; but she out her poverty put in all she had to live on"* (Luke 21:4). The Twelve were doubtlessly flabbergasted. They thought amount matters. It doesn't. Willingness does. When we give willingly, we have learned the secret of stewardship.

THE PURPOSE OF GIVING

One question remains when it comes to learning what it takes to get good at giving. It's basic. Why does God want us to give away our money in the first place? And, what for? He doesn't need it. But someone else does.

As we've seen, Paul was raising money. And yes, he was putting some subtle, but palpable, pressure on the Christians in Greece to help out their impoverished brothers and sisters in Palestine. He was collecting as much money as he could. He was a purpose-driven pastor. He tells the Corinthians what he was up to. *"Our desire is not that others might be relieved while you are hard pressed, but that there might be equality"* (2 Corinthians 8:13).

God is egalitarian; he's committed to equality among his people. Some of us should not have too much, while others don't have enough. That was the theme of Ronald J. Sider's book, *Rich Christians in an Age of Hunger – Moving From Affluence to Generosity.*[187] Economic equality is a biblical priority in both Testaments.

Though they were just getting by themselves, the Grecian Christians still had a surplus, while their Judean counterparts were operating on a deficit. It was an inequitable situation. *"At the present time your plenty will supply what they need, so that in turn their plenty will supply what you need. The goal is equality, as it is written: 'The one who gathered much did not have too much, and the one who gathered little did not have too little'"* (2 Corinthians 8:14-15). Paul is harking back to Exodus 16:18. God provided manna for his people's daily sustenance. Not more than they needed. Not less. Just enough. Hoarding was strictly forbidden.

Jesus's parable about the farmer who built bigger barns to store his surplus crops is properly called "The Rich Fool." The man was selfish. And foolish. *"You fool! This very night your life will be demanded from you. Then who will get what you have prepared for yourself?"* (Luke 12:20). The farmer's big mistake was that he was *"not rich toward God"* (Luke 12:21).

Jesus told that story to bolster his counsel about people's attitudes toward money and things. *"Watch out! Be on your guard against all kinds of greed; life does not consist in an abundance of possessions"* (Luke 12:15). Christ was an advocate of simple faith, and a simple life. *"Therefore, I tell you, do not worry about your life, what you will eat or drink; or about your body, what you will wear. Is not life more than food, and the body more than clothes?"*(Matthew 6:25) *"Do not worry about tomorrow, for tomorrow will worry about itself. Each day has enough trouble of its own"* (Matthew 6:34). *"Do not store up for*

---

187 Sider, Ronald. *Rich Christians in an Age of Hunger – Moving From Affluence to Generosity.* Nashville, TN: Thomas Nelson, 2005.

yourselves treasures on earth...but store up for yourselves treasures in heaven" (Matthew 6:19-20). When we forget these principles, or don't practice them, we get selfish. Like Jesus, Paul wants Christians to be rich toward God. We don't have more than we need so we can keep stockpiling it. Instead, along with meeting our needs, let's concern ourselves with meeting the needs of others too.

One morning I was having coffee and a cinnamon roll in the patio of a local bakery. All of a sudden, a dirty and ragged young man started making his way through the tables, asking the patrons for a handout. As he headed toward me, I reached into my backpack for some ready cash. I found a couple of $1 bills. I gladly handed them to him.

Who knows? Someday, those of us with more than we need may find ourselves in a situation with less than we need. Paul reasoned along those lines with the Corinthians. *"At the present time your plenty will supply what they need, so that in turn their plenty will supply what you need. The goal is equality"* (2 Corinthians 8:14). The purpose of grace-driven giving is equality. If and when we can, we lend other people a hand.

Paul has been teaching us the theory of biblical stewardship — the motivation, secret, goal, and purpose of giving. Now, he's going to shift from the why to the how of becoming the stewards of our money God intends us to be.

GIVING EAGERLY

I agree with the observation that when it comes to giving, money isn't the problem; motivation is. Most people have some disposable income. The question is, to whom or to what will they give it, and when? A fundraising professional admitted to me once, that he hates to see money "walk out of the room." Neither is the Apostle Paul hesitant to solicit people's financial contributions for a profitable purpose.

It's demonstrable that once people are persuaded of the worthiness of a cause, they will consider contributing to it. Charities understand this presupposition. Why else would World Vision publish the pictures of needy children? They could just describe impoverished and deplorable situations around the world. But, a photo of an adorable child in need stirs emotions. And generates contributions. Motivation matters. It was true of the Macedonians in Paul's day. *"Entirely on their own, they urgently pleaded with us for the privilege of sharing in this service to the Lord's people"* (2 Corinthians 8:3-4). They wanted to give. And they gave. The Corinthian Christians were eager to give too.

> *There is no need for me to write to you about this service to the Lord's people. For I know your eagerness to help, and I have been boasting about it to the Macedonians, telling them that since last year you in Achaia were ready to give; and your enthusiasm has stirred most of them to action.* (2 Corinthians 9:1-2)

Enthusiasm to give is contagious. One person gives and it invigorates others to do the same. In this circumstance, it was reciprocal; the Christians in Macedonia inspired the Christians in Achaia. And vice-versa. Eagerness makes things happen. Grace understood and experienced generates excitement. Let's enthuse others with our enthusiasm.

GIVING GENEROUSLY

One Christmas a Texas businessman bought himself a Santa suit and headed for New York City. He walked up and down the busy streets of the Big Apple, handing a $100 bill to anyone who would take it. Refusing to identify himself to the press, he said he never had so much fun in his entire life.

The Bible talks about being open-handed when it comes to giving. For example, the virtuous woman of Proverbs 31 is described like this: *"She opens her arms to the poor and extends her hands to the needy"* (Proverbs 31:20). If we are willing to hug people in need and easily touch them, we won't hesitate to reach for our wallet or purse to give them a few bucks when they need it. It's part of being right with God. *"The wicked borrow and do not repay, but the righteous give generously"* (Psalm 37:21). The operative word here is *"generous."* To be generous is to be free from smallness of mind or character. Generosity is an obligation for Christ's followers. Paul told Timothy once,

> *Command those who are rich in this present world not to be arrogant nor to put their hope in wealth... Command them to do good, to be rich in good deeds and to be generous and willing to share. In this way they will lay up treasure for themselves as a firm foundation for the coming age, so that they may take hold of the life that is truly life.* (1 Timothy 6: 17-19)

In 1966, film producer, Dino De Laurentiis, took on the ambitious project of portraying the first nineteen chapters of Genesis in a film entitled, *The Bible: In the Beginning,*[188] directed by John Huston. In one scene Huston portrays Cain and Abel bringing their offerings to the Lord. Abel, a shepherd, offers one of his sheep. God was pleased. Cain, a farmer, offers some grain. Without explaining why, the Bible states that God did not *"look with favor"* on Cain's offering (Genesis 4:5). In the movie, Cain brings a basket of grain to God. He pours the whole thing out on the ground. Then he has second thoughts. Furtively looking around, he scoops a few handfuls of his offering back into the basket and hurries off. Generous givers do not give as little as they can; they give as much as they can. And, gladly. When that happens, there's always more than enough. Money isn't the problem; motivation is the problem. And, the solution.

---

[188] De Laurentiis, Dino. *The Bible: In the Beginning.* 20th Century Fox, 1966.

Being generous is giving more than enough. Charles Dickens' Ebenezer Scrooge was a miserly old codger who reluctantly counted out a few shillings on payday to his impoverished employees. God wants us to be like Scrooge — after he saw the ghosts of Christmas — showering gifts to people on the street and buying a big fat Christmas dinner goose for Bob Cratchit and his family, including Tiny Tim.

There's a reliable principle involved in generous giving. What we sow, we reap. *"Remember this: Whoever sows sparingly will also reap sparingly, and whoever sows generously will also reap generously"* (2 Corinthians 9:6).

I learned this lesson as a young homeowner. It was our first house. I envisioned a lush green lawn out front for all the neighbors to admire. At the same time, I didn't have much money to make it happen. So, I went to Home Depot and bought the minimum amount of seed for the square feet I needed to cover. And, for the lowest possible price. My wife warned me that my dreams of a nice thick lawn were not going to come true. I ignored her. I spread my cheap seed as thin as I could and waited to see the results. Well, let's just describe what eventually did sprout as a horticultural version of male pattern baldness. My wife was right. I got sparse, not lush. While getting is never the proper goal for giving, the truth remains that what we give is what we get.

GIVING CHEERFULLY

Back in the day, Fram Automotive Products ran a memorable commercial on TV for their oil filters. In the 30 second spot, they subtly challenged car owners to ask themselves a couple of questions: Will we change our oil when our vehicle needs it? And, will we use high-quality American-made products? Fram answered the question for us. If we procrastinate or cut corners in the amount of money it takes to keep our cars in good shape, we may be sorry.

The ad featured two no-nonsense auto mechanics. One was doing the talking, while the other was rebuilding an engine on a workbench behind him. The first mechanic, holding a familiar orange Fram filter, said, "You can pay me now." Then, the one rebuilding the engine quipped, "Or pay *me* later."

Apprehension is not the incentive God chooses to use in motivating us to give our money for people or causes that he cares about. To the contrary, he wants us to be eager, generous, and happy when we give. Paul proclaims, *"God loves a cheerful*[189] *giver"* (2 Corinthians 9:7). Paul says that God is particularly fond of hilarious givers. Evidently, there's a special place for us in our heavenly Father's heart when we have to keep from cracking a smile, or getting giggly, when we give our money to him. That means that when the offering plate comes our way at church next weekend, we will experience some exuberant merriment. My wife and I still have a grin on our faces when we think of Lindsay Smith.

GIVING FEARLESSLY

From the time they were little we taught our five kids to give some of their money to God. Once, when our oldest son was about ten, he was saving every dime he had to buy a new bicycle. One Sunday on our way to church, we were talking about putting our offerings in the collection plate. In childlike honesty, he blurted out, "Dad, if I give my money to God, even some of it, how will I ever have enough to buy a bike?" Good question. Think fast, Pop! I said, "That's where faith comes in, son. You give some of your money to God—money you could use to get something you want—and you just have to believe that God will notice. Maye he will make it possible for you to

---

[189] Greek: "hilaros" (ἱλαρός). Our word "hilarious" is the transliteration of this Greek term. It describes any cheerful, joyful, and typically spontaneous action.

give and get at the same time." My son said, "Ok, I'll give my money to God. And, if he wants me to have a new bike, I will."

Little did I know at the time the wisdom of my own words. The next week, I got a phone call from one of the men of the church. His son had outgrown his bicycle. It was in good condition—and way cool. Did I know any boy in the church who might want it? For free! My son and I drove over to his house right after school that day to pick it up. Lesson happily learned.

Money relieves our fears. When we've got a steady job, the bills are paid, the savings account is growing, and the stock market is on the rise, we feel good—safe and secure. Reverse those fortunes and we get scared. "What's going to happen to us?!" My mother used to talk about ending up "in the poor house." I wasn't sure just what a poor house was, but I knew it couldn't be a good thing. Mom was exaggerating, but she was also a tad bit fearful about our financial well-being.

When we worry about what might happen to us, we become afraid. Often our concerns are imaginary. Sometimes, they're not. Fear is a distressing emotion aroused by impending danger, whether or not the threat is real. Money alleviates fear. Surely, we can't risk giving any significant amount of it away! What might happen to us if we do? Enter faith. God's on record about it. *"And God is able to bless you abundantly, so that in all things at all times, having all that you need, you will abound in every good work"* (2 Corinthians 9:8). Giving is a test of faith. But, notice, Paul promises that God is able to make sure that in all things we have all that we need, at all times. There you go.

When faith triumphs over our fears about giving, we re-experience the dependable and lavish provision of God. Not only for what we need, but even for what we want. God broadcasts financial blessings upon us like a farmer sows seed in his field. *"Now he who supplies seed to the sower and bread for food will also supply and increase your store of seed and will enlarge the harvest of your righteousness"* (2 Corinthians 9:10). The cliché is true; you can't out-give God. The more we sow, the more he gives us to sow. The more our resources are depleted, the more he renews them. Our oil jar[190] may not always be full, but it will never be empty. Money is the seed, but the harvest is righteousness — a right relationship with God and others.

Advocates of the Prosperity Gospel bank on what Paul says next. *"You will be enriched in every way"* (2 Corinthians 9:11). Just name it and claim it. After all, Jesus himself promised that if we leave houses and lands for his sake, we will receive a hundred times as much in this life and eternal life to boot (Mark 10:29-30).

Is that what Paul promises here? Let's read the whole sentence. *"You will be enriched in every way, so that you can be generous on every occasion, and through us your generosity will result in thanksgiving to God"* (2 Corinthians 9:11). There's a two-fold purpose represented in the phrase, *"so that."* God bestows material blessings on us for a couple of reasons. First, so that we will have the resources to be generous with what he provides. And second, so that he will be thanked and praised in the process. Both results are others-oriented, not self-centered. When we commit ourselves to this divine purpose, we will have what we need. We can be fearless about it.

GIVING FAITHFULLY

My wife and I are proud to sponsor six needy children around the world — two in Africa, two in India, one in Columbia, and one in Vietnam. Our monthly contributions are managed by World Vision and Compassion International. We've been committed to these youngsters and their families for years now. It's long distance stewardship, with occasional letters being exchanged between us.

Paul's fundraising efforts were a kind of long distance sponsorship too, minus the glossy photos of the beneficiaries on the

---

[190] See 2 Kings 4:1-7.

refrigerator. In those days, Palestine was a world away from Greece. The Grecian Christians were giving their money to people they'd never met, nor would ever see. Ultimately though, the experience would draw both giver and receiver together in gratitude to God. *"This service that you perform is not only supplying the needs of the Lord's people but is also overflowing in many expressions of thanks to God"* (2 Corinthians 9:12). Giving and receiving bonds the people involved to each other and to God — all in an attitude of gratitude. *"And in their prayers for you their hearts will go out to you, because of the surpassing grace God has given you. Thanks be to God for his indescribable gift!"* (2 Corinthians 9:14-15).

Giving is not only an act of faith, it is evidence of faith. When we give, we prove ourselves to be authentic Christians. What stronger evidence could there be for the power of the gospel? Paul confirms this spiritual truth when he compliments the Corinthians. *"Because of the service by which you have proved yourselves, men will praise God for the obedience that accompanies your confession of the gospel of Christ, and for your generosity in sharing with them and with everyone else"* (2 Corinthians 9:13). Spiritual leaders with integrity welcome the opportunity to teach these biblical principles of financial stewardship.

One day, we got a thank you note from Lindsay Smith. She wrote: "Just imagine my complete and utter astonishment when I received your card and check when I came to work today at KFC. You were complete strangers who did a kind deed." God's grace makes us all good at giving.

THINK

1. Why does Paul repeatedly call giving an act of *"grace"*? (2 Corinthians 8:1, 6, 7). What is the essential connection between grace and giving?

2. Giving is part of the larger concept of stewardship. Please explain.

3. Many pastors shy away from preaching about money unless they're desperate for it. Why?

4. What does God want before you give him your money?

5. What is the secret of Christian giving?

6. What's the purpose of Christian giving?

7. Where does the motivation to give away some of our money come from?

8. What is our goal when it comes to giving?

9. Is there always an element of receiving in the act of giving?

10. How would you rate your eagerness to give away your money?

ACT

1. Carry some extra cash. When the chance to give some of it to a total stranger comes along, do it.

2. Eliminate the word "tithe" from your fund-raising vocabulary.

3. Practice *"hilarious"* giving. The next time the offering plate goes by, let yourself chuckle a little as you put your money in it.

4. Purpose to increase the amount of money you give to God every year. Be specific about the percentage.

5. Put God to the test. Give away the money you are saving for something you want. And then, wait and see what he does.

Chapter 13

Brave Enough to Be Bold

2 Corinthians 10:1-18

When a young couple asks me to officiate at their wedding ceremony, I take it as a compliment. But, I don't say yes right away. I suggest that we get together and talk about their plans. My main concern is not for the ceremony itself, but for the lifetime of togetherness that will follow it. My purpose is to find out whether they should get married in the first place. After chatting with them for a while about their relationship, if I think there is a reasonable possibility for a successful marriage, we set up some counseling sessions to consider further their chances for a happy future as husband and wife. One of my priorities is to evaluate their mental, emotional, and spiritual health to help ascertain their compatibility as a couple. Compatibility is key. If they are compatible enough, I will do the ceremony. If they aren't, then I point out the things they need to work on before they set their wedding date. The first thing I have them do is take the Taylor-Johnson Temperament Analysis.[191]

Individual temperament is a crucial element in interpersonal compatibility. Each of us has a temperament. It's the combination of

---

[191] The Taylor-Johnson Temperament Analysis measures nine personality traits and their opposite characteristics: Nervous ↔ Composed, Depressive ↔ Lighthearted, Active-Social ↔ Quiet, Expressive-Responsive ↔ Inhibited, Sympathetic ↔ Indifferent, Subjective ↔ Objective, Dominant ↔ Submissive, Hostile ↔ Tolerant, Self-disciplined ↔ Impulsive. The test consists of 180 questions providing an evaluation in graph form that portrays each respondent's feelings about themselves. In premarital counseling, each person can also answer the questions as they apply to their intended life-partner.

our mental and emotional characteristics. When people around us don't seem to be adjusting well to others or their circumstances, we call them "temperamental." Temperament reveals our essential psychological outlook on life and how we tend to respond to the variety of situations we find ourselves in.

Since the days of Hippocrates (460–370 BC) it has been theorized that people fall into one of four categories of personal disposition: sanguine, choleric, melancholic, or phlegmatic. What determines temperament is debatable. Is it nature or nurture? Whatever the cause, our temperament is pretty much fixed. It reveals who we are.

In a balanced blend of personality traits, spiritual leaders with integrity share a common characteristic — they are bold. In the closing chapters of Second Corinthians this attribute will surface again and again.[192]

When we are bold we do not hesitate to act, even at the risk of potential conflict. When necessary, a bold leader is zealous, courageous, forceful, and even confrontational. "Conflict Avoidance" is the clinical term used to describe the absence of this important characteristic. Avoiding conflict is not good. When situations call for it, we all need to be brave enough to be bold.

Being bold is an art. It's a skill that has to be learned. If we are not bold in a biblical way we are going to hurt people and be less than useful in accomplishing God's purposes. In short, we need a Christ-like boldness. We need an apostolic boldness. We need to be unhesitatingly fearless in the face of danger, like they were — gently, forcefully, confidently, and even pridefully.

---

[192] We come now to the third distinct section of Second Corinthians. In chapters 10-13, Paul vigorously defends his integrity, standing up to the defiant minority in the Corinthian congregation, led by recently arrived rabble-rousers who were challenging his apostleship.

BEING BOLD GENTLY

For two thousand years the Apostle Paul has been every Christian's hero. We admire him. We respect him. We love him. It's shocking then for us to realize that back when he was here not everyone felt that way. Some disliked him. Some were doubtful of him. Some were disrespectful and even defiant of him.

Picture the Corinthian church as a pie chart. Three-fourths of the diagram represents the people who eventually came to re-appreciate, respect, and submit to Paul as their pastoral leader. I call them the Compliant Majority. The other quarter of the graph represents the parishioners who were dead-set against him. They rejected his spiritual authority. I call them the Defiant Minority.

To make matters worse, some self-appointed, strong-willed, and outspoken newcomers had wormed their way into the congregation. They had stoked the dissatisfaction of Paul's detractors and sowed doubt about him in the minds of everyone else. Such a situation demanded a response from a decidedly courageous leader.

As has been noted, the last four chapters of Second Corinthians are irrefutably different from the rest of the letter. The change in tone is so abrupt that some scholars think that it was, indeed, a separate letter altogether and later appended to the first nine chapters. Whether or not that hypothesis can be demonstrated is debatable. What is beyond doubt is the fact that up until now Paul has been firm, but cordial and conciliatory, with the Corinthian congregation. From here on though, he is combative and confrontational. It's as though he was addressing a separate group of people. He was. So far, he has been talking to the Compliant Majority, with the Defiant Minority listening in. Now, it's the opposite.

But even in his boldness, the apostle is gentle. *"By the humility[193] and gentleness Christ, I appeal[194] to you"* (2 Corinthians 10:1). Boldness

---

[193] Greek: "prautēs" (πραΰτης). This term connotes a mild and gentle friendliness. From classical times in Greece it was a highly valued social

has a purpose—to salvage and restore damaged or at-risk relationships. It's a Christ-like zeal. Unyielding, but gracious. It's meekness.

Some people mistake being meek for being weak. To the contrary, meekness speaks of strength under control. It was a word farmers and animal trainers used to describe a powerful creature, like an ox or horse, whose innate strength was brought into submission with just a word, a whisper, or a glance. Jesus was the embodiment of meekness. He made nearly everyone he met feel comfortable to be around him. Men, women, children, the rich, the poor, the socially connected, and the disenfranchised—all of them felt at ease in his presence. They weren't fearful that he would turn them away or put them down. He was meek, but never weak.

Like Christ, Paul was meek. He was strong, but he refused to overpower people. At the same time, he didn't hesitate to stand up to his opponents in Corinth. He threateningly pleads with them. *"I beg you that when I come I may not have to be as bold as I expect to be toward some people who think we live by the standards of this world"* (2 Corinthians 10:2).

An essential element to boldness has to do with speech. A bold person holds nothing back. What needs to be said, is said. The defiant ones in Corinth were relentlessly verbal in their attacks on Paul's character. Word has gotten back to him of what they've been saying. He alludes to their criticisms. *"I, Paul, who am 'timid'*[195] *when face to face with you, but 'bold' when away"* (2 Corinthians 10:1). His

---

virtue, the opposite of brusqueness and quick anger. It was the way friends treated one another. Judges with this proclivity tended to issue more lenient sentences. Jesus used the word to describe himself when he said *"I am gentle and humble in heart"* (Matthew 11:29).

[194] Greek: "parakaleō" (παρακαλέω). This verb means to call to one's side, the result of which is comfort, counsel, encouragement, or instruction.

[195] Greek: "tapeinos" (ταπεινός). This word means "not rising far from the ground." Metaphorically, it denotes being of a low degree. In a bad sense, of deferring to others in a servile way.

rivals were charging him with duplicity; saying that he was double-dealing and dishonest. They alleged that he was *"bold"* from a distance, but that in person he was the opposite. Paul is aggressive in responding to such slander, but he doesn't get brash or blustery. He stays meek.

BEING BOLD FORCEFULLY

In 1901, then Vice President, Theodore Roosevelt, gave a speech about foreign policy in which he coined the phrase, "Walk softly, and carry a big stick." The Apostle Paul took the same approach toward *"some people"* in Corinth (2 Corinthians 10:2). Like all good shepherds, he had a staff for the sheep and a rod for the predators threatening the flock. Being forceful is a simple concept: you will be assertive, if necessary. It's Big Stick Diplomacy.

Being forcible as a Christian leader is important—and complex. One thing's for sure though, it's not a worldly show of strength. We don't fight with anger, cunning, power, or positon. After all, we are in this world, but not of it. *"For though we live in the world,*[196] *we do not wage war as the world does"* (2 Corinthians 10:3). This is spiritual warfare.

> *The weapons we fight with are not the weapons of the world. On the contrary, they have divine power to demolish strongholds.*[197] *We demolish arguments and every pretension that sets itself up against the knowledge of God, and we take captive every thought to make it obedient to Christ.* (2 Corinthians 10:4-5)

---

[196] Greek: "sarx" (σάρξ). Literally, this word means "flesh." The term identifies the physical origin of something, the sensuous element of human nature; or human nature itself, apart from divine influence. It is the way of the world. Paul repeats the term twice in this sentence.

[197] Greek: "ochurōma" (ὀχύρωμα). This term is found only here in the New Testament. In the Greek translation of the Old Testament it was used to describe a fortress, as in Proverbs 21:22. *"One who is wise can go up against the city of the mighty and pull down the stronghold in which they trust."* It is in that sense that Paul employs it here.

I watched a fascinating documentary on PBS once. Modern day engineers made the attempt to design, construct, and operate a massive catapult like the ones used in medieval warfare. They built the catapult and its target—a wall hundreds of yards away, on the opposite side of an open field. Finally, the time came to test their ingenuity. A huge boulder was launched. Bam! The wall was demolished by its impact. The catapult proved itself a worthy facsimile of its prototypes. Paul's catapult has divine power to *"demolish strongholds."* His single objective was *"to take captive every thought to make it obedient to Christ"* (2 Corinthians 10:5).

Conflict is intimidating. It takes courage to fight for what is right. There will be casualties. In Stephen Crane's civil war classic, *The Red Badge of Courage,* boys became men.[198] When they signed up for battle they were filled with bravado, little knowing the horror ahead of them. Despite their mothers' tears, they marched off to war. But, with the cannons booming, the bullets flying, and their buddies dying on every side, their courage was sorely tested. Those who survived found out what they were made of. Many of them were grievously wounded. They came home with a bloody medallion for their bravery.

Spiritual conflict calls for fortitude. Daring people do brave things, despite their fears. That's what heroes are made of. They are willing to fight. *"We will be ready to punish every act of disobedience, once your obedience is complete"* (2 Corinthians 10:6).

In the original Gulf War, President George H. W. Bush squared off with Saddam Hussein. He drew a line in the sand. If the Iraqis invaded Kuwait, they would be up against the military might of the United States of America. In 100 hours, the "Mother of all Battles" was over. Hussein's Republican Guard was decisively defeated.

---

[198] Crane, Stephen. *The Red Badge of Courage.* New York: D. Appleton & Company, 1895.

When President Bush took that courageous stand against tyranny, he was channeling John F. Kennedy's resolve in his 1961 inaugural address when he said, "Let every nation know that we shall pay any price, bear any burden, meet any hardship to assure the survival and success of liberty."[199] The Apostle Paul's determination to stand up to spiritual aggression against the Kingdom of God was equally resolute. He was brave enough to be bold.

BEING BOLD CONFIDENTLY

Paul's enemies in Corinth had badly misread him.

> *You are judging by appearances. If anyone is confident that they belong to Christ, they should consider again that we belong to Christ just as much as they do. So even if I boast somewhat freely about the authority the Lord gave us for building you up rather than tearing you down, I will not be ashamed of it.* (2 Corinthians 10:7-8)

The fundamental misjudgment Paul's adversaries made was that they thought he was merely one of them. They didn't acknowledge the fact of his God-ordained spiritual authority. They were merely *"judging by appearances"* (2 Corinthians 10:7). Leaders with integrity know that God has appointed them to be over others. They are overseers. This doesn't mean, though, that we think of ourselves as superior to those we superintend. To the contrary, we consider ourselves ordinary Christians. At the same time, the title we wear is more than just a designation; it's an office. It's a post that God has called us to hold. We are humble about it. But we are certain about it too. Such certainty contributes to our confidence.

Leaders designated by God do not pull rank. Nor do we appear to be intimidating. *"I do not want to seem to be trying to frighten you*

---

[199] ourdocuments.gov/doc.php?doc=91. Accessed March 16, 2016.

with my letters" (2 Corinthians 10:9). Of course, this was precisely what Paul's critics were accusing him of. He knew what they were saying. *"For some say, 'His letters are weighty and forceful, but in person he is unimpressive and his speaking amounts to nothing'"* (2 Corinthians 10:10).

These days, too many of us have bought into the idea that image is everything. Paul challenges that conclusion. The apostle was not intimidated by the standards of his rivals, even if he fell far short of their expectations. *"Such people should realize that what we are in our letters when we are absent, we will be in our actions when we are present"* (2 Corinthians 10:11). Despite the fact that ancient tradition says he was short, bald, with a hooked nose and a unibrow, Paul knows who he is.[200] His self-esteem is established. The *"surface of things"* doesn't count.

BEING BOLD PRIDEFULLY

Christians mistakenly think that pride is always bad. After all, God resists the proud and gives grace to the humble (Proverbs 3:34; James 4:6; 1 Peter 5:5). So, pride is wrong, right? It depends what you are proud of. And why. Granted, there's a fine line between self-appreciation and arrogance. Healthy pride comes from knowing that you did something well or that you are a good person. It's self-respect. That kind of pride is proper. And prerequisite, to spiritual boldness.

How can we be bold if we think too little of ourselves? Positive self-esteem is not the result comparing yourself to someone else, but of measuring what you've done and who you are by the standard of your own aptitude and potential. Paul has it worked out. *"We do not dare to classify or compare ourselves with some who commend themselves. When they measure themselves by themselves and compare themselves with*

---

[200] newworldencyclopedia.org/entry/Acts_of_Paul_and_Thecla. Accessed April 11, 2016.

themselves, they are not wise" (2 Corinthians 10:12). There is no ambivalence here — Paul is castigating his critics.

Admittedly, there is such a thing as false pride. True pride, by contrast, comes appropriately from things we've actually accomplished. Under attack, we may need to remind people of them.

> *We, however, will not boast beyond proper limits, but will confine our boasting to the sphere of service God himself has assigned to us, a sphere that also includes you. We are not going too far in our boasting, as would be the case if we had not come to you, for we did get as far as you with the gospel of Christ. Neither do we go beyond our limits by boasting of work done by others. Our hope is that, as your faith continues to grow, our sphere of activity among you will greatly expand, so that we can preach the gospel in the regions beyond you. For we do not want to boast about work already done in someone else's territory.* (2 Corinthians 10:13-16)

Paul could certainly speak highly of his work in Corinth. Without him, the church wouldn't even exist. Still he keeps who is and what he's done in perspective. He repeats Jeremiah's admonition: *"Let anyone who boasts boast in the Lord"* (Jeremiah 9:23-24; 2 Corinthians 10:17).

Ultimately, none of us generates anything; we reflect it. When we are complimented it's okay to say "Thank you." But, we know that apart from God we can do few things truly worthwhile — or for the right reasons. *"For it is not the one who commends himself who is approved, but the one whom the Lord commends"* (2 Corinthians 10:18). How crucial it is, then, that we see ourselves as commended by Christ. That's something we can be properly proud of. It's foundational and fundamental to our boldness.

What are the characteristics of your temperament? That's what the Taylor-Johnson Temperament Analysis is designed to discover. The T-JTA comes with a graph, so that once you've taken the test, you can have a visualization of your disposition. The healthiest graph is in the middle range. No extremes between Nervous and Composed, Lighthearted and Depressive, Active and Quiet, Expressive and Objective, Hostile and Tolerant, Self-Disciplined and Impulsive, Submissive and Dominant. For leaders with integrity, boldness is in the mix. When circumstances dictate it, we are fearless, forceful, and zealous. Speaking the truth in love, we hold back on nothing that needs to be said. Or done. We are brave enough to be bold.

THINK

1. Have you ever taken a personality test of any kind? What did you learn about yourself?

2. What is boldness? Rate your own degree of boldness.

3. Being bold is a skill. True or False?

4. A person should be bold all the time. True or False?

5. What was especially challenging for the Apostle Paul about the church in Corinth that called for boldness on his part?

6. How can you be bold and meek at the same time?

7. What is the connection between being meek and being gentle?

8. Rate your own degree of meekness and gentleness.

9. What role does confidence play in being bold when you need to be?

10. Do you have spiritual authority? Where did you get it? What's it for?

ACT

1. Contact a qualified psychological therapist to set up an appointment to take the Taylor-Johnson Temperament Analysis and discuss the results.

2. Ask a few trusted friends if you are "conflict avoidant."

3. Identify a situation you are facing right now that calls for boldness. Make up your mind to deal with it forcefully, but gently. Begin conversation with the people involved.

4. What accomplishments and/or personal characteristics do you have that can you be legitimately proud of? Make a list and look at it once a week, thanking God that you can humbly take pride for what he has done in your life.

5. The next time someone compliments you, just politely say "Thank you." To yourself say: "God be praised!"

Chapter 14

To Protect and Serve

2 Corinthians 11:1-15

I was visiting my home town once when one of the local police patrol cars drove by. There on the front door, beneath the city's logo, was this insignia: "To Protect and Serve." I have since realized that this is a common motto of law enforcement. It's an appropriate reminder too for those of us in spiritual leadership.

When it comes to watching over God's people, there is biblical reason why we are called shepherds. The Greek word from which we get the title "pastor" means shepherd. We lead, we feed, we protect. And, every good shepherd has two tools to go along with a watchful eye. A staff and a rod are always at hand. The usefulness of each these implements is unique. The staff is for the gentle guiding of the sheep. With or without a crook, this stick is used to nudge the rams, ewes and lambs in the right direction. The rod, on the other hand, is a weapon. It is not a gentle gadget. To the contrary, it is to club predators to death, if that's what it takes to protect the sheep. When it's called for, pastors also have to be fierce in watching over their flocks. That means we may need to be "menacingly wild, violent in force and intensity, furiously eager."[201] When necessary, spiritual leaders with integrity are ferocious.

In these last four chapters of Second Corinthians, the Apostle Paul is wielding a club. He has no choice. Dangerous carnivores have already penetrated the perimeter of the Corinthian congregation. They are poised to ravage the flock. Like any shepherd

---

[201] dictionary.com/browse/fierce. Accessed April 1, 2016.

worthy of the name, Paul is vigilant and quickly springs into action. A shepherd who won't engage those threatening his sheep is merely a hired hand.[202] For them, shepherding is just a job; they high-tail it at the first sign of trouble. Not true shepherds. Like the Good Shepherd himself, we lay down our lives for the sheep. We protect the people we serve. We keep them from harm and injury.

It's not certain just who the predators were, eager to devour God's people in Corinth. It is quite likely though that these assailants were outsiders, stirring up the disgruntled members of the congregation we are calling the Defiant Minority. Smelling blood, they were moving in for the kill. Their every intention was to supplant Paul as the spiritual leader of the church. He labels them *"false apostles, deceitful workers, masquerading as apostles of Christ"* (2 Corinthians 11:13).

Paul is perceptive when it comes to spiritual impersonators. He is acutely aware of the subtle but serious threat they pose for any local church. Shortly after leaving Corinth the first time,[203] he admonished the elders of the church in Ephesus,

> *Keep watch over yourselves and all the flock of which the Holy Spirit has made you overseers. Be shepherds of the church of God...I know that after I leave, savage wolves will come in among*

---

[202] *"I am the good shepherd. The good shepherd lays down his life for the sheep. The hired hand is not the shepherd and does not own the sheep. So when he sees the wolf coming, he abandons the sheep and runs away. Then the wolf attacks the flock and scatters it. The man runs away because he is a hired hand and cares nothing for the sheep"* (John 10:11-13).

[203] Luke reports in Acts that after a year and a half of teaching the Corinthians the word of God (Acts 18:11), Paul stayed a little longer and then abruptly *"left the brothers and sisters and sailed for Syria accompanied by Priscilla and Aquila"* (Acts 18:18). On the way, he stopped off in Ephesus, leaving his companions there, while he returned to his home church in Antioch, Syria. Sometime later, Paul embarked on his third church planting trip and established a long-time and deep fellowship with the congregation in Ephesus (see Acts 18:18 - 20:38).

you and will not spare the flock. Even from your own number men will arise and distort the truth in order to draw away disciples after them. So be on your guard! (Acts 20:28-31)

The Apostle Paul practiced what he preached. As an attentive shepherd he can hear wolves howling from miles away. In Corinth, the snarling was close at hand. Paul doesn't hesitate to beat back the attackers. In doing so he models the characteristics of shepherds who protect their flocks at the risk of their own lives. In this case, Paul is hundreds of miles away, so he uses his pen as a rod.

His opening foray smacks of foolishness, and he acknowledges it. *"I hope you will put up with me in a little foolishness. Yes, please put up with me"* (2 Corinthians 11:1). Of course, there's a distinct difference between appearing foolish and being foolish. Paul is no fool, but he is willing to take the chance of looking like one in order to ward off the predators threatening the well-being of those under his care. As we shall now see, good shepherds share several crucial characteristics when it comes to watching over their flocks. It starts with a unique kind of zeal.

JEALOUS

Paul plainly says, *"I am jealous[204] for you"* (2 Corinthians 11:2). There's a place for jealousy in spiritual leadership. In fact, being jealous is biblical, good, and essential when circumstances call for it. To protect their people, Christian shepherds are jealous. In transliterating the original Greek word into English, there's just a one letter difference between jealous and zealous. Jealous is being zealous. Zeal is fervor, for a person, object, or cause.

Zeal is good. It's what impelled Jesus to make a whip one time and drive the money changers from the Temple. Jesus was ferocious

---

[204] Greek: "zēloō" (ζηλόω). This term means to be heated or to boil with emotion. It could be envy, anger or hatred. In the defense of righteousness, the word connotes zeal—to desire earnestly, to pursue or strive after.

that day. His actions made a vivid and lasting impression on the Twelve. Remembering the event some sixty years later, the Apostle John recalls their reaction, quoting Psalm 69:9, *"Zeal for your house will consume me"* (John 2:17). When it came to the threat of spiritual encroachment in Corinth, Paul was consumed too. It was a *"godly jealousy"* (2 Corinthians 11:2). Just like Jesus.

Clearly, most of our relationships with other people should be inclusive. When we resent someone in our circle of friends for one reason or another, or we feel threatened by the attention they are receiving at our expense, then that's ungodly jealousy. If distrust compels a husband to keep track of his wife's every move, then that's ungodly jealousy. It is, indeed, a green-eyed monster—the dark side of jealousy, rooted in self-centered insecurity.

Still, some relationships are meant to be exclusive. They are too sacred to be shared. Two's company, three's a crowd. It should not surprise us that God doesn't tolerate competitors for the affections of his people. He is jealous. It was his stated reason for the first two of the Ten Commandments—no other gods and never any idols. *"For I, the LORD your God, am a jealous God"* (Exodus 20:5). Yahweh was unbending about it. When the Israelites entered Canaan, God told Moses, *"Break down their altars, smash their sacred stones and cut down their Asherah poles. Do not worship any other god, for the LORD, whose name is Jealous, is a jealous God"* (Exodus 34:13-14).

In synagogue school Paul became familiar with such edicts. He embraced them. He embodied them. He declares his jealousy— zealously. No apologies. No hesitancy. *"I am jealous for you with a godly jealousy"* (2 Corinthians 11:2).

When it came to the Corinthians, Paul had good cause to be jealous. He was their spiritual father and reminds them of it. *"In Christ Jesus I became your father through the gospel"* (1 Corinthians 4:15). He has betrothed the Corinthians to Christ. True to ancient custom, he had arranged the marriage. *"I promised you to one husband, to Christ, so that I might present you as a pure virgin to him"* (2 Corinthians 11:2). Unmarried though he was, Paul was the father of the bride. And this bride-to-be was misbehaving. Paul views the Corinthians' dalliance with spiritual impostors as nothing short of unfaithfulness to Jesus. It is never right for a fiancé to be flirtatious.

One spring semester in the school where I teach, two students got engaged. We all celebrated their blossoming love. Then, the boy was called to tend to a family emergency back home in Argentina. He ended up being gone far longer than he planned. During his absence, his intended began to spend an inordinate amount of time with another young man on campus. It got to the place where they were practically inseparable. It wasn't scandalous, but it was inappropriate. Everyone was thinking, and whispering, "She's engaged!"

In his book, *The Four Loves*, C.S. Lewis makes the point that anyone can fall in love with any one, at any time.[205] We have to be alert about our loyalties, guarding our hearts as Proverbs counsels.[206]

Well, the Corinthians were anything but discreet. They were unguarded and vulnerable. Paul was rightly concerned, pointing out their embarrassing unfaithfulness. He was more than apprehensive; he was afraid. *"But I am afraid[207] that just as Eve was deceived[208] by the*

---

[205] Lewis, C. S. *The Four Loves*. London: Geoffrey Bles, 1960.

[206] *"Above all else, guard your affections. For they influence everything else in your life"* (Proverbs 4:23, Living Proverbs 1986).

[207] Greek: "phoboumai" (φοβοῦμαι). This term is the source of our word "phobia," which describes a persistent, irrational fear of a specific object, activity, or situation that leads to a compelling desire to avoid it. Not all fears are irrational though; some are quite solidly founded in reality. In this case, spiritual infidelity.

[208] *"Then the LORD God said to the woman, 'What is this you have done?' The woman said, 'The serpent deceived me and I ate'"* (Genesis 3:13).

serpent's cunning, your minds[209] *may be led astray from your sincere and pure devotion to Christ"* (2 Corinthians 11:3).

Spiritual leaders today would do well to recognize the serious danger some of their people have put themselves in. It's not the time to look the other way or whistle in the dark. The careless young Christians at Corinth were flirting with false teachers. Like naïve adolescents, they didn't recognize their own peril. They were not being careful about who they were spending time with. They were being seduced, and didn't know it. And the devil was in the mix. Satan's assault on Eve was not sexual as some rabbinic texts suggest.[210] It was even more consequential — he raped her mind. Paul was determined to not let that happen to his daughters and sons in Corinth.

Like he did to Eve in Eden, the devil — snake that he is — was mesmerizing the Corinthians. Paul tells them that they have been *"led astray from your sincere and pure devotion to Christ"* (2 Corinthians 11:3). Once the mind is corrupted, devotion is compromised. Ever the master of deception, Satan has mugged many Christians nowadays. He has coiled himself around them. That's where we come in — we uncoil him. And then, we stomp him underfoot.[211]

ALERT

Christians are often clueless about the religious predators all around them. False prophets don't usually look dangerous. What's to fear about a nicely dressed family knocking on our front door, even if

---

[209] Greek: "noēma" (νόημα). This word describes our perceptions and thoughts. It is used six times in the New Testament, and only by Paul. Five of the six times are in Second Corinthians. In 2 Corinthians 2:11 of the *"schemes"* of the devil; in 3:14 of *"minds"* made dull; in 4:4 of the blinded *"minds"* of unbelievers; in 10:5 of taking every *"thought"* captive to Christ. The sixth use is in Philippians 4:7 of the peace of God guarding our hearts and *"minds."*

[210] jwa.org/encyclopedia. Accessed April 6, 2016.

[211] See Romans 16:20.

we're not sure just what they've got in those briefcases? And, surely, polite young men with nice haircuts, riding bicycles through the neighborhood represent no threat to anyone's spiritual well-being. They have name tags on their dress shirt pockets, but no warning labels that read "Dangerous Heretic." The church at Corinth was being influenced by some very charming and convincing cultists. But, the Corinthians were oblivious about the predicament they were in. They were not alert. Paul was. He intervenes.

The Christ followers in Corinth were trifling with disaster. The danger was real. The apostle attempts to snap them to attention. *"For if someone comes to you and preaches a Jesus other than the Jesus we preached, or if you receive a different spirit from the Spirit you received, or a different gospel from the one you accepted, you put up with it easily enough"* (2 Corinthians 11:4). This is nothing less than a biblical description of a cultist—a different gospel, a different spirit, a different Jesus. These are not minor doctrinal disparities. They are lethal alternatives to the truth.

When it comes to the essential nature of the gospel, I ask this question: "How wrong can you be about Jesus, and still be right with God?" Saboteurs had slipped into the Corinthian congregation with a Jesus so foreign to the apostolic standard that Paul had to call him, *"a Jesus[212] other than the Jesus we preached"* (2 Corinthians 11:4).

The members of The Church of Jesus Christ of Latter Day Saints commonly say to evangelicals, "We are Christians too." They aren't. The Jesus of Joseph Smith is not the Jesus of the Apostle Paul. "Christian" cults share one thing in common; they always do something to downgrade the biblical deity of Christ. That is heresy.

---

[212] It is impossible for us to know in what particular ways the Jesus advocated by the false teachers in Corinth was an aberration of the truth. If the supposition that Paul's competitors were triumphalists, then the Jesus they represented was one of exclusive power and glory, with no room for humiliation and suffering.

Nothing could be more dangerous. A gospel with that kind of Jesus is not Good News.

No details are given as to the specific identities of the instigators of the false doctrine in Corinth. As it turned out, the arch-enemies of early Christian orthodoxy were the Gnostics; i.e., "the knowing ones." In their gospel, Jesus and the Christ weren't even the same person. God wouldn't and didn't become a man. There was no incarnation. Flesh is evil. Spirit is good. Gnostic salvation was through secret knowledge and intricate rituals by which the initiated were to work their way up a spiritual ladder suspended between earth and heaven. Whether or not the cultists in Corinth were precursors to second century Gnostics, we can't say. But they were heretics none the less, *"masquerading as servants of righteousness"* (2 Corinthians 11:5). They didn't look dangerous. But they were deadly.

Again, Paul springs into action. He's a good shepherd. He's jealous. He's zealous. It's not the first time he has had to act ferociously. It was a few years earlier with a similar group of unsuspecting and misguided new believers—the Galatians. Flabbergasted at their foolishness, he wrote,

> *I am astonished that you are so quickly deserting the one who called you by the grace of Christ and are turning to a different gospel – which is really no gospel at all. Evidently some people are throwing you into confusion and are trying to pervert the gospel of Christ – which is really no gospel at all.* (Galatians 1:6-7)

Not mincing his words, Paul declares, *"But even if we or an angel from heaven should preach a gospel other than the one we preached to you, let him be under God's curse"* (Galatians 1:8). Cultists are going to hell. The reason they are so damnable is that the message they preach isn't good news. Their gospels preclude the salvation of their converts. Leaders with integrity will do anything within their power to defeat such emissaries of Satan.

It's not that cultists aren't sincere. Most, surely are. But that's just the point; they deceive because they have been deceived.[213] Joseph Smith was known to stretch the truth before he concocted Mormonism, but I don't doubt that he encountered an angel on September 21, 1823 — and on several subsequent occasions. I'm equally certain that the angel he saw wasn't from God. "Moroni" was a Satanic apparition. Young Joseph was taken in. And now, his followers are taking in millions more.

There is a winsomeness about Mormonism when it's at its best. But, the spirit of that religious system is not the Holy Spirit. It is, as Paul puts it, *"a different spirit"* (2 Corinthians 11:4).[214] Unless we are willing to be convinced of that, and have the courage to say so, we won't be good shepherds of God's flock.

We live in tolerant times. Too tolerant. The apostles, by contrast, were not hesitant to speak the truth. They were willing to identify something by its real name. To be candidly explicit, a false teacher, sincere or not, is an antichrist. John, traditionally known as the Apostle of Love, was still a son of thunder[215] in his old age. He said, *"Who is the liar? It is whoever denies that Jesus is the Christ. Such a person is the antichrist — denying the Father and the Son"* (1 John 2:22). Paul

---

[213] Paul will later tell Timothy: *"Evildoers and impostors will go from bad to worse, deceiving and being deceived. But as for you, continue in what you have learned and have become convinced of, because you know those from whom you learned it, and how from infancy you have known the Holy Scriptures, which are able to make you wise for salvation through faith in Christ Jesus."* (2 Timothy 3:13-15)

[214] The spirit the Corinthians received when they obeyed the gospel was none other than the Holy Spirit, not *"the spirit of the world"* (1 Corinthians 2:12). He lived within them (1 Corinthians 3:16; 6:19). He was the source of power with which Paul carried out his ministry among them. *"My message and my preaching were not with wise and persuasive words, but with a demonstration of the Spirit's power"* (1 Corinthians 2:4). Whatever the energy was that influenced the false apostles in Corinth, it wasn't the Holy Spirit.

[215] See Mark 3:17.

would vigorously agree. And, so should we. Leaders with integrity are alert. And, because of that, they speak the truth. In love.

CONFIDENT

Cult leaders typically share another alarming characteristic. Charismatic and charming; they exude self-confidence. This empowers them to be persuasive. How else did Joseph Smith talk his young wife, Emma, into welcoming a sister-bride into their home and bedroom? How else did David Koresh get idealistic Branch Davidian devotees to become his wives? How else did Sun Young Moon sway thousands of marriageable young Koreans to let him pick their spouses for them? How else did Jim Jones beguile nine hundred and sixteen of his devoted followers to leave San Francisco and live together in an isolated compound in the tropical jungles of Guyana? These men were delusionally self-confident.

Moroni told Joseph Smith, "All the churches are wrong." Then he proceeded to inform him that he had been chosen to restore the true church of Jesus Christ, lost since the days of the apostles.[216] Anyone who is convinced of that kind of calling has the confidence to persuade others to share his destiny. Within five years there were thousands of Mormons. Today, there are thirteen million of them worldwide.

Paul's opponents in Corinth were equally self-confident. They dubbed themselves *"super apostles"* (2 Corinthians 11:5). What do we do when we are up against such blatant braggadocio? If we show the least bit of self-doubt, look out! We have to be confident enough to put up a fight.

Cult leaders are narcissistic. They are inordinately fascinated with their own attributes. By contrast, authentic leaders acknowledge their weaknesses and limitations. Paul admits his apparent deficiencies. He says, *"I may indeed be an untrained speaker"*

---

[216] mormonthink.com/moroniweb.htm. Accessed April 8, 2016.

(2 Corinthians 11:6).[217] He'll grant his opponents that much; they were better communicators than he was; at least by the standards of classical Greek oratory.

Even if Paul wasn't as eloquent as his antagonists, he does know what he is talking about. After all, what you know is vastly more important than being able to express it with panache. *"I may indeed be an untrained speaker, but I do have knowledge"*[218] (2 Corinthians 11:6).

If the Corinthians would just shake themselves into sobriety for a minute, they could have seen the truth of what Paul was saying. *"We have made this perfectly clear to you in every way"* (2 Corinthians 11:6). His confidence is intact. *"I do not think that I am in the least inferior to those 'super-apostles'"* (2 Corinthians 11:5). This is how leaders with integrity see themselves. And conduct themselves.

UNSELFISH

The rudimentary characteristic of spiritual leaders who fearlessly protect those they watch over is selflessness. That's what makes us so fierce when our people are being threatened. Instinctively, we are willing to risk our lives to protect them.

I was watching a nature program on TV once about bears. The host of the show was the famous zookeeper and animal activist, Jack Hanna. He was in Alaska accompanied by a professional guide. With cameras rolling, they were paddling around rivers and lakes, looking for bears. And, they found them. Hanna was a little nervous

---

[217] Paul is not acknowledging that he is a poor preacher. While in the Galatian city of Iconium, Luke reports of him and Barnabas that *"They spoke so effectively that a great number of Jews and Gentiles believed"* (Acts 14:1). In the adjacent town of Lystra, the crowd thought that Paul was the Greek god, Hermes—the spokesman of the gods (Acts 14:12).

[218] Greek: "gnōsis" (γνῶσις). This word describes general intelligence, understanding or a deeper, enlarged knowledge of something. The Gnostics, i.e., "the knowing ones" became the major Christian heresy of the second century. Gnosticism's predecessors were challenging apostolic orthodoxy, even in Paul's day.

about how close they were getting to some pretty big specimens. Watching them as they foraged for food, slapping huge Sockeyes out of the white water, he said to the guide, "Isn't this a bit risky, to get this close to hungry bears while they are eating?" The guide replied, "Not to worry, bears aren't interested in people, or afraid of them. Leave them alone, they will leave you alone." But, there is one well-known exception to that rule—a mother bear with her cubs. Get any closer than fifty yards and she will not only not leave you alone, she will come after you. And, don't bother to run; she'll outrun you. Grizzlies have been clocked running at twenty-five miles per hour, for over two miles. If and when that mother bear does catch you, the best chance you've got is to cover your face and to act as dead as you can—or you will be. Spiritual leaders are like mamma bears. Fearless and fierce.

I'm glad to see the beloved old hymn, *Come Thou Fount of Every Blessing,* in vogue with yet another generation of Christians. I love the line that says, "Jesus sought me when a stranger, wandering from the fold of God; he, to rescue me from danger, interposed his precious blood." Amen! And, we can do no less for those we serve. Shepherds lay down their lives for their sheep. Pastors do that for their people. Seldom, if ever, will we have to spill any blood, but it does mean being selflessly brave.

Predators can be vicious. So can disgruntled church members. One day a pastor friend of mine got an anonymous letter from somebody in his congregation, complaining that his wife was becoming an embarrassment to the church. She needed some new clothes, they said, advising him to buy her something decent to wear.

It's shocking what some Christians will do once they take up a rebellious attitude toward their spiritual leaders. The Defiant Minority in Corinth, and the intruders agitating their dissatisfaction, were nasty in their defiance of Paul. They made all sorts of slanderous accusations against him. In a fiendish twist of logic, they even took the fact that he ministered in Corinth at his own expense and turned it against him. Paul's sarcasm in defending himself reveals how hurt he was by this indictment.

> *Was it a sin for me to lower myself in order to elevate you by preaching the gospel of God to you free of charge? I robbed other churches by receiving support from them so as to serve you. And when I was with you and needed something, I was not a burden to anyone, for the brothers who came from Macedonia supplied what I needed. I have kept myself from being a burden to you in any way, and will continue to do so.* (2 Corinthians 11:7-9)

Later he will sarcastically say, *"How were you inferior to the other churches, except that I was never a burden to you? Forgive me this wrong!"* (2 Corinthians 12:13).

Leading, feeding, guiding, and protecting God's people is our priority. Paul was proud of his unselfishness, awkward as he was at verbalizing it. *"As surely as the truth of Christ is in me, nobody in the regions of Achaia will stop this boasting of mine"* (2 Corinthians 11:10).

The apostle was embarrassed to be drawing so much attention to himself. But, even in his boasting, love was his incentive. *"Why? Because I do not love you? God knows I do!"* (2 Corinthians 11:11) When we are sure enough of ourselves to call God to the witness stand in our defense, we are sure of ourselves. Love is the fire of ferocity. It is the fuel of zeal. It constrains us to be jealous, alert, confident, unselfish — and determined.

DETERMINED

A young woman made an appointment for an interview with a prestigious corporation. She asked if she could get into their highly respected training program. The very busy personnel manager, overwhelmed with a pile of applications, facetiously responded, "That's impossible right now. Come back in about ten years." The determined applicant replied, "Would afternoon or morning be best?"

Paul was resolute about protecting God's people. He was unintimidated and contentiously determined. *"And I will keep on doing what I am doing in order to cut the ground from under those who want an opportunity to be considered equal with us in the things they boast about"* (2 Corinthians 11:12).

These days, political correctness has been beatified. All beliefs are equally valid. Nonsense! X cannot be non-X. It's the law of contradiction. Two antithetical propositions cannot both be true. All logic depends on this simple principle. Paul and his adversaries in Corinth can't both be authentic apostles. This conflict has to be resolved. Someone will win. Someone will lose. This is not a defeat Paul will concede. He is flatly intolerant of the intruders at Corinth.

When it comes to heretics, we must all be un-forbearing and un-forgiving. It is not time to be magnanimous. We are oppositional to anything or anyone who leads people away from the simple and definitive truth of the gospel. We will cut the ground out from under their feet. We will protect the people we serve.

THINK

1. Are we each responsible to protect one another from spiritual danger? List five people God expects you to watch out for.

2. What part does jealousy play in motivating us to be vigilant in protecting those we love?

3. Explain the connection between being jealous and being zealous.

4. Did Paul have cause to be worried about the Christians at Corinth?

5. Why are cultists dangerous?

6. What does a *"different Gospel"* look like?

7. What was the basis of Paul's spiritual confidence?

8. How hard is it these days to stay determined to protect those we love from spiritual danger?

9. If we don't protect people who need it, what will happen to them?

10. Selfish people make lousy spiritual shepherds. True or False?

ACT

1. Take out a piece of paper, or open up a Word document, and write a few paragraphs in answer to this question: "How wrong can you be about Jesus and still be right with God?"

2. Are there any spiritual predators threatening the flock you tend, or are a part of, right now? If so, draw up a plan for confronting the perpetrators. Then do it.

3. Church members are often naïve about the dangers of cultists. Create a course of study on the significant cults in your area and teach your people about the beliefs and practices of these organizations. Forewarned is forearmed.

4. Candor and civility are crucial to speaking the truth in   love. In anticipation of situations when you will have to disapprove

someone's convictions and/or conduct, script out what you will say, being both firm and loving.

5. Make a list the things you need to do better in fulfilling your duties to lead, feed, guide and protect the flock of God's people you tend.

Chapter 15

Practicing Self-Defense

2 Corinthians 11:16-33

He came to be called "the subway vigilante." In 1985, Bernard Goetz, an ordinary work-a-day New Yorker, was riding the subway home from his job, just like hundreds of thousands of his fellow citizens that evening. Then it happened. Goetz was assaulted by four teenage thugs looking to shake him down for any money he might have. They harassed him. They attacked him. But, it turned out to be a bad decision on their part. Bernard Goetz was carrying a gun. He was armed in anticipation of the very situation he found himself in that night. To ward off his assailants, Goetz started shooting. He shot all four of the ruffians, one of them five times, leaving him alive but partially paralyzed and brain damaged.

In an astonishing aberration of justice, Bernard Goetz ended up on trial for protecting himself. This, despite the fact that in most states, including New York, self-defense is warranted even if you cause bodily injury or the death of someone trying to rob or harm you. But, there's one crucial stipulation: you cannot use more force than is necessary to resist the assault. Bernard Goetz was charged with attempted murder. He had the legal right to protect himself, but was he within those rights when he pumped five bullets into the body of one of his muggers? Had he used excessive force in his self-defense?

As spiritual leaders, the odds that any of us will be physically attacked are minimal. More likely, we will be the victims of verbal assault. We will be the casualties of psychological brutality. Do we have the right to defend ourselves against those who choose to slander our good name? Jesus seems to discourage it. *"You have heard it said, 'Eye for eye, tooth for tooth.' But I tell you, do not resist an evil person. If someone slaps you on the right cheek, turn to him the other cheek also"* (Matthew 5:38-39). Some take Christ's advice quite literally. You don't react when attacked. And yet, that's precisely what the Apostle Paul did when he was bushwhacked by his enemies in Corinth.

Generally speaking, turning the other cheek is a good idea. It forestalls the escalation of a conflict. Paul advocated it himself. When someone violates our personal rights, he asks, *"Why not rather be wronged? Why not rather be cheated?"* (1 Corinthians 6:7) The principle is practical. It's usually good to value personal relationships over personal rights. If I insist on maintaining my rights, I will most likely damage or ruin the relationship I have with the person who has violated them. Jesus also said, *"Love your enemies and pray for those who persecute you"* (Matthew 5:44). It's a Christ-like thing to do. *"When they hurled their insults at him, he did not retaliate; when he suffered, he made no threats. Instead, he entrusted himself to him who judges justly"* (1 Peter 2:23). Again, Paul himself was a champion of such interpersonal pacifism. *"Do not repay anyone evil for evil... If it is possible, as far as it depends on you, live at peace with everyone"* (Romans 12:17-18).

So, is there ever an exception to the rule of turning the other cheek? In a word, yes. There are times when it is not only okay to practice self-defense, it's necessary. Here it is: if and when our positive influence in the lives of people who look to us for spiritual leadership is threatened, it is mandatory to defend ourselves. Not for our sakes, but for theirs.

I learned this lesson once in the twenty years I pastored a local church. Significant attacks on my integrity as a pastor, and a person, were instigated against me by some members of the defiant minority in our congregation. Along with the elders, I was charged with altering the legal documents of the church for personal gain.

Now, let's suppose that I left those charges unanswered. Let's imagine that I turned the other cheek, saying nothing, while my critics made false accusations against me. There was more up for grabs than just my reputation. The well-being of the entire congregation was at risk. In that kind of circumstance, we fight. We defend ourselves. Sure, we will feel foolish. But, let's not hesitate.

Paul's integrity was under fire at Corinth. Insolent members of the congregation, goaded by opportunistic outsiders, were attacking his credibility. He answers back. He shows us how to do the same.

FOOLISHLY

In this last section of Second Corinthian, Paul talks a lot about foolishness. He has had to take the risk of appearing to be foolish. His antagonists have compelled him to play the game by their rules. Paul appeals to the congregation. *"I hope you will put up with me in a little foolishness"* (2 Corinthians 11:1). Self-consciously, he says it again. *"I repeat: Let no one take me for a fool.*[219] *But if you do, then tolerate me just as you would a fool, so that I may do a little boasting"* (2 Corinthians 11:16). Paul was being forced to boast about himself. To him, this was patently ludicrous. But, there was no alternative. The Corinthians had been swayed by the claims of his adversaries.

Most of us have known a few fools; we may even be related to one or two. The most disconcerting thing about every fool you meet is that they are seemingly the only ones who don't realize they are a fool. They are blind to the fact that nearly everybody has them pegged. A fool is a self-absorbed person. And, rebellious.

---

[219] Greek: "aphrōn" (ἄφρων). This is the description of someone who is senseless or stupid, who speaks or acts rashly, without reflection or rationale.

Paul's no fool. But, he's acting like one. He has to. The Corinthians suffer fools all too gladly (2 Corinthians 11:19). The interlopers in Corinth had hoodwinked them. So, Paul plays the fool in the hope that he can prod the credulous Corinthians back to reality. He's following Solomon's mocking advice, *"Answer a fool according to his folly or he will be wise in his own eyes"* (Proverbs 26:5).

The apostle is well aware of the built-in risk of this tactic. But, he has to do what he has to do, to salvage his reputation with the Corinthians, restore their confidence in him, and persuade them to reject his detractors. If he fails, the church is lost. The cultists take over.

A fool's stock in trade is boasting. Fools are braggarts. They are never far from talking about all the great things they have done. They epitomize excessive, exaggerated, and unfounded pride. Only occasionally are they puzzled by the realization that no one seems to recognize just how exceptional they are.

Paul knows how unlike Christ it is for him to even play the fool. He admits his discomfort. *"In this self-confident boasting I am not talking as the Lord would, but as a fool"* (2 Corinthians 11:17). He knows he's not doing what Jesus would do. Christ never met his critics on their level—not the Pharisees, the Sadducees, Pilate, Herod, or anyone who challenged his authenticity. Paul knows that. He admits that he isn't emulating his Lord. But, he proceeds to do it any way. Out of necessity.

Let's repeat the principle: self-defense is warranted when our positive influence in the lives of people who look to us for spiritual leadership is threatened. But, we must only use enough force to incapacitate our assailants. Even a thug doesn't need to be shot five times.

The apostle's foes have been trumpeting their accomplishments. Such behavior doesn't come naturally or easily to Paul, but now he must itemize his own achievements. He has to match his competitors claim for claim, awkward as he feels about it. *"Since many are boasting in the way the world does, I too will boast"* (2 Corinthians 11:18).

The word *"world"* is used in both positive and negative ways in the New Testament. In a positive sense, it describes the human presence on planet earth. *"For God so loved the world"* (John 3:16). More often than not, though, the term is used negatively, to identify the system of thinking and behaving that is in opposition to God. *"He was in the world, and though the world was made through him, the world did not recognize him"* (John 1:10). Jesus warned his disciples about the world. *"If you belonged to the world, it would love you as its own. As it is, you do not belong to the world, but I have chosen you out of the world. That is why the world hates you"* (John 15:19). He prayed, *"I have given them your word and the world has hated them, for they are not of the world any more than I am of the world"* (John 17:14).

Decades later, the Apostle John was explicit about the dangers of the world-system.

> Do not love the world or anything in the world. If anyone loves the world, love for the Father is not in them. For everything in the world – the lust of the flesh, the lust of the eyes, and the pride of life – comes not from the Father but from the world. (1 John 2:15-16)

John adds, *"Everyone born of God overcomes the world. This is the victory that has overcome the world, even our faith. Who is it that overcomes the world? Only he who believes that Jesus is the son of God"* (1 John 5:4-5). James asks, *"Don't you know that friendship with the world means enmity against God?"* (James 4:4). Paul testifies. *"May I never boast except in the cross of our Lord Jesus Christ, through which the world has been crucified to me, and I to the world"* (Galatians 6:14). It is in contradiction to that commitment that he now defends his apostleship.

Acting out of character, Paul resorts to irony in his attempt to correct his easily misled converts. *"You gladly put up with fools since you are so wise!"* (2 Corinthians 11:19) It was huckster P.T. Barnum who supposedly quipped, "There's a sucker born every minute." Well, in Corinth, there was a church full of suckers. They welcomed the influence of fools and were paying the price for their tendency to believe everything they were told.

Increasing the sarcasm, Paul taunts *"In fact, you even put up with anyone who enslaves you or exploits*[220] *you or takes advantage of you or puts on airs or slaps you in the face"* (2 Corinthians 11:20). The victims of cultists characteristically fall under a spell—and suffer all manner of indignities in the process.

Cult leaders imprison their followers psychologically. Sometimes, they do it literally. Devotees to Sun Yung Moon—the Moonies—used to lure their victims with offers of free food and shelter in their isolated compounds in the redwood forests of northern California's Mendocino County. But, try to leave once you got there. Forget it. Your parents will have to contract a deprogrammer to rescue you and try to restore you to your right mind.

Cult leaders manipulate people. A woman visiting the congregation I pastored was looking for a new church home. One of her first questions to me was to ask whether or not she could wear purple. Her name was Polly. Polly loved purple. Most of her clothes were in some shade of purple. She explained that the church she was currently a member of told her that purple wasn't a godly color. It was too much like Babylon the Great, the Mother of Prostitutes (Revelation 17:3-5). They insisted she couldn't wear purple if she was going to be part of their fellowship. Cult leaders enslave people.

---

[220] Greek: "katesthiō" (κατεσθίω). This term means "to consume by eating." It implies being forcibly devoured. By extension, it can mean to demand payment, or to strip someone of their possessions.

They endeavor to control their minds, decisions, and life-style. By contrast, the true gospel sets people free. Authentic spiritual leaders respect your individuality and your right to make your own decisions. If you like purple, wear it!

Cult leaders exploit people financially. Sooner or later they will separate you from your money. Another time, a couple visited our worship service. Afterwards, they introduced themselves. It was a reunion of sorts; I had known the woman when we were children at church camp. Her father was a respected pastor in our denomination. But, for years she and her husband had been involved with a cult-like sect that eventually persuaded them to sell their house and donate the proceeds to the organization. They did it because their leaders told them to.

Cult leaders are persuasive. How else could the likes of Joseph Smith, Vernon Howell, (aka. David Koresh), and David Berg (aka. Moses David) induce unsuspecting young women into becoming their sex partners? Mormonism is still trying to distance itself from the polygamous practices of its founders. I have a book in my library called *The Twenty-seventh Wife* by Irving Wallace. It's the story of Ann Eliza Young, one of Mormon prophet Brigham Young's fifty-five "sister-brides."[221] She divorced him in 1873 to lead in the fight against polygamy. Still, it's stupefying to see what ordinarily sane individuals will do once they are in the clutches of a manipulative religious leader.

Cultists are vicious. It's hard to know whether Paul meant to be taken literally or not, when he says that the false apostles in Corinth slapped the Corinthians in the face. But, figuratively or literally, they had been abused. And, evidently, without complaint. Paul scornfully separates himself from such spiritual imposters. *"To my shame I admit we were too weak for that!"* (2 Corinthians 11:21) The apostle

---

[221] Irving, Wallace. *The Twenty-seventh Wife*. New York: Signet, 1962.

proudly asserts his lack of nerve to mistreat people. Worldly weakness is always a sign of spiritual strength.

In her 1979 book, *Six Years with God*, former member of San Francisco's Peoples Temple, Jeanine Mills, tells of public spankings that were administered by her increasingly deranged pastor, Jim Jones.[222] When your spiritual leader insists on being called God, all kinds of cruelty may be heading your way. You better run while you can, elsewise you may find yourself impounded in the jungles of Guyana. In 1978, the drug-addled and delusional Jones shot himself to death after convincing over nine hundred of his followers to commit suicide with arsenic-laced Kool-Aid.

BOASTFULLY

Paul provides a further example of how to practice Christian self-defense. The self-appointed *"super apostles"* (2 Corinthians 11:5) in Corinth were talking up their accomplishments in order to sway the Corinthians to surrender to their authority. To counter that tactic, Paul was obliged to itemize his own impressive exploits.

He is no fraudulent pretender. He knows that. God knows that. The Corinthians, on the other hand, who should know that, aren't convinced. Some of them were vacillating, still undecided about just who was the real deal when it came to pastoral leadership. Since none of them was standing up for him; Paul had to stand up for himself. It doesn't come naturally though. He admits his discomfort, again. *"Whatever anyone else dares to boast about – I am speaking as a fool – I also dare to boast about"* (2 Corinthians 11:21).

The apostle lists his credentials, one at a time. He starts with his pedigree. *"Are they Hebrews? So am I. Are they Israelites? So am I. Are they Abraham's descendants? So am I"* (2 Corinthians 11:22). These claims indicate that Paul's adversaries were Jewish. Messianic Jews.

---

[222] Mills, Jeanine. *Six Years with God: Life Inside Reverend Jim Jones's Peoples Temple*. New York: A & W Publishers, 1979.

Sort of.[223] They were unduly proud of their heritage. To their way of thinking, circumcision was the sign of the New Covenant as well as the Old. Paul, vehemently disagrees; he considers it putting confidence in the flesh. Later, he will forcefully tell the Philippians,

> *Watch out for those dogs, those evildoers, those mutilators of the flesh. For it is we who are the circumcision, we who serve God by his Spirit, who boast in Christ Jesus, and who put no confidence in the flesh — though I myself have reasons for such confidence. If someone else thinks they have reasons to put confidence in the flesh, I have more: circumcised on the eighth day, of the people of Israel, of the tribe of Benjamin, a Hebrew of Hebrews; in regard to the law, a Pharisee; as for zeal, persecuting the church; as for righteousness based on the law, faultless.* (Philippians 3:2-6)

Paul has the qualifications that his competitors prescribe, but he is reluctant to talk about them. Anytime you argue for your credibility based on ancestry, well, that's a fool's game. Still, under assault Paul is forced to mention his heritage.

Continuing to play the fool, the apostle further pats himself on the back. *"Are they servants of Christ? (I am out of my mind to talk like this) I am more"* (2 Corinthians 11:23). Paul is the real McCoy. His detractors are the pretenders.

---

[223] These individuals were professing Christians, proponents of a hybrid gospel of grace, faith, and good works. Their main concern was conformity to the Law of Moses. "Judaizers" is the term sometimes used to describe these men. Paul and his associates have been confronting them for decades. The first incident of it was in Acts 15, where Luke records, *"Certain people came down from Judea to Antioch and were teaching the believers: 'Unless you are circumcised, according to the custom taught by Moses you cannot be saved'"* (Acts 15:1). Luke adds, *"This brought Paul and Barnabas into sharp dispute and debate with them"* (Acts 15:2). Though they professed to be Christians, they were still Pharisees (Acts 15:5). Despite the fact that the Jerusalem council flatly rejected their convictions, the discord didn't stop. Paul would later call them *"the circumcision group"* (Titus 1:10). It's not clear that Paul's opponents in Corinth fit this profile, but there is no doubt that they prided themselves in their Jewish heritage, making it a priority of apostolic authenticity.

The apostle's claims to credibility are indisputable. He continues. *"I have worked much harder, been in prison more frequently, been flogged more severely, and been exposed to death again and again. Five times I received from the Jews the forty lashes minus one. Three times I was beaten with rods, once I was pelted with stones"* (2 Corinthians 11:23-25). Compared to Paul, his foes in Corinth were neophytes. As far as we know, they had never even been arrested for being Christians, much less imprisoned, beaten, or left for dead under a pile of bloody rocks (Acts 14:19).

Paul continues to enumerate his heroic adventures.

> *Three times I was shipwrecked, I spent a night and a day in the open sea, I have been constantly on the move. I have been in danger from rivers, in danger from bandits, in danger from my fellow Jews, in danger from Gentiles; in danger in the city, in danger in the country, in danger at sea; and in danger from false believers.* (2 Corinthians 11:25-26)

Only a limited number of these harrowing experiences can be corroborated from the Book of Acts and Paul's other epistles, but happen they did. Still, he's not finished. *"I have labored and toiled and have often gone without sleep; I have known hunger and thirst and have often gone without food. I have been cold and naked"* (2 Corinthians 11:27).

At this point, Paul's contenders in Corinth have got to be feeling a bit like a prize fighter on the canvass after a sharp right hook to the jaw. Once back on their feet, Paul lands a final punch. *"Besides everything else, I face daily the pressure of my concern for all the churches"* (2 Corinthians 11:28).

Parishioners typically don't appreciate the burden their spiritual leaders bear. Those of us under it, do. It's not quite the weight of the world, but sometimes it feels like it. Paul knows. He asks, *"Who is weak, and I do not feel weak? Who is led into sin, and I do not inwardly burn?"* (2 Corinthians 11:29) He agonized over the failure of others.

278

He felt moral indignation when they were spiritually abused. He resonated with the righteous anger of Christ when he said,

> If anyone causes one of these little ones – those who believe in me – to stumble, it would be better for them to have a large millstone hung around their neck and to be drowned in the depths of the sea. Woe to the world because of the things that cause people to stumble! Such things must come, but woe to the person through whom they come! (Matthew 18:6-7)

No one could rightly question the Apostle Paul's compassion. When his people hurt, he hurt. When they got tangled up in sin, he suffered heartburn. Spiritual leaders with integrity know exactly what he's talking about.

Paul felt clumsy telling the Corinthians what an exceptional pastor he was. But, we understand why. His spiritual influence was being challenged. When that happens, we defend ourselves. Paul models one last way in which it should be done.

HUMBLY

A humble bragger? It's tricky. Laying aside the fool's persona, Paul unpretentiously speaks in character. Like all truly great people, he doesn't see himself as great. Greatness was the result, not the goal, of his life. *"If I must boast, I will boast of the things that show my weakness"* (2 Corinthians 11:30). He's humble. And truthful. *"The God and Father of the Lord Jesus, who is to be praised forever, knows that I am not lying"* (2 Corinthians 11:31).

After Sunday School one morning, two brothers were discussing their life goals. The first brother's ambition was to be rich and famous. The other's was to follow Christ to the fullest. The second boy went on to fulfill his intentions; his name was David Livingston, the renowned medical missionary to 19th century Africa. His brother achieved his goals too. But, his fame was borrowed. The epitaph on his tombstone read: "Here lies the brother of David Livingston."

Far from being a triumphalist like his adversaries in Corinth, the Apostle Paul freely acknowledged humiliating circumstances he's had to endure. In self-deprecating candor, he divulges an experience that he could have easily kept to himself. *"In Damascus the governor under King Aretas had the city of the Damacenes guarded in order to arrest me. But I was lowered from a window in the wall and slipped through his hands"* (2 Corinthians 11:32-33).

Paul had gone to Damascus as an inquisitor, riding on a horse,[224] with a small army of men behind him. They were on their way to arrest, incarcerate, and extradite Christians back to Jerusalem for trial. Luke summarizes the episode by saying, *"Saul was still breathing out murderous threats against the Lord's disciples"* (Acts 9:1). Instead, he got saved. *"Saul spent several days with the disciples in Damascus. At once he began to preach in the synagogues that Jesus is the Son of God"* (Acts 9:19-20). His influence and reputation burgeoned. *"Saul grew more and more powerful and baffled the Jews living in Damascus by proving that Jesus is the Messiah"* (Acts 9:22).

The embarrassed Jews didn't like the way Paul made them look. Not one bit. Luke adds, *"After many days had gone by, there was a conspiracy among the Jews to kill him, but Saul learned of their plan. Day and night they kept close watch on the city gates in order to kill him. But his followers took him by night and lowered him in a basket through an opening in the wall"* (Acts 9:23-24). Paul came to Damascus on a charger; he left in a hamper. Humiliating.

---

[224] An ancient tradition says that Paul was riding a horse on his way to Damascus. Several paintings have depicted it as such, most notably Caravaggio's *Conversion On The Way To Damascus*, 1601. But nowhere in the three New Testament references to Paul's conversion (Acts 9:23-24; 22:6-7; 26:12-14) is there a mention of a horse. It's a remote possibility, but still creates a dramatic image.

Ronald Reagan once said that, "there is no limit to what a man can do, if he doesn't mind who gets the credit."[225] In Second Corinthians Paul violates that principle. Temporarily. What else could he do? If the shepherd is struck down, the flock is in serious danger. To defend them, we must defend ourselves.

As you might imagine, the shy and retiring middle-aged New Yorker, Bernard Goetz, became a folk hero in "the city that never sleeps". He stood up to some thugs who threatened his right to peace and safety. Insult to injury though, he was brought to trial two years after the incident in which he shot his attackers in self-defense. One of the muggers, Darrell Cabey, had been left paralyzed and partially brain-damaged by the five bullets that Goetz left embedded in his body that night on the subway. The jury was unsympathetic to Cabey's case; they acquitted Goetz of the charges. Nine years later, Cabey filed another lawsuit against Goetz. This time he wanted $50 million, charging that the shooter acted recklessly and deliberately, inflicting physical and psychological distress on his attacker. This time the jury agreed. They awarded Cabey $43 million in damages. Not able to pay such an amount, Bernard Goetz's wages were garnished for the next twenty years, to cover at least a portion of the settlement. But, was justice done?

Self-defense is legal. We are perfectly within our rights to use whatever force necessary to resist someone threatening us, our loved ones, or our property. The one stipulation though is that we not use more force than is necessary to protect ourselves.

In this case, Paul was using the force required to rescue the Corinthians from their spiritual assailants. He was knowingly ignoring his Savior's advice to turn the other cheek. But, the suspension of that precept was justified because the circumstances demanded it.

---

[225] quoteinvestigator.com/category/ronald-reagan. Accessed March 12, 2016.

Jesus understood. He'll understand too, if and when, we need to do the same.

THINK

1. When is self-defense justified? Shouldn't personal insults be ignored?

2. In this section Paul admits he's acting foolishly. How so?

3. Against whom is Paul defending himself? Who are his accusers? What are their accusations?

4. In 2 Corinthians 11:20 Paul summarizes the abuses that have characterized the tactics of many cult leaders over the centuries. Can you think of any contemporary examples?

5. In defending himself against his cult-like opponents in Corinth, Paul resorts to sarcasm. Is such a tactic justified?

6. Should you ever try to match an adversary boast for boast? What good would that do?

7. Are you foolish if you know you are acting foolishly? What is foolishness?

8. Is hard work a legitimate credential of spiritual integrity?

9. Paul suffered physically as a servant of Christ. How did that authenticate his spiritual leadership?

10. If you haven't suffered for Christ, are you still qualified to represent him?

ACT

1. Do you have opponents in your ministry right now? Make a list of their names. Next, follow Christ's advice to pray for them (Matthew 5:44).

2. On a personal level, are you willing to be cheated or wronged by others? (1 Corinthians 6:7) Reflect upon situations in which you were able to do that. What was the outcome?

3. On a scale of 1-10, rate your degree of courage when called upon to defend yourself and the integrity of your ministry. If you are on the weak end of the spectrum, solicit the support of some reliable colleagues to help you stand up to the charges being leveled against you.

4. Take a moment to jot down the accomplishments and character-building experiences you've had that you could use to bolster your credibility if you should ever come under attack by rebellious church members. Then remind yourself that boasting about such things is foolish and should be avoided if at all possible.

5. Tell God that you really don't care if you get the credit for the things you accomplish for him.

Chapter 16

Transformed from Weakness to Strength

2 Corinthians 12:1-10

One summer, a few years back, I had a mountaintop experience. Literally. Along with eight other people, I backpacked to the top of a huge, treeless precipice in Yosemite National Park called Cloud's Rest. Cloud's Rest is north-east of Half Dome, and higher. It was the first and only time in my life that there was nothing above my own head. I could see the arc of the horizon. The nighttime sky was a domed vault. I'd never seen so many stars.

I've had some other mountaintop experiences that had nothing to do with actual mountains. When I was just twenty-four years old, I flew to Minneapolis, Minnesota for a pastors' conference hosted by the Billy Graham Association. There were about three thousand of us from across the country and around the world. As we sang God's praises together and listened to some thrilling preaching, it was a like a preview of eternity.

To speak of such spiritual highs as mountaintop experiences is firmly established in Christian parlance. We all know what someone is saying when we hear the phase. I'm not sure just why we equate rapturous personal experiences with being on top of a mountain. Perhaps it goes back to Sinai, when Moses spent more than a month alone with God. Maybe it calls to mind the afternoon Peter, James, and John witnessed Jesus in the sky talking with Moses and Elijah on the Mount of Transfiguration. Or, it could be that we are just trying to describe something that is otherworldly and exhilarating.

Mountaintop experiences are rare. They vary in intensity, but are always memorable, and are typically challenging to describe. More often than not, words escape us. In this section of Second Corinthians, Paul speaks of the ultimate in mountaintop experiences; he tells us that he has been to Heaven.

The apostle's rivals in Corinth have been bragging about some ecstatic experiences of their own, as if such things were prerequisite to credible spiritual leadership. Paul has been matching their claims boast for boast. They will have a tough time topping this one. *"I must go on boasting. Although there is nothing to be gained, I will go on to visions and revelations*[226] *from the Lord"* (2 Corinthians 12:1).

EXULTING IN ECSTACY

Let's imagine that today you could take a round trip to Heaven. Knowing that you would have to come back, would you still go? Evidently, Paul wasn't given a choice. He was snatched away. *"I know a man*[227] *in Christ who fourteen years ago was caught up*[228] *to the third heaven"* (2 Corinthians 12:2).

If you leave this earth without dying, you are in elite company indeed. It's the most exclusive club in the world. Enoch was the first. The Bible says, *"Enoch walked faithfully with God; then he was no more, because God took him away"* (Genesis 5:24). Elijah was next. One day the aged prophet was walking with his successor, Elisha, when it happened—a fiery exit. *"As they were walking along and talking*

---

[226] Grammatically, this is a hendiadys; i.e., when two words are joined by "and" to express a single idea—in this case *"visions and revelations."* If there is a distinction here, it would be that the first word describes the experience and the second, the content of the experience.

[227] Paul is speaking of himself, not someone else. It is curious as to why he uses the third person, but most likely he does so to underscore his reluctance to draw attention to himself in what he has already described as the foolishness of boasting. He repeats this awkward phrase two times.

[228] Greek: "harpadzō" (ἁρπάζω). This verb means to seize or carry off by force; to be suddenly snatched out of, or away, from something. It is the same word used in Acts 8:39. *"When they came up out of the water, the Spirit of the Lord suddenly took Philip away, and the eunuch did not see him again, but went on his way rejoicing."*

together, suddenly a chariot of fire and horses of fire appeared and separated the two of them, and Elijah went up to heaven in a whirlwind" (2 Kings 2:11). Paul was the third.

The brevity with which the apostle describes his celestial adventure testifies to its authenticity. He admits to some uncertainty about it as well. *"And I know that this man — whether in the body or apart from the body I do not know, but God knows — was caught up to Paradise"* (2 Corinthians 12:3-4).

Paul acknowledges the mystery of his apparent out of body roundtrip to Eternity. He doesn't know whether he was actually teleported to Paradise, or the whole experience was simply an intense dream. Somehow, he had been spirited away. Paul uses the same word to describe The Rapture.

> *For the Lord himself will come down from heaven, with a loud command, with the voice of the archangel and with the trumpet call of God, and the dead in Christ will rise first. After that, we who are still alive and are left will be caught up together with them in the clouds to meet the Lord in the air. And so we will be with the Lord forever.* (1 Thessalonians 4:16-17)

Swoosh! We're gone! One day we will all be whisked away to Heaven. Paul had a preview of that gravity-defying departure. It was a one man rapture. But, he was not gone *"forever."* He had to come back.

The apostle uses two apparent synonyms to describe the destination of his travels. First, he calls it *"Paradise"*[229] (2 Corinthians 12:4). Jesus used the same word when he told the thief on the cross,

---

[229] Greek: "paradeisos" (παράδεισος). This term is transliterated into English as "paradise." It had a variety of meanings in the ancient world. It was used to describe a grand enclosure, preserve, or park with shade trees and well-watered shrubs and flowers. Some Jews considered it to be part of Hades, where the souls of the righteous dead stayed until the resurrection. Others understood it to be the upper regions of the heavens.

"Today you will be with me in paradise" (Luke 23:43). Previously, Paul had designated it as *"the third heaven"*[230] (2 Corinthians 12:2).

This is a mysterious phrase. The simplest explanation of what the apostle is talking about, from a tiered cosmology perspective, is that what we commonly call the atmosphere is the first heaven; i.e., the sky, where the birds fly and the clouds drift by. The next layer is the stratosphere or Space — planets, stars, galaxies, and quasars. This is the second heaven. And beyond that, in a separate dimension altogether, is the third heaven. Or, what we commonly refer to as Heaven. One Greek word describes all three. Context determines the meaning. Paul is saying that he went to Heaven, or dreamed he did. He's not sure. But, *"God knows"* (2 Corinthians 12:2, 3).

The one thing the apostle was certain about regarding his heavenly excursion was that he was not allowed to talk about it. Speaking again in the third person, to deflect attention from himself, he says that he, *"heard inexpressible things, things that no one is permitted to tell"* (2 Corinthians 12:4).

It was not uncommon in biblical times for God to instruct his prophets to keep quiet about the things he revealed to them. In Revelation, for example, the Apostle John hears *"seven thunders"* speaking. He reports, *"And when the seven thunders spoke, I was about to write, but I heard a voice from heaven say, 'Seal up what the seven thunders have said and do not write it down'"* (Revelation 10:4). By contrast, in the last chapter of the Apocalypse, John is told, *"Do not seal up the words of the prophecy of this book because the time is near"* (Revelation 22:10).

---

[230] Greek: "ouranos" (οὐρανός). This word describes the vaulted expanse of the sky and all the things visible in it, day and night. By extension it can refer to space and ultimately the dimension of Heaven itself. There is a parallel passage in the apocryphal book, *The Apocalypse of Moses,* where God hands Adam over to the archangel Michael and says, "Lift him up into Paradise unto the third heaven." Both Paul and his readers were most likely familiar with that reference.

Likewise, Paul was initially forbidden to talk about what he saw and heard in Heaven. But now, he has evidently been released to do so. Still, he doesn't say much. He simply reports that he went and came back. And, even if he was inclined to give us some of the details, he didn't have the vocabulary to do so. They were *"inexpressible things"* (2 Corinthians 12:4).

C.S. Lewis summarized the impossibility of describing the real Narnia. "Even the common orange, you know: no one could have imagined it before he tasted it. How much less Heaven."[231]

Paul exults in the ecstasy of his brief visit to the other side—sort of. *"I will boast about a man like that, but I will not boast about myself"* (2 Corinthians 12:5). Unlike most braggarts, however, he is not embellishing his claims. *"Even if I should choose to boast, I would not be a fool, because I would be speaking the truth"* (2 Corinthians 12:6). In this disclosure, the apostle breaks a fourteen-year silence (2 Corinthians 12:2). But, he would soon learn that there was a price to be paid for his heavenly privileges.

PRAYING FOR DELIVERANCE

God had a plan to forestall any pride that might arise within Paul regarding his visit to Heaven. *"In order to keep me from becoming conceited I was given a thorn[232] in my flesh"* (2 Corinthians 12:7). Once back on terra firma, Paul soon discovered that he didn't have the time, inclination, or energy for hubris. He was, instead, preoccupied with chronic pain. From God! He doesn't identify the affliction; but we are curious. Was it migraine headaches, malaria, failing eyesight,

---

[231] Lewis, C.S. *Collected Letters of C. S. Lewis, Volume 3.* New York: Baxter Street, 2011.

[232] Greek: "skolops" (σκόλοψ). This term paints vivid images of a sharp wooden stake, a splinter, a thorn, or fishhook. The word turns up in the LXX, the Greek translation of the Old Testament. *"But if you do not drive out the inhabitants of the land, those you allow to remain will become barbs in your yes and thorns in your sides"* (Numbers 33:55). *"No longer will the people of Israel have malicious neighbors who are painful briers and sharp thorns"* (Ezekiel 28:24).

or epilepsy? All have been suggested. The apostle leaves us to guess at a diagnosis. Whatever it was, it was debilitating.

I have a scar on the underside of the middle finger on my left hand. I got it one day playing volleyball. I went up to spike the ball and caught a branch of a hawthorn tree on the down stroke. Feeling an instantaneous throbbing, I turned my wounded hand palm-up and watched a big black thorn bury itself into my flesh. Thankfully, the host of the party was a medical doctor. He took me inside the house and with a scalpel and surgical tweezers extracted the thorn from my finger. I've still got the scar, but the pain is long gone. Paul's pain was not gone. It would be an ongoing agony.

Everything in our lives, perceived by us to be good or bad, was ordered or allowed by God. At the least, his sovereignty lets things happen to us. Directly mandated or merely permitted, Paul had a serious malady that he attributes to God. And, as you might expect, Satan parlayed the pain to his own advantage.

The apostle recognizes the similarities between himself and Job. He says plainly that his suffering was *"a messenger from Satan to torment me"* (2 Corinthians 12:7). God intended the pain to prevent Paul from pride; the devil used the torment to make his life miserable. God wanted Paul to succeed; the evil one wanted him to fail. The trial was definitely a test—a test Paul did not want to take. He says, *"Three times I pleaded with the Lord to take it away from me"* (2 Corinthians 12:8). He prayed for deliverance.

What should we do when body and soul are in aguish, allowed by God and aggravated by the devil? In a word—pray. If you are dealing with unrelenting, debilitating pain, petition God to take it away. Ask for deliverance.

Nowhere in Scripture are we promised exemption from suffering. And, nowhere in Scripture are we expected to accept it as inevitable. Don't surrender too soon.   Paul didn't. On three desperate occasions he begged for mercy.

The apostle says he asked *"the Lord"* for relief (2 Corinthians 12:8). When Paul says *"the Lord,"* most scholars presume that he was speaking to Christ. Needless to say, Jesus knew exactly what Paul was going through. It was in Gethsemane that he himself begged three times: *"Abba, Father...everything is possible for you. Take this cup from me"* (Mark 14:36). Earlier, Mark reports that *"He began to be deeply distressed and troubled. 'My soul is overwhelmed with sorrow to the point of death'"* (Mark 14:33-34). Matthew includes more of the excruciating details. *"Going a little farther, he fell on his face to the ground and prayed, 'My father, if it is possible, may this cup be taken from me'"* (Matthew 26:39). Luke adds, *"And being in anguish, he prayed more earnestly, and his sweat was like drops of blood falling on the ground"* (Luke 22:44). All three Synoptic Gospels verify that Jesus implored God for deliverance three times. He set the precedent — Paul followed it. The apostle pleads his case. He is hoping for a Yes, but prepared for a No.

ACCEPTING DISAPPOINTMENT

You'd think that when the Son of God prayed, his Father would always grant his requests. He didn't. You'd think that when a saint like Paul prayed, God would grant his requests too. He didn't.

It seems that every life has at least one Gethsemane. God doesn't always grant a positive answer to our cries for deliverance from the suffering we face. To the contrary. No was the reply Jesus got. It was the reply Paul got. It may be the reply we get. It has nothing to do with our sincerity. Or, our faith. It has everything to do with God's will.

What should we do when God's will isn't ours? Again, Jesus sets the example. He prayed for deliverance three times. *"Take this cup from me."* But, when it was clear that he would have to drink it, he acquiesced, *"Yet not what I will, but what you will"* (Mark 14:36). Now, Paul petitions Christ himself for the same relief. The answer

Jesus gives is the answer he himself had received—no. *"But he said to me, 'My grace is sufficient for you'"* (2 Corinthians 12:9).

God's grace enables us to accept God's will. In the midst of our foibles, failures, and innate depravity, his fatherly compassion prevails. Such grace is multifaceted. For everyone there is common grace—the rain falls on the just and the unjust. *"He causes his sun to rise on the evil and the good, and sends rain on the righteous and the unrighteous"* (Matthew 5:45). It's the general benevolence of God toward humanity itself. Then, there's saving grace. *"For it is by grace you have been saved through faith—and this not from yourselves, it is the gift of God"* (Ephesians 2:8). Finally, there is enabling grace. *"And God is able to bless you abundantly, so that in all things at all times, having all that you need, you will abound in every good work"* (2 Corinthians 9:8). In other words, the suffering God doesn't take away, he enables us to endure.

God has a reason for human suffering, especially if it is undeserved, unexpected, or unrelenting. How else could he perfect his power in us? When we are weak, he is strong. His strength and our weakness coexist. It's simultaneity: existing, occurring or operating at the same time. When we are weak, God is strong—both at once. The implication is that when we are strong, God's power is not easily discerned. Or, at least, it is not immediately obvious just where our strength is coming from. When we have no strength and are still strong; it's all God.

My wife and I were once acquainted with a woman who was diagnosed with breast cancer. She opted for a double mastectomy. Soon thereafter, her husband of many years opted to leave her, for another woman. It was a one-two punch, straight to the solar plexus. We were impressed with the aplomb, and even joy, with which she endured the double dose of trouble. It was not strength she had in herself. And, she was the first to acknowledge it. In time, she fully recovered from her surgery. The heartbreak took a little longer. She's a living example of simultaneity; when we are weak, God is strong. This strength-in-weakness principle enables us to not only accept our disappointment, but to take pride in our pain.

BOASTING OF WEAKNESSES

Paul had taken his case all the way to the supreme court. The judgment did not go his way. But, once God's gavel fell, the apostle declined to be bitter about the verdict. Nor, would he let himself lapse into negativity. He refused to sulk about circumstances he couldn't control. Instead, he chose to glory in God's grace. *"Therefore I will boast all the more gladly about my weaknesses, so that Christ's power may rest[233] in me"* (2 Corinthians 12:9).

Paul's attitude reminds me of evangelist David Ring. David Ring has cerebral palsy. He can't completely control his body or his speech. When he preaches, he sounds like he's disabled or drunk. And, here's the kicker—from boyhood, all he wanted to do was be a preacher. But, how can you preach when you can barely make yourself understood when you talk? Well, if you have ever heard David Ring preach, then you know it can be done. You have to listen carefully. But when you do, you will hear the voice of God.

David Ring uses his considerable limitations to glorify the Lord. He says he wouldn't trade places with anybody. He is proud of his handicap because it is such a profound display of Christ's power.

Paul says, *"I will not boast about myself, except in my weaknesses"* (2 Corinthians 12:5). Sounds foolish, doesn't it? Boasting in weakness. Who does that?! David Ring is the kind of person ill-bred numbskulls mockingly mimic. But, it's clear; they are the ones to be pitied.

---

[233] Greek: "episkēnoō" (ἐπισκηνόω). This verb referred to setting up a tent, or a military bivouac. It's an unusual word, appearing only here in the New Testament, not at all in the Septuagint, and rarely in classical Greek.

DELIGHTING IN DIFFICULTIES

Paul takes the strength-in-weakness precept a step further. If human weakness serves to release Christ's power in us, let's be quick to comply. Then, we can actually delight in our difficulties — exuberantly! *"That is why, for Christ's sake, I delight[234] in weaknesses, in insults, in hardships, in persecutions, in difficulties"* (2 Corinthians 12:10). The apostle rejoices in experiences the rest of us tend to run from. We've got a lot to learn. Maybe we should make his testimony our own. *"For when I am weak, then I am strong"* (2 Corinthians 12:10).

Cloud's Rest is a granite crag. Its surface is about the size of a football field. And straight down on all sides. At 9,931 feet, it is over a thousand feet higher than Half Dome itself. Being afraid of heights, my experience of it that day was both exhilarating and terrifying.

Spiritual mountain tops often have the same effect. When we encounter the presence of God, it is overwhelming. More than ever before, we recognize our human fragility and God's divine power. And, in the experience we are transformed from weakness to strength.

THINK

1. Have you ever had a mountaintop experience? Describe it.

2. In what sense was the Apostle Paul's experience, described in 2 Corinthians 12:1-10, the ultimate spiritual high?

3. Though Paul was reluctant to speak of his visit to Heaven, he still did. Why?

---

[234] Greek: "eudokeō" (εὐδοκέω). This verb means to think of something as good; to prefer, to feel favorably inclined toward, or to take a high degree of pleasure in something.

4. Spiritual highs are always followed by spiritual lows. True or false?

5. Can you verify contemporary claims to *"visions and revelations"* from God?

6. God protected Paul from spiritual conceit. How?

7. What was Paul's *"thorn in the flesh"*? Was it from God or the devil?

8. If you suffer from chronic pain, what should you do about it?

9. If we have faith, God will always deliver us from painful experiences. True or false?

10. Paul boasts about his weaknesses. How do you do that? Why would you do that?

ACT

1. Write out a page or two memoir of your most dramatic spiritual mountaintop experience.

2. Discuss with some good friends whether or not you would you take God up on the offer for a short round trip to Heaven, presuming too, that like Paul, you could not talk about it to anyone when you got back. And that you would have to live with a God-given disability to keep your pride in check.

3. Do you have a *"thorn in the flesh"*? If you have not pleaded with God to take it away, do so. Three times.

4. Itemize your weaknesses. Ask God for opportunities to boast about them at every appropriate opportunity. Then do so.

5. Google David Ring and watch one of his sermons.

Chapter 17

Spending and Being Spent

2 Corinthians 12:11-21

Late, one especially cold night, I went into the backyard to check on our family dogs and there on the lawn was our oldest son, age 16, unconscious. I ran into the house to get my wife. When she saw him, she thought he was dead. He looked dead. He was hardly breathing. He didn't respond to our efforts to rouse him. I called 911.

By the time the medics arrived, he was cognizant and sitting up on the grass. It turns out that he had been drinking whisky with his friends and passed out before he could sneak back into his room. Sadly, it was the latest in a long list of episodes in which our son had put us through the wringer emotionally. We wondered what he could possibly do next to break our hearts.

When we are having our babies and starting our families, we never imagine that those innocent little children have the potential to grow up and hurt us. It doesn't always happen; some parents are blessed with compliant, cooperative kids. But, it seems that they are the exceptions to the rule.

As John White points out in his book, *Parents in Pain,* parental pain is a unique kind of sorrow.[235] It's so unanticipated; the little ones we sacrificed so much for, and loved so unselfishly, stop loving us in return. Instead of the respect and affection we rightly deserve, we get indifference, ingratitude, and at times, hostility. The same thing can happen to spiritual parents. God uses us to help someone

---

[235] White, John. *Parents in Pain.* Downers Grove, IL: InterVarsity Press, 1979.

be born again. We invest ourselves in the early months and years of their spiritual growth. Then something happens and they start to misbehave. As their Christian parents, we exercise our right, and accept our responsibility, to step in and do something about it. However, instead of appreciation for our concern, they react to it. And, to us. It hurts. But, just because our children stop loving us, doesn't mean we stop loving them. They take, we give. They don't care, we do. It's all about spending and being spent on their behalf.

With parental devotion, the Apostle Paul affectionately addresses the Corinthians as, *"my dear children"* (1 Corinthians 4:14). And then, he reminds them of how they became Christians in the first place. *"Even though you have ten thousand guardians in Christ, you do not have many fathers, for in Christ Jesus I became your father through the gospel"* (1 Corinthians 4:15). Love speaks the truth. Tenderly.

In his book, *The Road Less Traveled,* psychiatrist Scott Peck defines authentic love as the willingness to extend ourselves for the spiritual well-being of someone else.[236] Peck disdains romance as a misleading substitute for the real thing. Love is not something you "fall" into. He reminds us that true love is effortful. Inevitably, it entails hard work, courage, and self-sacrifice. In other words, energy must always be expended. And, there's the risk that the person loved will not return the devotion. Hence, the need for courage. Finally, authentic love knows well that self-denial is essential. Sacrifice is required.

When we love others this way, we are willing to expand our ego boundaries[237] to include people who aren't lovable, or are unwilling

---

[236] Peck, Scott. *The Road Less Traveled.* New York, NY: Simon & Schuster, 1978.

[237] Ego boundaries represent the mental and emotional distinction between ourselves and others. They serve as psychological protection to prevent us from being hurt. But, they also isolate us from other people and hinder us from taking the chance to love them.

to be loving themselves. Surprisingly, there's joy in the risk of doing that. Peck maintains that it is impossible to truly love others without loving ourselves at the same time. It is, in fact, a tangible way of doing so. He also contends that human beings are entitled to be loved. We then, are obligated to love them. They need it. We give it—even if our devotion is not reciprocated. Paul serves as a role model in showing us how to enlarge our ego boundaries.

AUDACIOUSLY

A group of rebellious church members at Corinth, agitated by some infiltrating outsiders, have forced Paul's hand. Gladly, after First Corinthians, a stern letter, and a painful personal visit, most of the congregation had belatedly repented of their insurgency against his spiritual leadership. We've been calling them the Compliant Majority. But there remains an unruly minority of the membership who did not share in that contrition. We've labeled them the Defiant Minority.

Paul has no choice but to be audacious; i.e., bold, daring, brave, and fearless. He has to say and do whatever it takes to prevent a hostile takeover of the church, instigated by the recently arrived intruders. In so doing, he has been forced to *"Answer a fool according to his folly or he will be wise in his own eyes"* (Proverbs 26:5). He knows the entire exercise is preposterous. If you are not a fool, it's onerous to act like one. Paul begins with an admission and an accusation. *"I have made a fool of myself, but you drove me to it"* (2 Corinthians 12:11).

Christian leaders should never have to speak pridefully of their own accomplishments. When they must, it's because their followers have failed to do so. If the Corinthians had stood up to Paul's opponents when they first arrived in town, stirring up those already at odds with his leadership, he wouldn't have to be standing up for himself now. Or at all. The apostle chastises them for such glaring neglect. *"I ought to have been commended by you"* (2 Corinthians 12:11).

Every leader has flaws. But hardworking, sincere servants of Christ should never have to defend themselves. Instead, their people should have zero-tolerance for rumors, gossip, or overt complaints about their spiritual shepherds. There's a script every church member should memorize, rehearse, and deliver—gently but firmly—in situations like this: "Listen, I don't want to hear your criticisms about our spiritual leaders. If you have a problem with them, go to them, not to me. If you want, I'll go with you. But it's not my place to pay attention to your grievances."

The Corinthian Christians were not mature enough to do that. They didn't stop the gossip, so it proliferated. *"Without wood a fire goes out; without gossip a quarrel dies down"* (Proverbs 26:20). The outside agitators in Corinth would still have been troublesome, but dissension soon dissipates when no one pays attention to it. Paul has to say for himself what they should have said for him. *"I am not in the least inferior to the 'super-apostles'"* (2 Corinthians 12:11).

Still uncomfortable with being the braggart, the apostle feels compelled to soften his boasting by saying, *"Even though I am nothing"* (2 Corinthians 12:11). Paul's self-esteem was well established. But, like all truly great individuals, he did not permit himself to see himself as great. Instead, he maintained his equilibrium by realizing that he was both a Nobody and a Somebody.

In an earlier effort to defuse the fervor of some of the Corinthians who proudly proclaimed, *"I follow Paul"* (1 Corinthians 1:12), he described himself as simply a seed planter. *"I planted the seed, Apollos watered it, but God has been making it grow. So neither he who plants nor he who waters is anything, but only God who makes things grow"* (1 Corinthians 3:6-7). He summarized his estimate of himself and his colleagues by asking a rhetorical question. *"What after all is Apollos? And what is Paul? Only servants through whom you came to believe—as the Lord has assigned to each his task"* (1 Corinthians 3:5).

This is the image of himself he kept in place. We would be wise to do the same.

Paul knew that Christ had tapped him on the shoulder for his life's work. At the same time, he was consistently conscious of the fact that he was once a notorious sinner, now saved by grace. He has already told the Corinthians, *"I am the least of the apostles and do not even deserve to be called an apostle, because I persecuted the church of God. But by the grace of God I am what I am, and his grace to me was not without effect"* (1 Corinthians 15:9-10). Later, he confesses to Timothy, *"Even though I was once a blasphemer and a persecutor and a violent man, I was shown mercy because I acted in ignorance and unbelief. The grace of our Lord was poured out on me abundantly"* (1 Timothy 1:13-14).

Though he has not forgotten his infamous past, Paul was equally cognizant of the reality that he was far from insignificant. He confidently calls himself God's *"co-worker"* (1 Corinthians 3:9). He describes himself as *"a wise builder"*[238] (1 Corinthians 3:10). He knew that he was chosen for his life's work before he was born, claiming that *"God set me apart from my mother's womb"* (Galatians 1:15). He had heard Christ himself say of him, *"This man is my chosen instrument"* (Acts 9:15). You can't be aware of all that and not conclude that you are somebody. Somebody, indeed.

The apostles were in a class by themselves when it came to spiritual authority. After all, they were handpicked by Jesus. Paul calls himself *"abnormally born"* but nonetheless, chosen (1 Corinthians 15:8). The cult-like usurpers at Corinth had appointed themselves as spiritual authorities. But, they weren't the *"super apostles"* they claimed to be; they were pseudo-apostles (2 Corinthians 11:5). They weren't commissioned by Christ. They weren't authorized by him to do anything. Paul speaks

---

[238] Greek: "architektōn" (ἀρχιτέκτων). This term is the origin of our word "architect;" a designer of buildings, who often supervises their construction.

disparagingly of them. *"For such men are false apostles, deceitful workmen, masquerading as apostles of Christ"* (2 Corinthians 11:13).

The apostle's opponents in Corinth had an unwritten list of standards in which they prided themselves and by which they measured themselves against everyone else. In order to demonstrate that he is not in the least inferior to any of them, Paul is now compelled to compare himself to them.

For example, his competitors claimed supernatural powers. Paul responds. *"I persevered in demonstrating among you the marks of a true apostle, including signs, wonders and miracles"* (2 Corinthians 12:12). Naturally, we are curious as to just what miraculous powers he's talking about. But, Luke's account of Paul's year and a half in Corinth includes no mention of miracles. Still, if they hadn't happened the apostle wouldn't be prompting the Corinthians to recall them. They were witnesses to the astounding things he had done.

When he wrote to the Romans, a few months later, Paul makes reference to *"What Christ has accomplished through me in leading the gentiles to obey God by what I have said and done — by the power of signs and miracles through the power of the Spirit of God"* (Romans 15:18-19). In Acts, Luke includes an astounding aside that reminds us of Paul's supernatural abilities. *"God did extraordinary miracles through Paul, so that even handkerchiefs and aprons that had touched him were taken to the sick, and their illnesses were cured and the evil spirits left them"* (Acts 19:11-12). What the imposters in Corinth claimed to be able to do, Paul did. The contrast was clear.

The apostle's adversaries couldn't invalidate his credentials, so in an end run they attacked his attitude toward the Corinthian church, claiming that he didn't love them like he did the rest of the churches he'd started. If he did, they insinuated, he would have charged them a fee for his services. Somehow, they persuaded the congregation that expecting payment would have proved that he loved them. It was a convoluted line of reasoning, but evidently the Corinthians were giving it some credibility. Now, they were feeling slighted by him, as his critics implied they should be. Exasperated, Paul exclaims, *"How were you inferior to the other churches, except that I was never a burden to you?"*[239] (2 Corinthians 12:13) When Paul speaks of being a burden, he's talking about money. He insists that it was never his intention to be a financial burden to them. Deeply wounded by this cruel allegation, the apostle makes a plea dripping with irony. He exclaims, *"Forgive me this wrong!"* (2 Corinthians 12:13)

ALTRUISTICALLY

Parental love, at its best, is essentially unselfish. Good parents are altruistic — they are consistently and selflessly devoted to the welfare of their kids. They do it by instinct. They do it characteristically and as a matter of course. After all, sacrifice is a fundamental element of authentic love. True love extends itself for the well-being of another.

In our family, my wife has lived a parent-shaped life. She gave herself to her children — planning and preparing daily meals, reading to them, rocking them to sleep, ironing clothes, cutting hair, making prom dresses, and attending countless soccer games, wrestling matches, school plays, and ballet recitals. She even baked cookies so that they were hot from the oven when the kids walked in the front door after school. And now, she's doing it all over again with her

---

[239] Just what churches he had in mind here, Paul does not say. He is known to have taken money on more than one occasion from the church in Philippi. He tells them, *"I thank my God every time I remember you. In my prayers for all of you, I always pray with joy because of your partnership in the gospel from the first day until now"* (Philippians 1:3-5). He adds, *"Moreover, as you Philippians know, in the early days of your acquaintance with the gospel, when I set out from Macedonia not one church shared with me in the matter of giving and receiving except you only; for even when I was in Thessalonica, you sent me aid again and again when I was in need"* (Philippians 4:15-16).

grandchildren. When they arrive at our house, she stops everything she's doing to give them her undivided attention. She's a parent, first and foremost. One of her most treasured possessions is a framed saying given to her by our youngest daughter that reads, "Mother, the world may never know that you cared more, gave more, loved more than ever was expected. But, Mother, I know." That sentiment is shared by all of our five children.

Loving parents live for their children. The last thing they want to be is a burden to their kids. Spiritual parents operate on the same benevolent principle. Again, the Apostle Paul sets the example. His intensions and actions were unselfish. *"Now I am ready to visit you for the third time,*[240] *and I will not be a burden to you, because what I want is not your possessions but you"* (2 Corinthians 12:14).

There may be some pastors in the ministry for money, but I've never met one. Not that money isn't important. Not that workers aren't worthy of their wages; that's scriptural.[241] Who doesn't deserve a fair wage? But, money is never a priority.

Once, I ran across the profile of "The Perfect Pastor." The Perfect Pastor preaches for no longer than thirty minutes. He condemns sin, but never makes anyone feel uncomfortable about their own sins. He works six days a week. He is on call twenty-four hours a day and sometimes doubles as the church custodian. He is young, with twenty-five years of experience. He's handsome, charming, patient, and sensitive. He loves teenagers and children. His kids are well-behaved and his wife is pretty. He wears fashionable clothes and drives a nice, but not new, car. He visits the sick and chats with the

---

[240] Paul's previous two visits were his pioneer missionary visit, recorded in Acts 18, and his *"painful visit"* (2 Corinthians 2:1). He mentions this intended third visit several times in this final section Second Corinthians (10:2; 12:20-21; 13:1; 13:10).

[241] Jesus said, *"The worker deserves his wages"* (Luke 10:7). Quoting Deuteronomy 25:4 and Leviticus 19:13, Paul told Timothy, *"For the Scripture says, 'Do not muzzle the ox while it is treading out the grain' and 'The worker deserves his wages'"* (1 Timothy 5:18).

older members of the church. He's always in the office and considerately available, especially if you drop by unannounced. He's glad to share his time with you when you have nothing else to do. He is grateful for his modest salary and gives twenty percent back to the church.

Of course, this kind of pastor doesn't exist. But, unselfish ones are out there. Lots of them. They are givers, not takers. In Paul's case, he didn't ask anything from the Corinthians. And, to their chagrin, he didn't take anything from them either. The principle he put into practice is simple: *"After all, children should not have to save up for their parents, but parents for their children"* (2 Corinthians 12:14).

We've all seen the expensive motorhome rolling down the road, occupied by a retired couple touring the country. The bumper sticker on the back reads, "Spending the kids' inheritance." The saying is funny because it is the reverse of how things usually work out. Parents are givers, children are takers. It's the way it is. It's the way it should be.

The dollar amount of what it costs to raise a kid from birth to 18 always needs to be adjusted for inflation, but it's pricey. As I write this paragraph, that figure is $304,480![242] Good parents pay that price. And then, they often send their kids to college too. That's what you do; you spend and expend yourself for your children. It's what Paul did. *"So I will very gladly spend[243] for you everything I have and expend[244] myself as well"* (2 Corinthians 12:15).

---

[242] huffingtonpost.com. Accessed February 5, 2016.

[243] Greek: "dapanaō" (δαπανάω). This verb means to incur an expense. In a negative sense it connotes consuming, wasting, or squandering. It appears several times in other parts of the New Testament and typically refers to spending money. It is used to describe the woman with unremitting menstrual bleeding who *"suffered a great deal under the care of many doctors and had spent all she had"* (Mark 5:26). Or the Prodigal Son, who *"spent everything"* (Luke 15:14). See also Acts 21:24 and James 4:3.

[244] Greek: "ekdapanaō" (ἐκδαπανάω). This verb shares the same root as "dapanaō" (δαπανάω). It appears only here in the New Testament and it

Spiritual leaders, like loving parents, give, give, give, and then give some more. They do it every day and usually fall into bed at night—exhausted. Then they get up the next morning, early, and do it all over again. Parenting is spending money, time, and energy for a long time. A lifetime!

Parents expend themselves. When you expend something you consume it. You use it up. You deplete it. Real love is effortful. It is consistently self-sacrificing. Loving parents are the ideal embodiment of such an expenditure. Wouldn't it be shocking if their children didn't appreciate such noble virtue? But sometimes they don't. Sometimes, the more you love your kids, the less they love you. You are a parent in pain. Paul was a parent in pain. He expresses his heartbreak. *"If I love you more, will you love me less?"* (2 Corinthians 12:15)

The apostle has been excoriated by his competitors. They've accused him of being conniving, duplicitous, and selfish; exploiting his spiritual children for personal gain. You can almost hear what they had been whispering. *"Crafty fellow that I am, I caught you by trickery!"* (2 Corinthians 12:16). Paul's detractors were accusing him of deceiving the Corinthians regarding the funds he was raising for the Christians in Judea. The inference was that he was skimming money off the top for himself.

Some things never change. Despite our most sincere and selfless intentions, people presume that pastors are after their money. Like Paul, we must do our best in word and deed to discredit such prejudices.

Paul argues that his refusal to take money from the Corinthians was evidence that he wasn't exploiting them. *"Be that as it may, I have not been a burden to you"* (2 Corinthians 12:16). That motivation was misconstrued by his opponents. But the truth will prevail. Paul was

---

means to exhaust one's resources. Paul is making a play on words. In his ministry to the Corinthians, he spent and was spent. Gladly.

innocent of these charges. And his colleagues were too. *"Did I exploit[245] you through any of the men I sent you?"[246]* (2 Corinthians 12:17)

Everyone associated with Paul was squeaky clean. His accusers couldn't refute that. *"I urged Titus to go to you and I sent our brother with him. Titus did not exploit you, did he? Did we not walk in the same footsteps by the same Spirit?"* (2 Corinthians 12:18) Paul is an adroit defense attorney. He challenges the prosecution to prove their charges. Of course, they can't. Case dismissed.

NON-DEFENSIVELY

How do you defend yourself without being defensive? The first is an action; the second is an attitude. Paul has been steadily defending himself, without being at all rancorous about it. Still, he doesn't want to leave any doubt in the jury's mind that he is innocent of the allegations being leveled against him. For the moment, he's setting aside a scriptural precept. *"Fools show their annoyance at once, but the prudent overlook an insult"* (Proverbs 12:16). Paul isn't agitated; but neither is he willing to tolerate insults. Besides, he knows another adage: *"In a lawsuit the first to speak seems right, until someone comes forward and cross-examines"* (Proverbs 18:17). The apostle cross-examines his accusers. It's not his ego he's defending; it's his reputation. Paul isn't reacting to his critics; he is responding to their charges.

If Paul doesn't prove himself innocent of the indictments against him in Corinth, the entire church will be won over by men who don't

---

[245] Greek: "pleonekteō" (πλεονεκτέω). This verb means to have more, or to take a greater part or share of something; hence, to gain an advantage over someone. It presumes selfish motivation.

[246] Paul has already stated his priorities in the administration of the monies entrusted to him. *"We want to avoid any criticism of the way we administer this liberal gift. For we are taking pains to do what is right, not only in the eyes of the Lord but also in the eyes of man"* (2 Corinthians 8:20-21).

have anyone's interests in mind but their own. The apostle's motive in defending himself was pastoral. He asks, *"Have you been thinking all along that we have been defending ourselves to you? We have been speaking in the sight of God as those in Christ; and everything we do, dear friends,*[247] *is for your strengthening"*[248] (2 Corinthians 12:19). Like a devoted parent, Paul is reassuring his beloved children in the faith. He is extending himself to them and expending himself for them.

RIGHTEOUSLY

People sometimes confuse love with cathexis. Cathexis is the investment of emotional energy in a person, object, or idea.[249] Cathexis looks like love, but it isn't. And for good reason; it is self-indulgent. Parental love is the opposite. It operates by an unselfish set of moral standards—an internal yardstick. Misplace that measurement and love is lost. What you've got left is sticky sentimentality. Or, what's even worse than that; self-serving permissiveness, in the name of love.

Paul is brother and friend to the Corinthians. He is also their parent. He is willing to act like a parent when they need it. He is intentional about maintaining the spiritual standards of the family. God's family. Parental love is tough love. It is a functional endeavor, not merely an emotional one.

A family is not an open society. Individual members cannot do whatever they want. There are codes of conduct to be accepted and conformed to. It is the parents' responsibility to define those

---

[247] Greek: "agapētos" (ἀγαπητός). This word means "beloved." It expresses the deepest kind of attachment anyone can have with another. It is beyond affection or familial connection. It speaks of the most special of relationships.

[248] Greek: "oikodomē" (οἰκοδομή). This term describes the construction of a building. Figuratively, it speaks of building something, or someone, up. Edification.

[249] merriam-webster.com. Accessed February 6, 2016.

standards and to enforce them. That's the role Paul was playing with the Corinthians.

He's concerned that what he'll find when he gets back to Corinth is a regression into the carnality that characterized the congregation in the past. *"For I am afraid that when I come I may not find you as I want you to be, and you may not find me as you want me to be. I fear that there may be discord, jealousy, fits of rage, selfish ambition, slander, gossip, arrogance and disorder"* (2 Corinthians 12:20).

Paul is fearful for them. And, he is fearful for himself. *"I'm afraid that when I come again my God will humble me before you, and I will be grieved over many who have sinned earlier and have not repented of the impurity, sexual sin and debauchery in which they have indulged"*(2 Corinthians 12:21).

The apostle knows well the kinds of sins some of the Corinthians were capable of committing. The congregation was peopled with former idolaters, adulterers, active and passive homosexual partners, alcoholics and thieves (1 Corinthians 6:9-10). He was frightened that he might find out that their celebration of recovery had suffered a relapse—that he could no longer say, *"But you were washed, you were sanctified, you were justified in the name of the Lord Jesus Christ and by the Spirit of our God"* (1 Corinthians 6:11).

Now was the time to deal with these dormant proclivities. Paul has previously expressed his angst about how this kind of conduct may force his hand. *"What do you prefer? Shall I come to you with a rod of discipline, or shall I come in love and with a gentle spirit?"* (1 Corinthians 4:21)

We take a calculated risk when we bring children into this world. The equation is filled with variables. We may be proud of our offspring, or they may embarrass us, or even call our reputations into question. There is no guarantee of untarnished success.

My wife and I have experienced our share of parental disappointment and pain. In the process, we have consoled ourselves with the fact that we gave all our kids the same familial climate in which to grow up. It was an atmosphere of love and honesty. Each of them was loved. Each of them had the same opportunity to learn of God and love him as we did. What they did with that nurturing up-bringing was their call.

Our oldest son caused us a considerable amount of grief in his teenage years. We tried all kinds of techniques to hold him accountable to the standards we set for our family. In an effort to do this we actually drew up written behavioral contracts with him. If he wanted to stay in our home, with us and his siblings, he would have to comply. It was understood that if he failed to live up to those stipulations he would forfeit his right to be part of the family. He signed those contracts. And, he broke them. When he reneged on his last and final agreement, we told him, in tears, that he could no longer live in the home where he grew up. We put him out.

There were times when we didn't know where he was, or even if he was dead or alive. All contact was lost. We had no idea of how things were going to turn out. We shed lots of tears, said lots of prayers, and paced lots of floors over him. But, we never stopped loving him.

I'm glad to report that, in time, he came back to us, and to Christ. There wasn't a dry eye in the place the Sunday in church when he stood up in front of the entire congregation and thanked his mom and me for loving him unconditionally. That day he publically apologized for all the pain he'd caused us. But, we just did what parents do. We work. We risk. We sacrifice. We extend ourselves and expend ourselves in love for our children. Spiritual leaders with integrity do too.

THINK

1. Being hurt by your children in an inevitable part of parenting. True or false?

2. Should spiritual parents expect mistreatment from those they give birth to as Christians?

3. Are you a spiritual parent?

4. In what ways might you have to appear foolish to demonstrate your love for someone?

5. Do church members sometimes turn against their spiritual leaders? If so, why?

6. Should parents expect anything from their children?

7. In 2 Corinthians 12:15, Paul uses two verbs to describe his unselfishness toward the Corinthians; *"spend"* and *"expend"*? What's the difference between the two words?

8. Children usually appreciate their parents' sacrificial love. True or false?

9. Should you ever defend yourself as a parent? Can you do that without being defensive?

10. Parents who don't have strict standards for their children are bad parents. True or false?

ACT

1. List the names of people who could be considered your spiritual children. Underline the ones who have broken your heart. Commit yourself to pray for them every day. In time, set up an appointment to meet with them and seek to reconcile your relationship with them.

2. Read Scott Peck's book, *The Road Less Traveled.*

3. Commit yourself to teach the members of your church to defend you and the other leaders of your congregation against unwarranted allegations.

4. Take the responsibility of making sure that the designated leaders of your church are squeaky clean when it comes to conduct of any kind. Agree to hold each other accountable.

5. List the names of individuals you are currently reacting to emotionally. Then stop it.

Chapter 18

Determined to be Decisive

2 Corinthians 13:1-14

I was counseling a young man in his late twenties once about his relationship with his wife. You could call it marriage counseling, but the truth was, his marriage was over. They had been together as a couple for several years. No kids. It was never an easy relationship. Three steps forward, two steps back. Finally, his wife ran out of energy. She said she was through. There was nothing he could say or do to change her mind. She moved out.

Like most husbands desperate to save their marriages, he pleaded and promised, coaxed and cajoled. But, to no avail. It was too late. She told him to forget it. They would never be husband and wife again. At last, he accepted that reality. In time, he began dating and eventually fell in love with another woman. They were talking about getting married. A wedding date was set. Then, he got a call from his estranged wife. She said she'd been doing a lot of thinking since they'd been apart. She realized now that she really loved him all along. She'd changed her mind about their marriage. If he was willing, she would like to work on being reconciled and remarried.

What was he going to do? In his heart, he still loved his wife. They were bonded. He was also in love with his fiancé. They were bonded too. He was double-bonded. And, in a bind. Now, he was going to have to decide between the two of them. He asked both women for time to think it through. They complied.

That's where I came in. He wanted to know what to do. My task was to help him sort out the alternatives. To me it was clear; he should be reconciled with his wife and re-establish their marriage.

But, it was his decision to make, not mine. Should he go forward and marry his fiancé? Or, should he go backward and try to untangle the problems that caused the breakup of his marriage in the first place? Old or new? Fresh start, or re-start?

He agonized over it. For months. The women waited, anxiously. Everyone was frustrated. Still, he couldn't choose between the two. The result? He lost them both. The message each woman got was simple: "He doesn't love me." He ended up with no wife.

By default, not making a decision is a decision. The consequences of indecision can be tragic. Leaders with integrity avoid being indecisive. They know that it's crucial to be pre-active, not re-active. They don't wait to see what happens and then whine and complain as they end up frustrated, defeated, and bitter.

Every day there are forks in the road; choices that have to be made. The direction of life itself can be reduced to the individual decisions we make along the way — big and small. If we're smart, we slow down. Maybe, we even pull over to check the map. We pray. We choose. We go left or right. Being decisive is being definite about what needs to be done. When a decision has to be made, we make it.

In the early 1970s Henry Kissinger was Richard Nixon's Secretary of State. Once in an interview with the news media, he was asked about a certain military operation currently under consideration. Would we take action or not? His answer was straightforward. He said, "Whatever must happen ultimately should happen immediately."[250]

With every important decision we make, timing is everything. But, putting off what we know must be done will usually make things worse. In short, we decide to be decisive. We gather

---

[250] brainyquote.com/quotes/quotes/h/henryakis115110.ht-ml. Accessed March 12, 2016.

information, weigh our options, make a decision, and carry it out. We are resolute. The people we lead are expecting it. They should.

A leader is a person who directs others by going before them, or alongside them, toward a specified destination. Leaders use their personality, knowledge, ideas, ingenuity and initiative, word and example, to take their followers somewhere. A leader projects a course of action and proposes solutions to problems. A leader organizes human and material resources. A leader gets people going and keeps them going toward an agreed upon and clearly articulated goal. No dillydallying. No flip-flopping. No meandering. Just a straight line in the right direction. With leaders like that, followers follow. Certain things are necessary, though, to make that happen. In this last chapter of Second Corinthians, Paul tells us how.

STAY STRONG

Fabled University of Minnesota football coach Bernie Bierman was sometimes asked how he found such big and strong young men to play for his teams. He purportedly responded by saying, "When I drive along country roads, I look for boys walking behind plows."

Dictionary definitions for the word "strong" include the following qualities: muscular, able, competent, capable, energetic, strenuous, vigorous, forceful, powerful, influential, authoritative, resourceful, aggressive, willful, clear, firm, tenacious, tough, unfaltering, solid, steady, durable, and robust. You get the idea.

When I was in high school, the pastor of our church was also a body builder. I remember walking into his home office one day to see shelves lined with all the trophies he'd won over the years. I was impressed. Underneath that long-sleeved dress shirt were some big guns. But, his spiritual power was even more impressive. Decisive leaders are strong—not always physically, but for sure, psychologically. And spiritually. They have to be. Because, sooner or later, that strength will be tested.

315

More than any other congregation he'd ever worked with, the Corinthian church tested Paul's mettle. It was a battle of wills. The tension between them was headed for a showdown. Paul anticipates the clash. *"This will be my third visit[251] to you"* (2 Corinthians 13:1).

The apostle pictures a court date in which his accusers will have to prove their allegations. Quoting Deuteronomy 19:15, he reminds them that, *"Every matter must be established by the testimony of two or three witnesses"*[252] (2 Corinthians 13:1). This stipulation of Old Testament jurisprudence was revered and practiced by the Jewish community in the first century. Paul's opponents were in full agreement with it. They could hardly argue with his insistence on it. Evidence, not rumors, will settle this case. His critics are going to have to "prove it." If they can't verify their accusations with at least two credible witnesses, then the charges must be dropped.

I was a member of a church board one time when a handful of congregants were careless in implying that the pastor was having an affair with a woman in the church. We met with him and asked if there was any truth to the things being said about him. He said no, there wasn't. Based on his testimony and the absence of any witnesses to the contrary, those responsible for the gossip were told to cease and desist. There was no case against him. Hearsay and suspicion do not a court case make. That's U.S. law. That's God's law.

Sometimes, you've got to call people's bluff. Paul warns the Corinthians, *"I already gave you a warning when I was with you the*

---

[251] This is the last of such pronouncements made by Paul in the final four chapters of Second Corinthians. See 10:2; 12:14, 20-21.

[252] Jesus himself included this rule of law in his instructions to his disciples about church discipline in Matthew 18:16. It is also referenced in other parts of the New Testament. See John 8:17; 1 Timothy 5:19; Hebrews 10:28; 1 John 5:8.

second time.[253] *I now repeat it while absent: On my return I will not spare those who sinned earlier or any of the others"*[254] (2 Corinthians 13:2).

In nearly every local church there is a Defiant Minority. These people are used to having things their way. When they don't like a direction the leaders of the church are taking, they make a fuss. Sometimes they attack the paid staff and, in particular, the lead pastor. Often, they prevail. One of the reasons this happens — and sometimes repeatedly — is because no one has the backbone to stop them.

Paul is tough enough to take the troublemakers to task. Combatively, he warns, *"Since you are demanding proof*[255] *that Christ is speaking through me"* (2 Corinthians 13:3). Paul is no High Plaines Drifter, looking for an excuse to be bloody. But, he's not backing down either. To restore law and order anywhere, you have to be strong, courageous, and decisive. If you are not quick on the draw, you'll be dead. And the townspeople in danger.

The Apostle Paul is strong, but he knows that his strength is not his own. It's Christ's. *"He is not weak in dealing with you, but is*

---

[253] Paul recalls his painful, and unproductive, emergency visit to Corinth between the writing of First and Second Corinthians. Here, he chooses the perfect tense of the verb when he talks about warning the Corinthians. It indicates a past event with continuing effects into the present. The threats he made then are still in force.

[254] It is impossible to reconstruct this situation to accurately identify who Paul is talking about, or their sins. The traditional view is that it has to do with the incestuous offender of 1 Corinthians 5 who became Paul's chief antagonist and publically attacked him in some dramatic way during the conflict that emerged from his emergency trip to Corinth in a vain attempt to resolve the situation (2 Corinthians 2:5; 7:12).

[255] Paul's opponents in Corinth have imposed upon him their own criteria for spiritual authority; things like personal charisma, impressive public speaking skills (2 Corinthians 10:10) and the performance of miraculous signs and wonders (2 Corinthians 12:11-13). The apostle doesn't object to such credentials, but he is definitely opposed to the public display of them for the purpose of establishing personal credibility.

powerful among you. For to be sure, he was crucified in weakness, yet he lives by God's power" (2 Corinthians 13:4).

Jesus set the example to be followed when it comes to being strong in spite of weakness. It was in his apparent fragility that God's power knew its finest hour. But, even God's power is not power for power's sake. It is power for love's sake, released on behalf of the very people who sometimes little understand or appreciate it. Paul is proud to share in such seeming helplessness, *"Likewise, we are weak in him, yet by God's power we will live with him in our dealing with you"* (2 Corinthians 13:4).

When I was eleven I saved my allowance and sent away to New York City for the Charles Atlas Muscle Building Course. The ad in *Boy's Life Magazine* showed a puny teenager at the beach, having sand kicked in his face by a rude ruffian as he took away the scrawny kid's girlfriend. "Don't be a 90 lb. weakling!" the ad chided. Do something about it. I did. I weighed about ninety pounds at the time myself and had no intention of letting some chiseled muscleman take away the girlfriend I didn't have yet. The exercise regimen — basic isometrics — arrived a few weeks later. You should see me now!

Paul isn't about to let some bullies in Corinth kick sand in his face and walk away with his church. He's not looking for conflict, but he's not afraid of it either. He's strong. And, he's definite about it.

BE INSISTENT

A wise seminary professor stunned our pastoral care class one day by telling us, "Problems are people." I never forgot that epigram. Like most proverbs, it's not the last word on the subject, but it's still true. In one way or another, most of the challenges we face in life are connected with other people. Few problems are people-free. Human beings are always in the mix somehow. To solve problems you have

318

to deal with people. Sadly, some spiritual leaders don't have the moxie for conflict. It's a shame. The bad guys win. The good guys lose. Innocent people in between, get hurt.

Leaders with integrity don't shy away from being assertive. If people are behaving badly, they call them out. Paul isn't hesitant to challenge the Corinthians to change their ways and do what is right. Even if they don't think it's any of his blankety-blank business. He's making their behavior his business. He's insistent about it.

Bird watchers say that when crows invade a corn field, they assign a few of their number to perch in a nearby tree to act as sentries to warn the rest of the birds of any threat that may come their way while they are feeding. The folk tales persist that if the sentry crows fail in their duties, the rest of the group will attack and kill them for their negligence. This may be why a flock of crows is often referred to as a "murder" of crows.[256]

Paul is not a distracted sentry. He's alert and vigilant. *"Examine yourselves to see whether or not you are in the faith; test yourselves"* (2 Corinthians 13:5). Critical people are preoccupied with the flaws and faults of others. What they should do instead, is take a long look in the mirror.

An indie Christian band in the 1990s named themselves *Plankeye*. They were reminding their fans of the parable Jesus told about people who are always volunteering to get the splinter out of everyone else's eye, while being blind to the 2x4 in their own. That describes the insurgents at Corinth. But, Paul's eyesight is excellent. He sees their faults clearly because he has dealt with his own.

Fearlessly, the apostle asks the Corinthians a pointed question: "Are you even Christians anymore?" He temporarily suspends his usual assurances of salvation by grace through faith. Instead, he throws some cold water in their faces. If their answer to that question about themselves isn't right, then that would explain why

---

[256] crows.net/mjw.html. Accessed March 18, 2016.

they are so wrong about him. After giving them a minute to think it over, Paul softens the insinuation. *"Do you not realize that Christ Jesus is in you?"* (2 Corinthians 13:5)

Paul has consistently addressed the Corinthians as Christians. He calls them *"the church of God in Corinth"* (1 Corinthians 1:2; 2 Corinthians 1:1). Corporately, he says, *"Do you not know that you yourselves are God's temple and that God's Spirit dwells in your midst?"* (1 Corinthians 3:16) Individually, he asks, *"Do you not know that your bodies are temples of the Holy Spirit who is in you, whom you have received from God?"* (1 Corinthians 6:19) Paul does not doubt the authenticity of their salvation. Still, he wants them to reconsider their current behavior in the light of the reality of their relationship with Christ. He presses them to do some serious introspection. *"Unless, of course, you fail the test"* (2 Corinthians 13:5). They need to ask themselves if they are they truly Christians. If so, are they acting Christianly? The Corinthians were integrity-deficient. They have yet to consistently live out what they said they believed in.

Paul next appeals to their sense of fair play. If they give themselves the benefit of the doubt, they should surely do the same for him. *"And I trust that you will discover that we have not failed the test"* (2 Corinthians 13:6). Paul is a true Christian. He is a spiritual leader with integrity. In their hearts, the Corinthians knew that the unverified charges against him were just that. As they were in the right to be gracious towards themselves, they should be equally big-hearted toward him and the rest of his apostolic team.

Resuming a conciliatory tone, Paul discloses that he's been praying for them and the tense situation they've created. *"Now we pray to God that you will not do anything wrong – not so that people will see that we have stood the test but so that you will do what is right even though we may seem to have failed"* (2 Corinthians 13:7). Again, as they acknowledge their own humanity, he appeals to them to acknowledge his. This is not an admission of guilt. Or failure. It is a courteous concession to encourage them to face up to their own faults. Their responsibility is to do the right thing. In the end, the proof of our leadership is the spiritual maturity of those we lead.

I recently read an anecdote about a young stay-at-home mom who was feeling frustrated because she had so many responsibilities as a parent. Then she saw a sign at a local childcare center that advertised: "Let us love your kids while you're at work." That changed her perception of her situation. From then on, she was grateful to have the opportunity to love her children herself.

As exasperating as the Corinthian church was, and as hard as they were to love, Paul welcomed the chance to try. His main concern was that they do what was right. He was decisive enough to be insistent about it. He's confident that in the end they will align themselves with the truth. *"For we cannot do anything against the truth, but only for the truth"* (2 Corinthians 13:8). Ultimately, truth triumphs; there is no alternative outcome. As Paul knows all too well, kicking against the goads is futile.[257] Now, to get the Corinthian Christians to realize it too.

Preoccupied with the well-being of his converts, Paul is willing to be misunderstood. What matters is their spiritual progress and maturity. He knows that in perceived weakness, God's power is released. We can rejoice in that too. *"We are glad whenever we are weak but you are strong; and our prayer is for your perfection"* (2 Corinthians 13:9, NIV 1984). Paul is willing to appear weak so that his followers may be strong. *"For we who are alive are always being given over to death for Jesus' sake, so that his life may be revealed in our mortal body. So then, death is at work in us, but life is at work in you"* (2 Corinthians 4:11-12). As Jesus said, *"Unless a kernel of wheat falls to the ground and dies, it*

---

[257] Knocked to the ground on the road to Damascus, Paul heard Jesus say, *"Saul, Saul, why do you persecute me? It is hard for you to kick against the goads"* (Acts 26:14).

remains only a single seed. But if it dies, it produces many seeds" (John 12:24).

Paul is hopeful for a harvest in Corinth. He won't be satisfied until he sees *"perfection"*[258] (2 Corinthians 13:9, NIV 1984). The original word suggests that something is broken and needs to be repaired. Something is damaged and needs to be restored. This is what ministry is all about.

Paul's preference is to be gentle, rather than stern. But, he does not hesitate to be strict when necessary. *"This is why I write these things when I am absent, that when I come I may not have to be harsh in my use of authority — the authority the Lord gave me for building you up, not tearing you down"*(2 Corinthians 13:10). Paul knows well the purpose of spiritual authority.

In his book, *Spiritual Authority,* Watchman Nee claims that many people in Christian leadership don't understand authority.[259] There are two serious consequences to such ignorance: leaders like that are not under authority, and they don't know how to be in authority either. Pity the church for whom that is the case.

Spiritual authority is an aptitude born of knowing the heart of God, the will of God, the Word of God — and the wisdom that comes from implementing it over and over again. Paul has a Ph.D. in spiritual authority. He knows that it's all about the edification of God's people. If that's not the result, spiritual authority is out of whack.

---

[258] Greek: "katartisis" (κατάρτισις). This term describes training, disciplining, instructing, strengthening, and perfecting. The RSV renders it "improvement" which may be closer to the idea Paul had in mind. The 2011 edition of the NIV says "fully restored." The ESV: "restoration." The NLT: "mature." The NASB: "complete."

[259] Nee, Watchman. *Spiritual Authority.* Washington, DC: Christian Fellowship Publishers, 1972.

KEEP OPTIMISTIC

You've probably heard that there are two kinds of people in the world: those who wake up every day and say "Good morning, Lord!" And those who get up and say, "Good Lord, it's morning!"

Or, how about this one: A traveling shoe salesman was assigned a new territory in the remote hollows of Appalachia. He immediately left a message with his boss, saying, "Don't send any shoes for me to try to sell; nobody wears shoes around here." Another salesman, assigned to the same region, wired the home office saying, "Send all the shoes you've got; nobody here has any!"

Okay, one more. A frazzled husband comes home after a long stressful day at the office. Seeing the fretful look on his wife's face when he walked in the door, he growled, "Everything's gone wrong today. If there's one thing I don't want to hear, it's more bad news!" His wife tartly replied, "In that case, dear, you'll be glad to know that three of your four children did not break their arms today."

Paul refuses to let the immaturity of his followers make him react negatively to them. No way is he going to end this epistle by sounding harsh and demanding. Instead, he says farewell with affection. *"Finally, brothers and sisters rejoice!"*[260] (2 Corinthians 13:11) Paul wishes them the joyful experience of God's grace.

Despite the real problems they have, and the unresolved tension between them, the apostle encourages the congregation to be happy. It's the same verb he uses in his well-known injunction: *"Rejoice in the Lord always. I will say it again: Rejoice"* (Philippians 4:4). For Christians, there is no room for gloom.

Paul continues his final exhortations. *"Listen to my appeal,*[261] *be of one mind, live in peace. And the God of love and peace will be with you"* (2

---

[260] Greek: "chairō (χαίρω). The root of the term means "grace." Used as a greeting, it is more like "grace to you."

[261] Greek: "parakaleō" (παρακαλέω). The verb is part of Paul's default vocabulary; he uses it a lot. It means to exhort, entreat, instruct, encourage as well as to console and comfort.

Corinthians 13:11, NIV 1984). Tranquility is a synergistic experience. If they'll give God a chance to work among them, he will.

Paul adds yet another word of encouragement to his extended farewell. He tells the Corinthians to express affection toward one another. *"Greet one another with a holy kiss"*[262] (2 Corinthians 13:12). Affection is a demonstration of love. It serves to ease tensions between people. Who knows, maybe if we act like we like someone we don't like that much, we will get to like them. Like they say in Alcoholics Anonymous — "Fake it, until you make it!"

I love to visit Chile. Christians down there don't let you wonder whether or not they are glad to see you. Go to church or Bible study, and perfect strangers will embrace you like a long-lost cousin. They hug you three times, kiss you on the cheek three times, and shake your hand like they mean it. That's what Paul is encouraging the Corinthians to do.

There's something special about Christian fellowship. Wherever you may be in this big wide world, when you are with other believers, there is love. We are part of a universal fellowship. *"All God's people send their greetings"* (2 Corinthians 13:13).

Paul closes his benediction with a soaring doxology. *"May the grace of our Lord Jesus Christ and the love of God and the fellowship of the Holy Spirit be with you all"* (2 Corinthians 13:14). This parting blessing is a classic example of what scholars refer to as Task Theology.[263]

---

[262] Scholars are challenged with how to translate statements like this; literally or conceptually? Most stick with *"kiss."* The NLT opts for "Greet each other with Christian love." In *The Message*, Eugene Peterson says "holy embrace." The admonition itself is often repeated in the New Testament. See Romans 16:16; 1 Corinthians 16:20; 1 Thessalonians 5:26 and 1 Peter 5:14.

[263] While the New Testament is chock-full of theology, it is not systematized. And, while the apostles think theologically, they are not theologians in the common sense of the term. They are instead, evangelists and pastors. Their theological thoughts are expressed in response to real-life situations in the experiences of the people they lead and serve. That is the essence of Task Theology. For a helpful discussion of this concept, see *How*

While the term "Trinity"[264] appears nowhere in Scripture, the concept of a three-person deity is presumed — as in the Great Commission, where the three persons share a single name. *"Go and make disciples of all nations, baptizing them in the name of the Father and of the Son and of the Holy Spirit"* (Matthew 28:19).

The term God, is a reference to deity in general. But, more specifically, it refers to God, the Father, Yahweh, or Jehovah, as in *"God so loved the world that he gave his one and only Son"* (John 3:16). Jesus, though usually described as Lord, is also occasionally referred to as God, as in *"Our great God and Savior, Jesus Christ"* (Titus 2:13). The terms are used interchangeably.

In Revelation, Father and Son, both call themselves *"the Alpha and the Omega"* (Revelation 1:8; 22:13). Their equality is presumed in the familiar verse, *"In the beginning was the Word, and the Word was with God, and the Word was God"* (John 1:1). Jesus himself declared that equality when he said, *"I and the Father are one"* (John 10:30). And, *"Anyone who has seen me has seen the Father"* (John 14:19). The writer of Hebrews adds, *"The Son is the radiance of God's glory and the exact representation of his being"* (Hebrews 1:3). In this closing blessing to the Corinthians, Paul presumes the inclusion of the Holy Spirit in the circle of Deity. The three are One. The One is three.

This concept is dramatically portrayed in the controversially provocative book by Paul Young, *The Shack.* Befuddled by his dreamlike weekend with the Trinity, the main character, Mack Mackenzie, blurts out, "So, you are all three God?!" "Yes," they say simultaneously. Laughing.[265]

I introduce all this theological exactitude to my students by telling them that when I spell the word GOD with all capital letters, I

---

to Read the Bible for All Its Worth, by Gordon Fee and Douglas Stuart, third edition, pages 86-87.

[264] The first known use of the term Trinity is attributed to Tertullian (165-220 AD).

[265] Young, William Paul. *The Shack.* Los Angeles: Windblown Media, 2007.

am referring to the Trinity; Father, Son and Holy Spirit. Ever One. Ever individual. Ever in relationship.

When I was growing up listening to sermons in church and at summer camp, Jim Elliot was one of the heroes of the faith that the preachers loved to talk about. Jim Elliot and four of his companions were missionary martyrs. On January 8, 1956 they met their deaths in a remote region of Ecuador at the hands of the Auca Indians they thought they had befriended. Their dead bodies were riddled with dozens of razor sharp arrows.[266] In time, the widows of the five men led the entire village to faith in Christ.

Years earlier, Jim Elliot had fervently prayed, "Father, make of me a crisis man. Bring those I contact to a point of decision. Let me not be a milepost on the road of their lives. Make me a fork in that road that men must turn one way or another when they face Christ in me."[267] That prayer was answered. Jim Elliot was decisive for Christ — a role-model for generations to come. May we be the same.

THINK

1. What's the distinction between making decisions and being decisive?

2. Would you describe yourself as decisive?

3. Have you ever been unable to make a decision? What happened?

4. To make no decision *is* a decision. True or false?

---

[266] crossroad.to/Victory/stories/missionary/11-auca. Accessed March 19, 2016.

[267] goodreads.com./541037-father-make-of-me-a-crisis-man. Accessed March 19, 2016.

5. What you know you will have to do ultimately, you should do immediately. True or false?

6. Can a person decide to be decisive?

7. Are you a strong person? Where does your strength come from?

8. How often should a spiritual leader have to talk like Paul does in 2 Corinthians 13:2?

9. How decisive are you about making sure people do what is right?

10. What's the purpose of spiritual authority?

ACT

1. What situation are you facing right now that calls for decisive action on your part? Make a decision and do it.

2. Would the people who know you consider you a strong leader? Ask them.

3. If problems are people, list yours.

4. Identify the Defiant Minority in your church. Now, begin to meet and pray with your leadership team to create a strategy for bringing them into harmony with the rest of the congregation.

5. Read Watchman Nee's book *Spiritual Authority*.

Postscript

The Bible isn't a book. It's a collection of books—a library of sixty-six individual volumes. Despite its remarkable cohesiveness, there is also wide diversity, expressed in at least ten literary genres: Old Testament Narratives, Law, Prophets, Psalms, Wisdom Literature, Gospels, Parables, Acts, Epistles and Revelation. Scripture is both easy to understand, and at times, quite complicated too. Several priorities have to be simultaneously kept in mind. And, in balance.

AUTHORIAL INTENTION

Of paramount importance in correctly interpreting and applying Scripture, is to find out what the biblical author intended to achieve by what he had to say. This is not always simple to do.

Sometimes, as in the case of the Corinthian correspondence, we can come close to Paul's authorial intention. With other letters, like Romans, that is not so easily done. In some instances, it is quite possible that an author had more than a single reason for writing. Still, our goal is to discern, as best we can, what the biblical writers meant to accomplish—the presumption being that what they intended to say is one in the same with what the Holy Spirit intended to be said. Their words become God's Word.

Ascertaining authorial intention is crucial in discovering the correct interpretation of any scriptural text. The question is, can this be done? In his book, *Elements of Biblical Exegesis*, Michael J. Gorman argues that it is presumptive to think so.[268] He suggests that a more realistic and worthy goal would be to achieve a coherent

---

[268] Gorman, Michael J. *Elements of Biblical Exegesis, Revised and Expanded Edition.* Grand Rapids, MI: Baker, 2009.

understanding of any given text on its own terms and in its original context.

In either case, it is incumbent upon us as exegetes to get as close as we can to what the Holy Spirit was inspiring the biblical writers to say in the first place. Only then, will the Bible speak to us in our contemporary context as it did to the original readers in theirs.

POLYVALENCE

What every sincere and serious student of Scripture is in pursuit of, then, is a definitive interpretation of God's Word; i.e., the intended meaning of the text. What we are often uncomfortable about in this imposing process is ambiguity. We don't want the Bible to seem to be saying more than one thing, much less contradictory things.

There are many possible causes for biblical ambiguity. It may be an absence of sufficient knowledge on our part about the historical circumstances of a particular passage. Or, the reason may be linguistic; we just don't understand the vocabulary or grammatical construction of the passage at hand. Sometimes, though, the ambiguity is built into the text. Maybe even intentionally so by the author himself. Deliberate ambiguity is good, in the sense that it prods us to think more deeply about what God seems to be saying.

Thus, while every passage of Scripture may have one true interpretation, it may also have a variety of meanings that are also quite legitimate. Each interpreter will see unique nuances in the text that are valid, even if they are secondary to the author's main idea.

In short, biblical texts are multidimensional. This is called polyvalence. After all, *"the Word of God is alive and active"* (Hebrews 4:12). Scripture itself is dynamic; it continues to speak in new and vibrant ways, with the single caveat that it can never mean what it never could have meant to the author or its original readers. That being understood, let's let God speak to us afresh from his Word.

In the process of writing this book, one of my colleagues was kind enough to read chapter nine, "Being Emotionally Consistent." Courteously, he raised the question as to whether moodiness was really the primary topic of that particular passage (2 Corinthians 6:1-13). I freely admitted that perhaps it wasn't. But, I maintained that while it may not have been the apostle's first concern, it is still a legitimate facet of what he was saying.[269]

EXTENDED APPLICATION

It's axiomatic that every generation of Christ followers shares a sense of immediacy with the Christians of the first century. Despite the expanse in time, language, and cultural circumstances between us, we have many things in common. This means that God's Word to them is God's Word to us.

That is especially true when our circumstances are similar to theirs. But what of situations that aren't similar to theirs? For example, we have acknowledged that Paul's admonition to the Corinthians to not be unequally *"yoked together"* with unbelievers (2 Corinthians 6:14), was about binding relationships with members of the various trade guilds in the city. It was not about Christians marrying non-Christians, as we commonly apply the passage to modern day audiences. But, are we in the wrong to do so?

One thing's for certain—responsible exegesis must prevail. We can't come to Scripture with only the here and now in mind. We must pay attention to the there and then, following the principle that application is based on interpretation. Inadequate interpretation is a foundation of sand. Nothing built on it will stand for long.

---

[269] A persistent fantasy of mine is to picture myself meeting the Apostle Paul in Heaven someday and sitting down to discuss my interpretations of his epistles. In general, of course, I hope he approves. In specific instances, I imagine him saying, "I didn't think of it exactly that way, but you do make a good point."

God's Word to us is limited to its original intention. To make sure we don't make the Bible say what we want it to say, requires that we consider other passages of Scripture in which our extended application is confirmed as valid in no uncertain terms.

The hermeneutical maxim is true—the Bible interprets itself. Can it be demonstrated, then, that God forbids marriage between his people and those who aren't his people? Emphatically, yes. Thus, if it can be shown that our proposed application of a given text is substantiated apart from the passage itself, then we are free to proceed. With caution.

In this volume I have superimposed upon Second Corinthians the construct of spiritual integrity. I think this thesis falls well within the boundaries of Paul's original intentions in writing the letter. And, that it is in harmony with the multidimensional nature of what he had to say— as well as being in keeping with the tenor of Scripture as a whole. It has been my goal to be pragmatic; dealing sensibly with real issues. I hope you have found it helpful.

Made in the USA
Columbia, SC
11 August 2019